THE BIG CON

THE
BIG CON

The True Story of How
Washington Got Hoodwinked
and Hijacked by
Crackpot Economics

JONATHAN CHAIT

HOUGHTON MIFFLIN COMPANY
BOSTON | NEW YORK
2007

For information about permission to reproduce selections from
this book, write to Permissions, Houghton Mifflin Company,
215 Park Avenue South, New York, New York 10003.

www.houghtonmifflinbooks.com

Library of Congress Cataloging-in-Publication Data
Chait, Jonathan.
The big con : the true story of how Washington got hood-
winked and hijacked by crackpot economics / Jonathan Chait.
p. cm.
Includes bibliographical references and index.
ISBN-13: 978-0-618-68540-0
ISBN-10: 0-618-68540-5
1. Lobbying — Moral and ethical aspects — United States.
2. Economists — United States — Political activity. 3. Political
corruption — United States. 4. Deception — Political aspects —
United States. 5. United States — Economic policy — Moral
and ethical aspects. I. Title.
JK1118.C43 2007
320.973 — dc22   2007014001

Printed in the United States of America

Book design by Victoria Hartman

QUM 10 9 8 7 6 5 4 3 2 1

To my two families—first, Mom, Dad, and Daniel, and now Robin, Joanna, and Benjamin. They have given me a life of boundless joy.

CONTENTS

ACKNOWLEDGMENTS

My life is hard to understand. I'm a compulsive procrastinator, I'm not particularly good-looking, and though I do a few things well, I do many others badly. And yet my life has gone far better than I ever could have hoped. I often puzzle over my inexplicable good fortune. The best explanation I can give is that at every stage of life I've been surrounded by people who saved me from my failings.

My parents, David and Ilene, have always been warm, encouraging, smart, and funny. My mother encouraged me to read, write, and think from an early age, constantly taking me to the library. My father explained to me history, politics, science, and almost everything under the sun in concise, entertaining ways. I only hope that as a parent I can give my children the warmth and generosity that my parents have shown to me. My brother Daniel would no doubt vouch for this. Daniel is brilliant and hilarious, a lifelong intellectual influence and a wonderful friend.

My childhood best friend, Michael Mullen, taught me a lot and — being far tougher than I — saved me from some beatings. In high school I became great friends with David Lenter and Joel Rubenstein, who debated politics with me and encouraged me (in vain, alas) to apply myself in school. In college I made lifelong friendships with Geoff Earle and Jay Mazumdar, who stood together with me at the *Michigan Daily* when it was not popular to do so. After college I was hired at the *American Prospect* by Jonathan Cohn, my first mentor, who remains a close friend and is one of the finest human beings I have ever met. At the *Prospect*, Paul Starr was a sharp and brilliant editor, and Robert Kuttner generously let me publish, even though I was, in his words, "a damn moderate."

After a year at the *Prospect* I came to *The New Republic*, my journalistic heaven. I learned much from every editor I worked with — Andrew Sullivan, the late (and mourned) Michael Kelly, Charles Lane, and Peter Beinart. When the current editor, Frank Foer, was first named, I was ecstatic. Frank is a great friend, and working under him has been the highlight of my career. All those editors were selected by Marty Peretz, who sustained this wonderful institution.

My close friends at *TNR* have included Michael Crowley (who started with me as an intern), Hanna Rosin (my second mentor), Margaret Talbot, Jonathan Cohn (again), David Grann, Ryan Lizza, Michelle Cottle, Noam Scheiber, Jason Zengerle, Leon Weiseltier, and John Judis. Michael Kinsley taught me a huge amount simply by publishing brilliant work. I enjoy the company of others whom I haven't known quite as long or as well, and I benefit from their brilliance every day. In fact, I wrote this book in *TNR*'s offices rather than holing up in isolation, as most authors do. If there's a more fun place to work, I haven't heard of it.

Chris Orr — a great friend and colleague — deserves special mention for helping me through every stage of this book. His imprint on it is profound. David Grann, Michael Crowley, Jonathan Cohn, Frank Foer, and Hanna Rosin provided valuable input. I hired the talented young writer Elspeth Reeve to do the endnotes, and she saved me from innumerable mistakes.

When I started this book, friends advised me that book editors do very little. Somehow I ended up with Webster Younce, a rare talent who poured himself into this project and helped shape every facet. My agent, Gail Ross, was one of the first to believe in me and did a fantastic job. (If you need an agent, look her up; several of my writer friends already have.)

I owe thanks as well to my loving grandparents Miriam Chait, who passed away a dozen years ago, and Bunny and Leonard Seidman. Arlene Swern, the best mother-in-law a guy could have, helped me find the time to write this book. (I cranked out the first outline in her guest bedroom while she entertained my young daughter.) My equally sweet father-in-law, David Grayson, caught a cringe-inducing mistake in the final drafts.

When I was young, I was terrified of and hopelessly inept with girls. By sheer good fortune I ended up with Robin, my beautiful, sharp, funny, oh-so-sweet bride. This was the greatest break of all. I still don't know quite how it happened, but I give thanks every day that I get to spend my life with her. The lesson here is that you don't have to be good, or even competent, at courtship — you just have to hit the jackpot once. Robin cheerfully indulged my many late nights spent making up for unproductive days. Our children, Joanna and Benjy, are a daily wonder. I boast about them constantly.

This acknowledgment is all too short, and I have probably left out important people. Here is why. I simply forgot to write one until, shortly before publication, it occurred to me that I should. I wrote this very quickly, and the publisher of this book heroically wedged it in at the last — the very, very last — minute. Nobody who knows me would find this the least bit surprising.

INTRODUCTION

I have this problem. Whenever I try to explain what's happening in American politics — I mean, what's *really* happening — I wind up sounding a bit like an unhinged conspiracy theorist. But honestly, I'm not. My politics are actually quite moderate. (Most real lefties, in fact, think I'm a Washington establishment sellout.) So please give let me a chance to explain myself when I tell you the following: American politics has been hijacked by a tiny coterie of right-wing economic extremists, some of them ideological zealots, others merely greedy, a few of them possibly insane. (Stay with me.)

The scope of their triumph is breathtaking. Over the course of the last three decades, they have moved from the right-wing fringe to the commanding heights of the national agenda. Notions that would have been laughed at a generation ago — that cutting taxes for the very rich is the best response to any and every economic circumstance, or that it is perfectly appropriate to turn the most rapacious and self-interested elements of the business lobby into essentially an arm of the federal government — are now so pervasive, they barely attract any notice.

The result has been a slow-motion disaster. Income inequality has approached levels normally associated with Third World oligarchies, not healthy Western democracies. The federal government has grown so encrusted with business lobbyists that it can no longer meet the great public challenges of our time. Not even many conservative voters or intellectuals find the result congenial. Government is no smaller — it is simply more debt-ridden and more beholden to wealthy elites.

And yet the right-wing ascendancy has continued inexorably despite continual public repudiation. The 2006 elections were only the latest electoral setback. The right has suffered deeper setbacks before, and all of them have proven temporary. In 1982, after the country had entered the deepest recession since the 1930s, Republicans were slaughtered in the midterm congressional races, losing twenty-seven seats in the House of Representatives. Ronald Reagan, whose election two years earlier had seemed to augur a new conservative era, trailed his likely 1984 Democratic challengers by double digits in the polls and seemed destined to be a lame duck. "What we are witnessing this January," wrote the esteemed *Washington Post* reporter David Broder in the first month of 1983, "is not the midpoint in the Reagan presidency, but its phase-out. 'Reaganism,' it is becoming increasingly clear, was a one-year phenomenon."[1] We know what happened the next year.

And the conservative revolution has had its obituary written many times since. In 1986, Republicans lost the Senate, and shortly thereafter Reagan saw his approval ratings sink as he became embroiled in the Iran-Contra scandal. In 1992, Democrats won back the White House along with both chambers of Congress, and there was widespread talk of "a conservative crackup." It happened again after the public turned on the Republicans following their 1995 government shutdown, and once more after the public rebelled against the Clinton impeachment. By the late 1990s, the Republican revolution had again been written off.

And yet the Republican right keeps coming back, and back, and back. Their fortunes rise and then dip, but each peak is higher than the last peak, and each dip is higher than the last dip. Consider the present situation. Things have gone about as badly as they could have in George W. Bush's second term. A Republican administration started and lost a major war in Iraq; presided over an economy that has failed to deliver higher wages for most Americans; contributed in the aftermath of Hurricane Katrina to the near-wipeout of a major American city; launched a failed assault on Social Security, the most popular social program in the history of the United States; and saw its members suffer an almost unprecedented string of sexual and financial scandals. Still, Democrats find themselves holding only the slimmest of majorities in the House and Senate. Even if they hold their majorities in Congress and win the White House in 2008, the structural forces in Washington will make it nearly impossible to roll back any significant chunks of the Bush tax cuts, let alone take on crises like global warming or the forty-five million Americans lacking health insurance.

Global warming, come to think of it, may offer the best metaphor for understanding the conservative ascent. If you look at the temperature of the earth from month to month, it bounces up and down as seasons change and heat spells or cold snaps come and go. If you look at it over the course of many years, however, it is clear that it is moving inexorably in one direction. The arrival of winter does not mean the end of global warming. To confuse the short-term blips with the long-term trend is to mistake the weather for the climate. The 2006 elections are one of those blips, a pause in the right's three-decade ascent.

Permanent *partisan* majorities are not possible in American politics. Power changes hands regularly. Sometimes the other party's president will preside over an economic boom or win a war. Sometimes yours will preside over a recession or sleep with an intern. Short-term fluctuations, often driven by events beyond the control of the party in power, are inevitable. So the way to win is not to win every election but to control the terms of the debate. The conservative movement's signal triumph is to have done just this, reshaping what is possible in American politics over the long term. This is not, therefore, a book about the political weather. It is a book about the political climate.

MOST PEOPLE UNDER forty fail to grasp how different American politics looked three decades ago. For me, there is no better evidence of the rightward lurch than recalling that my father used to be a Republican. A liberal Republican, to be sure, but a Republican. By the time I was old enough to understand anything about politics, he had long since abandoned the GOP, and at first his former affiliation puzzled me. In the political world in which I came of age — Ronald Reagan left the White House during my junior year of high school — it seemed inconceivable that someone like my dad, who today resides well within the center of the Democratic Party, could identify in any way with the Republicans.

But, of course, as someone my age could not have guessed, the parties of a generation ago bore only a faint resemblance to their modern versions. After World War II, the Republicans accepted the new role of government in American life ushered in by Franklin Roosevelt. The decades after the war saw a great American consensus. Democrats were a bit looser with the purse strings, Republicans a bit tighter, but their general vision of the country was the same. This vision was expressed by the Republican president Dwight Eisenhower just before his inauguration when he declared, "There is, in our affairs at home, a middle way between untrammeled freedom of the individual and the demands for the welfare of the whole nation. This way must avoid government by bureaucracy as carefully as it avoids neglect of the helpless." This credo was the credo of the Republican Party my dad could identify with. He looked up to GOP moderates like Nelson Rockefeller and William Milliken, the long-time governor of our home state of Michigan — men born to privilege who used their power for the benefit of all, not just their own class.

Eisenhower left the top tax rate at a staggering 91 percent, and he repeatedly preached the virtues of budget balance. (When a colleague complained about this confiscatory rate, his treasury secretary, a wealthy former steel executive, replied acidly, "I pay 91 percent, and yet I don't complain and you do all the time."[2] His line reflects a sense of social obligation totally alien to today's GOP.) This tradition of moderate Republicanism remained strong well into the 1970s. A Republican president, Gerald Ford, actually vetoed tax *cuts* proposed by Democrats as fiscally irresponsible.

There were, of course, Republicans of a more conservative bent in those days as well, but conservatism meant something altogether different from what it does today. Indeed, the whole face of American politics has changed. Opposition to deficits, which once made up the right wing of the partisan debate, is now closer to the left wing. ("I hope you're all aware we're all Eisenhower Republicans," Bill Clinton once noted wryly in a Cabinet meeting. "We stand for lower deficits and free trade and the bond market.") Today's right-wing position — upper-bracket tax cuts wherever and whenever possible — was off the right edge of the political spectrum three decades ago.

The ground has shifted very far under our feet, and its manifestations are everywhere. In 1979, the highest-earning one-tenth of 1 percent of all taxpayers — the richest of the rich — took home only 3 percent of the national income. Today they take home 10 percent. And over that same span, their average tax rate has dropped from 32 to 23 percent. The minimum wage has lost nearly half its purchasing power. The health care plan proposed by Richard Nixon in 1974, if introduced in Congress today, would be considered radically liberal and probably could not gain the support of any but a handful of the most left-wing Democrats.

American politics has been transformed, yet in this change lies the deeper mystery. The public has not clamored for it. While it is true that, starting around the late 1960s, polls showed a growing backlash against the welfare state, that backlash petered out during the 1980s and actually began to reverse itself a few years later. Which is to say, the public has actually grown *less* receptive to conservatism in general, let alone the particular upper-class variety practiced by today's GOP.

How do I know this? Here's one example. The National Election Survey has been asking voters for many years whether they would prefer a larger government with more services or a smaller government with fewer services. In 1982, the first year of the poll, 32 percent favored smaller government, and 24 percent preferred larger government (with the remainder right in the middle or expressing no opinion). By 2004, it had completely flipped, with 43 percent preferring bigger government and just 20 percent wanting a smaller one. Other polls have showed that the public has turned away from its antigovernment mood of the 1970s and favored a more active government and more progressive taxes. The public has been moving steadily left for twenty years, while Washington has lurched rapidly in the opposite direction.

This isn't supposed to happen. Abraham Lincoln once said, "Public sentiment is everything. With public sentiment, nothing can fail. Without it, nothing can succeed." This is the core of the American civic religion. But over the last thirty years, something has happened that strikes at that core. The underpinnings of American democracy have slowly frayed, and in the place of the great moderate consensus that once prevailed we have seen the rise of an American plutocracy.

ONE POPULAR EXPLANATION for the triumph of right-wing economics, familiar to readers of Thomas Frank's *What's the Matter with Kansas?*, is that cultural issues have obscured pocketbook ones.

Conservatives have tricked the masses into voting on the basis of social issues, thus ignoring their economic self-interest. It is certainly true that tens of millions of potential Democratic voters support the Republican Party on the basis of its opposition to abortion, gays, and the like. But the phenomenon of conservative elites using culture and patriotism to win support from the masses is an old one. Left-wing populism of the kind that Frank and others favor may have failed to take root because of working-class social conservatism. This does not, however, explain a slightly different question: how and why the economic right has gained so much strength over the last three decades. After all, by nearly any measure, the American public has grown more socially liberal over this span. Since 1977, the proportion of Americans believing gays should be allowed to teach in elementary school has doubled, from 27 to 54 percent. Those favoring gay adoption has risen from 14 to 49 percent.[3] Since 1976, the proportion of Americans who believe women deserve an equal role in business and political life has nearly doubled, from 30 to 57 percent. The proportion who believe that a woman's place is in the home has collapsed from 10 to 2 percent.[4]

If the public is not moving right on economics, and if it is not even moving right on social issues, then we cannot explain the rise of right-wing economics by looking at the voters. We can only understand it by examining Washington.

THIS BOOK HAS two parts. The first half explains how the Republican Party my father admired, the party of social and fiscal responsibility, was transformed into the party of class warfare. It is an astonishing tale, and it begins in the mid-1970s with the rise of a sect of pseudo-economists known as the supply-siders. This small cult of fanatical tax-cutters managed, despite having been proven decisively wrong time after time, to get an iron grip on the ideological machinery of the conservative movement. The supply-siders were not maverick conservative economists, as you might assume; they were amateurs and cranks, convinced that their outsider status enabled them to reach conclusions that had escaped the scrutiny of professional economists. The most prominent among them spent their lives advocating a number of patently ludicrous ideas. (One supply-side guru compared Slobodan Milosevic to Abraham Lincoln. Another said that American upper-class women "are averse to science and technology and baffled by it.") While their other preposterous ideas went nowhere, the equally preposterous notion of supply-side economics took the political system by storm. Why? Because it attracted a powerful constituency: the rich.

An almost theological opposition to taxation quickly took hold within the GOP, opening up the opportunity for business lobbyists to hijack the party's agenda. And so they did, as described in chapter 2. Far from being ideological fanatics, these were the most coolly calculating men. Their distinguishing quality was cynicism. Some of them were flamboyant crooks, like the gangster wannabe Jack Abramoff. But most were crooks of a more respectable variety — the kind with seven-figure salaries and offices at prestigious law firms. All of them understood that the destruction of the old Republican ethos of restraint opened up the public coffers to them, and they have availed themselves and their clients of a massive looting of the Treasury.

Their takeover of the Republican Party took years to complete. The supply-siders and the business lobbyists had two internal obstacles to overcome before they could take full control: the Republican rank-and-file voting base, and the old Republican Washington establishment, both of which still clung to the old ethos of fiscal responsibility and public-mindedness. To deal with them there arose a new breed of ideological enforcer — propagandists, party organizers, lobbyists, or often (as in the case of prototypes like Grover Norquist and Ralph Reed) all of these things at once. They drove out the old party establishment and created a new party line that fused in a seamless web supply-side ideology with their own financial interests.

There is something distinctly cultlike about their thinking. Their canon is presumptively infallible, and any apparent failure must instead be seen as an impetus to recommit themselves to doctrinal purity. Last spring, in an example typical of this thinking, the *Wall Street Journal* columnist Kimberly Strassel diagnosed the Republican Party's ailments thusly: "The base is in the dumps, disenchanted with a party that has lost sight of its economic moorings." The solution? Tax cuts, and lots of them. Strassel ran through how all the leading Republican presidential candidates had pledged their fealty to the governing supply-side faith. Each of them promised to make permanent all of Bush's tax cuts, but of course this was a given. The competition was between which candidate would promise even *deeper* cuts in upper-bracket rates.

As a diagnosis of what ails the Republicans today, this was, of course, insane. Bush signed a major tax cut each of the first six years of his presidency. Whatever the GOP's political liabilities may be, an insufficient commitment to tax-cutting is obviously not among them. To propose that the road to victory lies in recommitting the party to even more upper-bracket tax cuts requires a detachment from reality that would have been the envy of the Manson gang. But this is the sort of thinking that now predominates in conservative and Republican circles, and the obeisance of all the leading GOP presidential hopefuls shows just how deeply it has sunk in.

For such a tiny claque to have conquered a major political party is remarkable in itself, but it is astounding that the extremism of their agenda did not doom the new GOP at the ballot box. Somehow it didn't, and the second half of the book explains why.

In a nutshell, the answer is that the culture of Washington failed. By "culture," of course, I don't mean the Washington Opera or the appalling dearth of good delis inside the Beltway. What I mean is that American politics is governed not only by a series of formal rules but also by a web of mores and beliefs held in place by a permanent establishment. During the bygone era of the great moderate consensus, this culture did a good job of ensuring that parties in power did not veer too far from the common good. The press corps trod a careful middle path between Republicans and Democrats, lending equal credence to each side's claims. The Washington elites made sure their leaders were men of sound character. They relied on each branch of government to limit overreach by the others, and they assumed a middle ground between the two parties would reflect a sensible consensus.

All these cultural norms made sense when the Republican Party was run by pragmatists driven by a strong sense of the public good. But they no longer apply because the plutocracy has perverted the ground on which those norms depend. It has made journalistic even-handedness into dishonesty's handmaiden. It has taken control of the way Americans see the personal character of their leaders and used that distorted lens to hide the unpopularity of the plutocratic agenda. It has abused the power of whatever branches of government it has controlled, and it has stymied any measures of accountability. And ultimately the cherished notions of moderation and bipartisanship have become tools of radicalism.

As I said at the outset, this is not a radical book. It is a book about the disappearance of the center and the triumph of the extreme. And it is not a conspiratorial book. Everything I describe here happened out in the open, in plain view. But it happened so slowly and with enough obscurantist jargon that it escaped the notice of nearly everyone. This is the story of how it happened.

PART I

THE TRANSFORMATION
OF THE
REPUBLICAN PARTY

1

CHARLATANS AND CRANKS

For many, many years, Republican economics was relentlessly sober. Republicans concerned themselves with such ills as deficits, inflation, and excessive spending. They did not care very much about cutting taxes, and (as in the case of such GOP presidents as Herbert Hoover and Gerald Ford) they were quite willing to raise taxes in order to balance the budget. By temperament, such men were cautious rather than utopian. Over the last three decades, however, such Republicans have passed almost completely from the scene, at least in Washington, to be replaced by, essentially, a cult.

All sects have their founding myths, many of them involving circumstances quite mundane. The cult in question generally traces its political origins to a meeting in Washington in late 1974 between Arthur Laffer, an economic consultant, Jude Wanniski, an editorial page writer for the *Wall Street Journal,* and Dick Cheney, then chief of staff to President Ford. Wanniski, an eccentric and highly excitable man, had until the previous few years no training in economics whatsoever, but he had taken Laffer's tutelage. His choice of mentor was certainly unconventional. Laffer had been an economics professor at the University of Chicago since 1967. In 1970 his mentor, George Shultz, brought him to Washington to serve as a staffer in the Office of Management and Budget. Laffer quickly suffered a bout with infamy when he made a wildly unconventional calculation about the size of the 1971 Gross Domestic Product. President Nixon seized on Laffer's number, which was far more optimistic than estimates elsewhere, because it conveniently suggested an economic boom under his watch. When it was discovered that Laffer had used just four variables to arrive at his figure — most economists used hundreds if not thousands of inputs — he became a Washington laughingstock. Indeed, he turned out to be horribly wrong. Laffer left the government in disgrace and faced the scorn of his former academic colleagues yet stayed in touch with Wanniski, (who died in 2005), whom he had met in Washington, and continued to tutor him in economics.[1]

Starting in 1972, Wanniski came to believe that Laffer had developed a blinding new insight that turned established economic wisdom on its head. Wanniski and Laffer believed it was possible to simultaneously expand the economy and tamp down inflation by cutting taxes, especially the high tax rates faced by upper-income earners. Respectable economists — not least among them conservative ones — considered this laughable. Wanniski, though, was ever more certain of its truth. He promoted this radical new doctrine through his perch on the *Wall Street Journal* editorial page and in articles for the *Public Interest,* a journal published by the neoconservative godfather Irving Kristol. Yet Wanniski's new doctrine, later to be called supply-side economics, had failed to win much of a following beyond a tiny circle of adherents.

That fateful night, Wanniski and Laffer were laboring with little success to explain the new theory to Cheney. Laffer pulled out a cocktail napkin and drew a parabola-shaped curve on it. The premise of the curve was simple. If the government sets a tax rate of zero, it will receive no revenue. And if the government sets a tax rate of

100 percent, the government will also receive zero tax revenue, since nobody will have any reason to earn any income. Between these two points — zero taxes and zero revenue, 100 percent taxes and zero revenue — Laffer's curve drew an arc. The arc suggested that at higher levels of taxation, reducing the tax rate would produce more revenue for the government.

At that moment, there were a few points that Cheney might have made in response. First, he could have noted that the Laffer Curve was not, strictly speaking, correct. Yes, a zero tax rate would obviously produce zero revenue, but the assumption that a 100 percent tax rate would also produce zero revenue was just as obviously false. Surely Cheney was familiar with communist states such as the Soviet Union, with its 100 percent tax rate. The Soviet revenue scheme may not have represented the cutting edge in economic efficiency, but it nonetheless managed to collect enough revenue to maintain an enormous military, enslave Eastern Europe, fund ambitious projects such as Sputnik, and so on. Second, Cheney could have pointed out that even if the Laffer Curve was correct in theory, there was no evidence that the U.S. income tax was on the downward slope of the curve — that is, that rates were then high enough that tax cuts would produce higher revenue.

But Cheney did not say either of these things. Perhaps, in retrospect, this was due to something deep in Cheney's character that makes him unusually susceptible to theories or purported data that confirm his own ideological predilections. (You can almost picture Donald Rumsfeld, years later, scrawling a diagram for Cheney on a cocktail napkin showing that only a small number of troops would be needed to occupy Iraq.) In any event, Cheney apparently found the Laffer Curve a revelation, for it presented in a simple, easily digestible form the messianic power of tax cuts. The significance of the evening was not the conversion of Cheney but the creation of a powerful symbol that could spread the word of supply-side economics. If you try to discuss economic theory with most politicians, their eyes will glaze over. But the Curve explained it all. There in that sloping parabola was the magical promise of that elusive politician's nirvana: a cost-free path to prosperity: lower taxes, higher revenues. It was beautiful, irresistible.

With astonishing speed, the message of the Laffer Curve spread through the ranks of conservatives and Republicans. Wanniski evangelized tirelessly on behalf of this new doctrine, both on the *Journal's* editorial pages and in person. As an example of the latter, one day in 1976 he wandered by the office of a young congressman named Jack Kemp. He asked to talk to Kemp for fifteen minutes, but he wound up expounding on the supply-side gospel to the former NFL quarterback for the rest of the day, through dinner, and late into the night. "He took to it like a blotter," Wanniski later recalled. "I was exhausted and ecstatic. I had finally found an elected representative of the people who was as fanatical as I was."[2] Adherents of supply-side economics tend to describe the spread of their creed in quasi-religious terms. Irving Kristol subsequently wrote in a memoir, "It was Jude [Wanniski] who introduced me to Jack Kemp, a young congressman and recent convert. It was Jack Kemp who, almost single-handedly, converted Ronald Reagan."[3]

The theological language is fitting because supply-side economics is not merely an economic program. It's a totalistic ideology. The core principle is that economic performance hinges almost entirely on how much incentive investors and entrepreneurs have to attain more wealth, and this incentive in turn hinges almost entirely on their tax rate. Therefore, cutting taxes — especially those of the rich, who carry out the decisive entrepreneurial role in the economy — is always a good idea. But what, you may ask, about deficits, the old Republican bugaboo? Supply-siders argue either that tax cuts will produce enough growth to wipe out deficits or that deficits simply don't matter. When Reagan first adopted supply-side economics, even many Republicans considered it lunacy. ("Voodoo economics," George H. W. Bush famously called it.) Today, though, the core beliefs of the supply-siders are not even subject to question among Republicans. Every major conservative opinion outlet promotes supply-side economics. Since Bush's heresy of acceding to a small tax hike in 1990, deviation from the supply-side creed has become unthinkable for any Republican with national aspirations. The full capitulation of the old fiscal conservatives was probably best exemplified by Bob Dole, the crusty old Kansan once thought synonymous with the traditional midwestern conservatism of the GOP. Early on, Dole had openly scorned the supply-siders. "People who advocate only cutting taxes live in a dream world," he said in 1982. "We Republicans have been around awhile. We don't have to march in lockstep with the supply-siders."[4] By the time he had risen high enough in the party to gain its presidential nomination, Dole had no choice but to embrace the Laffer Curve. He chose Jack Kemp, an original supply-side evangelist, as his running mate and made a 15 percent tax cut the centerpiece of his campaign.

George W. Bush's fidelity to tax-cutting runs even deeper. He took as his chief economic adviser Larry Lindsey, a fervent supply-sider, whose book *The Growth Experiment* defended Reagan's tax cuts. He picked as his running mate yet another original supply-sider in Cheney, who summed up the new consensus by declaring (according to the former treasury secretary Paul O'Neill), "Reagan proved deficits don't matter."[5] Bush has poured every ounce of his political capital into cutting taxes, having signed four tax cuts during his administration; when fully phased in, they will reduce federal revenues by about $400 billion a year. Bush and his staff repeatedly tout tax cuts as an all-purpose cure-all. Bush can endorse even the most radical supply-side claims — "the deficit would have been bigger without the tax-relief package," he asserts regularly — without raising eyebrows.[6] So deeply entrenched is the devotion to supply-side theory that even in the face of large deficits and a protracted war, not a single Republican of any standing has dared broach the possibility of rolling back some of Bush's tax cuts.

CRANKERY MADE UNDERSTANDABLE

Like most crank doctrines, supply-side economics has at its core a central insight that does have a ring of plausibility. The government can't simply raise tax rates as high as it wants without some adverse consequences. And there have been periods in American history when, nearly any contemporary economist would agree, top tax rates were too high, such as the several decades after World War II. And there are justifiable conservative arguments to be made on behalf of reducing tax rates and government spending. But what sets the supply-siders apart from sensible economists is their sheer monomania. Indeed, the original supply-siders believed — and many of them, including their disciples at places like the *Wall Street Journal* editorial page, continue to believe — that they have not merely altered established economic thinking but completely overturned it.

Let me explain this as quickly and painlessly as possible. Traditional (or, as it was called, "neoclassical") economics held that markets were perfectly rational and inherently self-correcting. According to this view, if the economy entered a recession, it merely reflected a needed correction by which wages would fall to their natural level, after which things would return to normal. During the Great Depression, this complacent view became less and less tenable. That's when John Maynard Keynes argued that recessions often reflect a failure of demand for goods and services. Keynes endorsed government measures — such as reducing interest rates or deliberate deficit spending — in order to put more money into circulation under such circumstances. Since then, traditional conservative and liberal economists have debated exactly what causes expansions and recessions, with different schools of thought placing more or less emphasis on different factors, like the money supply, deficits, the global economy, and so on.

Pure supply-siders, on the other hand, see changes in tax rates as the single driver of all economic change. What caused the Great Depression? Mainstream economists blame different factors to various degrees, but supply-siders insist that the single cause was the 1930 Smoot-Hawley Tariff. (The tariff surely added to America's economic woes, but to blame a higher tax on imports, which accounted for just 6 percent of the economy, for causing the entire economy to contract by a third is just plain loopy.) Likewise, most economists pinned the 1991 recession on mistakes by the Federal Reserve, but supply-siders blame George H. W. Bush's tax hike. Bush raised the top tax rate from 28 to 31 percent. To think that a three-percentage-point jump in the top tax rate would discourage entrepreneurs and investors enough to tip the entire economy into recession requires attributing to tax rates powers bordering on magical.

Indeed, it doesn't take a great deal of expertise to see how implausible this sort of analysis is. All you need is a cursory bit of history. From 1947 to 1973, the U.S. economy grew at a rate of nearly 4 percent a year — a massive boom, fueling rapid growth in living standards across the board. During most of that period, from 1947 until 1964, the highest tax rate was 91 percent. For the rest of the time, it was still a hefty 70 percent. Yet the economy flourished anyway.

None of this is to say that those high tax rates *caused* the postwar boom. On the contrary, the economy probably expanded despite, rather than because of, those high rates. Almost no contemporary economist would endorse jacking up rates that high again. But the point is that, whatever negative effect such high tax rates have, it's relatively minor. Which necessarily means that whatever effects today's tax rates have, they're even *more* minor.

This can be seen with some very simple arithmetic. As just noted, Truman, Eisenhower, and Kennedy taxpayers in the top bracket had to pay a 91 percent rate. That meant that if they were contemplating, say, a new investment, they'd be able to keep just 9 cents of every dollar they earned, a stiff disincentive. When that rate dropped down to 70 percent, our top earner could now keep 30 cents of every new dollar. That more than tripled the profitability of any new dollar — a 233 percent increase, to be exact. That's a hefty incentive boost. In 1981, the top tax rate dropped again to 50 percent. The profit on every new dollar therefore rose from 30 to 50 cents, a 67 percent increase. In 1986, the top rate dropped again, from 50 to 28 percent. The profit on every dollar rose from 50 to 72 cents, a 44 percent increase. Note that the marginal improvement of every new tax cut is less than that of the previous one. But we're still talking about large numbers. Increasing the profitability of a new investment even by 44 percent is nothing to sneeze at.[7]

But then George Bush raised the top rate to 31 percent in 1990. This meant that instead of taking home 72 cents on every new dollar earned, those in the top bracket had to settle for 69 cents. That's a drop of about 4 percent — peanuts, compared to the scale of previous changes. Yet supply-siders reacted hysterically. The *National Review*, to offer one example, noted fearfully that, in the wake of this small tax hike, the dollar had fallen against the yen and the German mark. "It seems," its editors concluded, "that capital is flowing out of the United States to nations where 'from each according to his ability, to each according to his need' has lost its allure."[8]

Here is where a bit of historical perspective helps. If such a piddling tax increase could really wreck such havoc on the economy, how is it possible that the economy grew so rapidly with top tax rates of 70 and 91 percent? The answer is, it's not. It's not even *close* to possible. All this is to say that the supply-siders have taken the germ of a decent point — that marginal tax rates matter — and stretched it, beyond all plausibility, into a monocausal explanation of the world.

CHARLATANS AND CRANKS

It is difficult for most of us to get our minds around the fact that American economic policy has been taken over by sheer loons. Economists, after all, are a fairly sober lot. Even if they're wrong, we tend to assume that their theories have at least undergone some fairly grueling academic scrutiny before they even reach the point of becoming a theory in the first place. So if supply-side economics is so off the wall, how could it have survived this review process in the first place?

The answer is, it didn't. In his excellent 1994 book, *Peddling Prosperity*, the Princeton economist Paul Krugman wrote: "Not only is there no major department that is supply-side in orientation; there is no economist whom one might call a supply-sider in any major [economics] department."[9] To be sure, economics departments are filled with conservatives who very much favor smaller government. But none of them share the basic supply-side view that tax rates, more or less alone, determine the fate of the economy. Nor do they believe that, in anything resembling the present environment, tax cuts can spur enough growth to pay for themselves. Conservative economists do believe that tax cuts can create some increase in growth, but that belief is almost always predicated on a corresponding cut in spending.

Perhaps the most aggressive support for tax-cutting from a bonafide economist comes from Greg Mankiw, a Harvard economist who led the Council of Economic Advisors under George W. Bush. Mankiw estimated that a perfectly crafted tax cut on capital, matched by spending cuts, could over the very long run encourage enough growth to pay for half its cost. This is far, far more modest than the supply-side claim that broad-based tax cuts, without corresponding spending cuts, can encourage enough growth to recoup their *entire* cost, *within a few years.*[10] Indeed, Mankiw himself wrote an economics textbook in which he discussed supply-siders in a chapter called "Charlatans and Cranks" and compared them to a "snake-oil salesman."[11]

So if supply-side economics did not come out of the economics profession, where did it originate? It emerged from the writings and discussions of Laffer, Wanniski, and the late *Wall Street Journal* editorial page editor Robert Bartley. Those three did not do the kinds of things that real economists do, such as write academic papers or submit their findings to peer review. Instead they wrote editorials and columns or sometimes longer articles for magazines like Irving Kristol's *The Public Interest*. Now, I'm a journalist myself, and obviously I see nothing wrong with journalists writing about economic policy. But Wanniski, Bartley, and their crowd were not merely commenting on economic policy; they were claiming to have disproven the collective wisdom of the economics establishment.

The sole true academic economist among the supply-siders is one Robert Mundell of Columbia. Mundell is undoubtedly brilliant; he recently won a Nobel Prize for his work on international currency exchanges in the 1960s. But he essentially withdrew from the normal academic channels before he began championing supply-side theory. As Krugman noted:

> The fact is that around 1970 Mundell veered off from conventionality in a number of ways. . . . Mundell dropped out of the usual academic round of conferences and seminars, and began holding his own conferences in a crumbling, half-habitable villa he owned near Siena. Most important, Mundell completely abandoned his former academic intellectual style; since 1970 he has written little, and what he has written tends to be marked by extravagant rhetoric, accusing his fellow economists of "sheer quackery" in espousing ideas that he himself had held when younger.[12]

The supply-siders allied with Mundell saw his renegade status not as a troubling sign of instability but as a mark of genius. "At a later White House meeting, Mundell tried to explain his policy mix to establishment economists, as he had earlier at a 1971 conference of economists in Bologna," Bartley later wrote. "But the ideas he expressed, recounted in this volume, were so out of the mainstream not even the most eminent economists could follow them." One suspects that the eminent economists actually *could* follow Mundell's ideas; they simply didn't accept them, though this possibility seems not to have occurred to Bartley. For supply-siders, the hostility of authorities merely deepens their own sense of certainty. While most people would regard with some distrust a theory that has been rejected by the experts but embraced by politicians, the supply-siders consider it a badge of honor. As Bartley boasted, "Economists still ridicule the Laffer Curve, but policymakers pay it careful heed."[13]

Aside from popular articles in places like the *Journal's* editorial page, two classic tomes defined the tenets of supply-side economics: Wanniski's *The Way the World Works* and George Gilder's 1981 manifesto, *Wealth and Poverty*. Both have had enormous influence, and both capture the feverish grandiosity that is the hallmark of the Laffer Curve acolytes. Here is what makes the rise of supply-side ideology even more baffling. One might expect that a radical ideology that successfully passed itself off as a sophisticated new doctrine would at least have the benefit of smooth, reassuring, intellectual front men, men whose very bearing could attest to the new doctrine's eminent good sense and mainstream bona fides. Yet if you look at its two most eminent authors, good sense is not the impression you get. Let me put this delicately. No, on second thought, let me put it straightforwardly: they are deranged.

Gilder was not an economist when he wrote *Wealth and Poverty*. Until then he was known primarily for having written a pair of antifeminist tracts, and his notoriety derived mainly from his penchant for making comments such as "There is no such thing as a reasonably intelligent feminist."[14] *Wealth and Poverty*, though, launched him as an eminent defender of supply-side economics just as adherents of the new creed had been catapulted into power. Gilder articulated the new philosophy of the Reagan era in admirably straightforward fashion. "To help the poor and middle classes," he wrote, "one must cut the taxes of the rich." In reflecting the new prestige Republicans wished to see afforded the rich, Gilder defended capitalists as not merely necessary or even heroic but altruistic. "Like gifts, capitalist investments are made without a predetermined return," he wrote.[15] In fact, while capitalists may not be sure of their exact return, they do expect to make more than they put in, which makes an investment *unlike* a gift in a fairly crucial way. Yet there was enough of an audience for such sentiments that Gilder's book sold more than a million copies. President Reagan handed the book to friends, and advisers such as David Stockman hailed its "Promethean" insight. "*Wealth and Poverty*," reported the *New York Times*, "has been embraced by Washington with a warmth not seen since the Kennedys adopted John Kenneth Galbraith."

From the beginning, Gilder betrayed signs of erratic thought, and not merely in his misogyny. In a 1981 interview with the *Washington Post*, he declared:

> ESP is important to me. I learned that it absolutely exists. A roommate and I were sharing an apartment, and another man in the building was a psychic. He taught me how to do it. The single most striking trick I learned how to do was cutting for the queen of spades in a deck of cards. I got so I could do it time after time. Once somebody put two queens in the pack, and it fell open to both of them. I had hundreds of experiences of that sort during that period. The trick is that you have to have faith.[16]

In the mid-1980s, Gilder's career took an abrupt turn. He became fascinated with microprocessors and took time off to learn the physics of the new technology. This led him, by the mid-1990s, to stake out a position as the most wild-eyed of the technology utopians who flourished during that period, and he ended up publishing a newsletter that offered stock tips. Some of his pronouncements were obviously crazy even at the time. These would include his advice to short Microsoft stock in 1997, his claim that Global Crossing (now bankrupt) "will change the world economy," and general techno-giddiness, such as his claim that, because of online learning, within five years "the most deprived ghetto child in the most benighted project will gain educational opportunities exceeding those of today's suburban preppy."[17]

In the fevered stock bubble of the 1990s, though, some of Gilder's prognostications seemed to pan out, at least for a while, and his newsletter attracted a subscription base of $20 million, making him fabulously rich. In 2000, Gilder used some of his lucre to purchase the *American Spectator,* a monthly conservative magazine best known for investigating the details of President Clinton's personal indiscretions, both real and imagined. Gilder turned the *Spectator* into a shrine to Gilderism, a fusion of supply-side utopianism and techno-utopianism. He installed his cousin as editor and ran both a lengthy excerpt as well as a favorable review of his own book.

The crowning touch of Gilder's ownership was a lengthy interview with himself in the June 2001 issue. Among other musings on display were Gilder's familiar ruminations on feminism: "Christie Whitman is an upper-class American woman . . . almost none of them have any comprehension of the environment. Almost all of them are averse to science and technology and baffled by it." His financial success seemed to have propelled Gilder to even greater heights of hubris, his Promethean insights greeted by his employees with awed deference:

> TAS: In the late 1970s and early '80s, you led the intellectual debate on sexual issues from the conservative side. In the 1980s your book *Wealth and Poverty* transformed the way people thought about capitalism. And then you wandered off to study transistors. Why did you do that?

GILDER: I thought I had won those debates. Whenever I actively debated anybody, they didn't have any interesting arguments anymore, so I thought I should learn something I didn't know about.

In presenting the interview with their boss, the *Spectator*'s editors promised: "An equally wide-ranging talk with George will be an annual event."[18] Alas, it never recurred. As the tech bubble burst, Gilder and his investors found their wealth spiraling downward. Despite Gilder's frantic reassurances — "Your current qualms will seem insignificant," he promised in mid-2001 — his subscribers deserted him. In 2002 he confessed to *Wired* magazine that he was broke and had a lien against his home.[19] "Most subscribers came in at the top of the market," Gilder later explained, "So the modal experience of the Gilder Technology Newsletter subscriber was to lose virtually all of his money. That stigma has been very hard to overcome." Nonetheless, Gilder soldiers on. Today he champions the theory of intelligent design. Once again, he can see the truth that has eluded all the so-called experts.[20]

Who could have foreseen such a tragic downfall? Actually, there was one man visionary enough to presage Gilder's fate: Gilder himself. In *Wealth and Poverty*, one of Gilder's arguments for more sympathetic treatment of the rich held that "the vast majority of America's fortunes are dissipated within two generations . . . In a partial sense, a rich man represents a gambler betting against the house."[21] This is a terribly inapt description of the American economy. (It is the rare homeless shelter that caters to descendants of the Rockefeller or Morgan family fortunes.) But it turned out to be a precise description of Gilder's own fortune. Wealth and poverty, indeed.

AS INFLUENTIAL AS Gilder and his book were, they were not nearly as influential in legitimating supply-side theory as Wanniski or his book. This isn't terribly reassuring, though, because Wanniski makes Gilder look like the model of sobriety. The literary and intellectual style of *The Way the World Works* is immediately familiar to anybody who has ever worked at a political magazine. It is the manifesto of the misunderstood autodidact — an essay purporting to have interpreted history in a completely novel and completely correct way, or to have discovered the key to eternal prosperity and world peace, or some equally sweeping claim. *The Way the World Works* fits precisely into this category, except that rather than being scrawled longhand on sheaves of notebook paper and mass-mailed to journalists, it was underwritten by the American Enterprise Institute, has been published in four editions, and features introductions attesting to its genius from such luminaries as Bartley and the columnist and ubiquitous pundit Robert Novak.

For supply-side evangelists, there is almost nothing that their theory cannot explain. For instance, in his book Wanniski uses the Laffer Curve as a model for all of human development, beginning with young babies:

> Even the infant learns to both act and think on the margin when small changes in behavior result in identifiable "price changes." The infant learns, for example, something that politicians and economists frequently forget, which is that there are always two rates of taxation that produce the same revenue. When the infant lies silently and motionless in his crib upon awakening, mother remains in some other room. The "tax rate" on mother is zero, yielding zero attentiveness. On the other hand, when the baby screams all the time demanding attention, even when fed and dry, he discovers that mother also remains in the other room and perhaps even closes the nursery door. The tax rate is 100 percent, also yielding zero attentiveness.

Parents, too, must abide by the Curve:

> The parent who does not understand that there are two tax rates that yield the same revenue is a poor political leader in the family unit, and should not be surprised if the prohibitively taxed infant

rebels in one way or another — becoming an incorrigible terror (revolutionary) or withdrawing into himself (the only form of emigration open to a child).

This thought produces a footnote: "The wise ruler will never surround his adversaries with 'no-nos.'" Wanniski then runs through a number of historical rulers wise and unwise, concluding with his observation that "Kennedy's determination to box in Cuba, which included plans to assassinate Fidel Castro, left Castro no avenue but the assassination of Kennedy."[22]

Apparently nothing in human history defies Wanniski's attempts to involve the Laffer Curve. He goes on to write: "When Hitler came to power in 1933, fascinated with Mussolini's syndicalist style, he — like Roosevelt — left tax rates where he found them." Can you see where this is going? Yes: "Although he left the explicit tax rates high, [Germany] did chip away at the domestic and international wedges. The economy expanded, but in so distorted a fashion that it compressed the tension between agriculture and industry into an explosive problem that Hitler sought to solve through *Lebensraum*, or conquest [*sic*]."[23] You, dear reader, may have thought that Nazi ideology led to the invasion of Poland, but thanks to Wanniski, you can see that the underlying cause turns out to have been high taxes. (It is amazing that Bill Clinton's tax hike did not lead him to invade Canada.)

Republicans did not find these obvious signs of wingnuttery troubling. Indeed, Wanniski's book hastened his astonishingly rapid rise. Five years before he wrote his book, Wanniski knew nothing about economics. Within a few years he had formulated a new creed and sold it to a series of powerful opinion leaders and politicians. By 1977, the Republican National Committee formally called for an across-the-board tax cut modeled on the one proposed by Wanniski's closest disciple, Jack Kemp. The next year, Congress enacted a capital gains tax cut that he lobbied for in the halls of the

Capitol and championed in the *Journal*'s columns. Two years after the publication of his book, Wanniski found himself advising Ronald Reagan, who ran for president on ideas Wanniski had devised. But in time the same qualities that made him such an effective evangelist for supply-side economics — his gregariousness, his naiveté, his absolute faith in his own correctness, and his ability to persuade others of the same — did him in. Wanniski gave an interview in 1980 about the battle for Reagan's mind among his advisers, all but openly saying that the candidate was a creature of his staff. This brought about his quick expulsion from the inner circle.[24] In 1995, fearing that the supply-side agenda was stagnating, Wanniski came up with the idea of persuading Steve Forbes, the millionaire publisher and Laffer Curve devotee, to run for president. After Wanniski lashed out at the Christian Coalition strategist Ralph Reed, though, he became a liability to the campaign he had created and was shut out. The next year, after the GOP nominee Bob Dole named his acolyte Jack Kemp to share his ticket, Wanniski again won a place of influence.

It was around this time that Wanniski's nuttiness began manifesting itself in ways that even conservatives could recognize. Wanniski began meeting with and defending Louis Farrakhan, the head of the Nation of Islam, explaining, "I expressed my belief that Jewish leaders fear he could lead the black electorate away from the Democratic Party and into opposition of support for Israel." And Farrakhan is far from the only unsavory character Wanniski embraced. He likened Slobodan Milosevic to Abraham Lincoln.[25] He met with the lunatic conspiracy theorist and convicted felon Lyndon LaRouche and hired a number of his followers at his economic consulting firm. ("[T]hey're not trained in demand-model economics," he explained to *Business Week* with undeniable logic.)[26] And Wanniski championed Saddam Hussein, even to the point of denying that the late Iraqi dictator had ever used chemical weapons against the Kurds. ("There is no possibility that Saddam gassed his own people," he wrote.)[27]

Such statements, combined with his erratic behavior, eventually made Wanniski an outcast within the GOP. His expulsion from the party's good graces was consecrated, in a sense, by a series of short editorial items in the conservative *Weekly Standard* in the mid-1990s, ridiculing his nutty views on Farrakhan and Iraq. But while Wanniski himself is remembered as a nut by most conservatives, his primary doctrine has lost none of its influence. The *Standard* continues to publish editorials saying such things as "the supply-side Laffer Curve has worked." So Wanniski is now viewed as a nut on all matters save the very thing that is the font from which all his nuttiness springs. His personal influence has never been lower, but his ideological influence has never been greater. "It is no exaggeration to say that the recent history of the United States would have been far different were it not for Jude Wanniski," wrote Novak.[28] The scary thing is that he's right.

HOW DID THIS HAPPEN?

The cartoonist Matt Groening wrote a book called *School Is Hell* in which he identified, among the various types of professors you encounter, the "Single-Theory-to-Explain-Everything Maniac." (Groening portrays a professor spouting: "The nation that controls magnesium controls the universe!") There are, and have long been, countless such cranks throughout the land insistently disseminating their monomaniacal theories. Why, though, did this *particular* monomaniacal theory — supply-side economics — move so rapidly from the fringes into the centers of power?

A few factors enabled this remarkable ascent. The first is fortuitous timing. From World War II until about 1973, Keynesian economics ruled almost unchallenged in a time of prosperity. Keynesians thought they had a strong handle on how the economy worked. One of their beliefs was that inflation and unemployment worked in opposite directions — when lots of people had jobs, they tended to bid up wages, causing general prices to rise. When employment fell, the opposite happened, and inflation tended to fall as well. Mainstream economists believed the correlation between the two was so strong that it could be measured almost scientifically. Managing the economy, therefore, was a relatively simple matter of steering a middle course between excessive inflation on the one hand and excessive unemployment on the other.

The 1970s, however, deeply shook this view. Unemployment and inflation began rising in tandem — a phenomenon called "stagflation." In hindsight, economists don't find this so puzzling anymore. Stagflation resulted from the confluence of a number of unfortunate events, most notably the oil shock after the 1973 Arab-Israeli war. But as a result, economists no longer have total confidence in their ability to measure the opposing effects of unemployment and inflation. They do, however, agree on a general relationship. That's why the Federal Reserve today still sets interest rates on the assumption that the economy should grow as fast as possible without triggering inflation. During the 1970s, though, stagflation threw into question the wisdom of the economics profession. The establishment had no answer for what was ailing the economy. Listening to a bunch of radicals who claimed that the economics establishment was completely wrong, then, didn't seem so crazy.

Second, supply-side economics offered Republicans a potentially very appealing way to win votes. Before supply-siders took control of the GOP in the late 1970s, Democrats tended to favor higher spending and lower taxes in the hopes of boosting growth while Republicans fretted about deficits and inflation. The Laffer

Curve held out the possibility of handing tax cuts to the voters without fretting about the resulting deficits. The GOP would be transformed into the party of Santa Claus, with Democrats, if they stood in the way, stuck playing the Grinch. The political seductiveness of this prospect meant that not all conservatives cared whether their new theory was actually true. Irving Kristol, the conservative intellectual who arranged funding for a number of supply-side tracts, including *The Way the World Works,* has been remarkably candid on this point, at least in retrospect. Kristol recalled that when Wanniski tried to convert him to supply-side economics, "I was not certain of its economic merits but quickly saw its political possibilities." And in 1995 Kristol breezily confessed in an article: "The task, as I saw it, was to create a new majority, which evidently would mean a conservative majority, which came to mean, in turn, a Republican majority, so political effectiveness was the priority, not the accounting deficiencies of government."[29]

Third, supply-side economics had a particular appeal for the rich, who stood to reap immediate dividends in the form of tax cuts. There's not a large natural constituency for a magnesium-centric view of the world. There are, however, lots of rich people, and they are in a position to publish newspapers and magazines promoting their point of view. The lesson for cranks everywhere is that your theory stands a stronger chance of success if it directly benefits a rich and powerful bloc, and there's no bloc richer and more powerful than the rich and powerful.

Finally, supply-siders benefited from the fact that few people understand economics. Utterly deluded though they may be, they express themselves in economic jargon that few Americans, even intellectuals, can judge. Debates between supply-siders and advocates of mainstream economics appear, to outsiders, like technical disputes between experts with equally valid points of view. Crackpot economic theories thus enjoy an inherent advantage over other sorts of crackpot theories because it's harder for ordinary people (or even elites) to recognize the lunacy.

DESPITE ALL EVIDENCE TO THE CONTRARY

The rise of supply-side economics, then, is remarkable enough. But the truly mind-blowing thing is its continued political vitality. After all, it's one thing to take a flier on an unproven new theory, especially when the status quo isn't working. It's quite another to embrace this theory ever more tightly when it has been conclusively disproven. Knowing what we do about the supply-siders, though, we shouldn't find this surprising. One of the hallmarks of cult thinking is, after all, an uncanny ability to explain away inconvenient facts.

The first such facts were the large deficits that appeared immediately after Ronald Reagan took office. The most confident supply-siders had predicted that Reagan's cuts would not cause a loss in revenue. As Gilder put it, "A cut in marginal rates, which Kemp-Roth [the basis for Reagan's tax cut] would accomplish, would generate enough new revenue to eliminate the deficit or reduce it to manageable size."[30] Even mainstream Republicans insisted that Reagan's numbers added up. No less an eminence than Alan Greenspan, even then respected for his sagacity, vouchsafed that "this is an exercise in reasonable budget making."[31] Very quickly, though, the deficit exploded — first past $100 billion, then past $200 billion — and those outside Reagan's budget process suspected a connection between the red ink and Reagan's mixture of tax cuts with higher defense spending. Indeed, many Reaganites did, too. David Stockman, Reagan's budget director, wrote in 1986: "By 1982, I knew the Reagan Revolution was impossible," at which point he addressed himself to "reducing the size of the nation's fiscal disaster."[32]

The true believers begged to differ. In fact, conservatives have constructed an entire cottage industry devoted to rehabilitating Reagan's fiscal record. The apologias, many of them running to book length, are tedious, but a few basic themes recur. First, they blame the deficits on a spendthrift Democratic Congress. The difficulty with this line of defense is that Congress spent virtually the same amount of money that Reagan proposed in his budgets. More problematically, conservatives also like to credit Reagan's tax cuts for reining in spending, which, obviously, is hard to reconcile with the high-spending Congress excuse.[33]

Next, conservatives insist that tax revenues actually did rise under Reagan. And in a literal sense this is true: as the *Wall Street Journal* editorial page writer and supply-side propagandist Stephen Moore triumphantly declared: "From 1982 to 1989 income tax receipts climbed from $298 billion to $446 billion — a 50 percent increase."[34] But this is like saying that your policy of feeding your children nothing but marshmallows for six months has been proven correct and healthful because your children have continued to grow. It's a meaningless measure. In any growing economy, tax revenues will tend to rise in nominal dollars — from inflation alone, if nothing else. The more accurate measure of revenue growth is as a percentage of the economy, and by that count revenues dropped under Reagan.

Supply-siders reply to this by insisting that the economy grew solely because of Reagan's supply-side magic. But the truth is that the economy wasn't actually all that impressive during the 1980s. Basically, the Federal Reserve, in a successful effort to break the back of inflation, hiked interest rates and induced a severe recession in 1982. The economy began recovering the next year and expanded steadily until around 1990. While conservatives portray this period as a kind of Eden of unprecedented prosperity, it was in fact just a normal business cycle recovery: the economy grew very fast mainly because the recession had been so severe. Idle employees and machines returned to work, but the underlying productivity growth — that is, how much each worker could produce, which is the main way living standards ultimately rise — didn't increase much over the bad old 1970s.

The supply-siders disagree because they fundamentally don't believe in the business cycle. They think booms and busts result from changes in tax policy — and only from changes in tax policy. So, ludicrous though this interpretation of the 1980s may be, in a funny kind of way it holds together. If you accept their irrational premises about the all-consuming power of tax rates, you can't help but conclude that Reagan's policies worked after all. The supply-side view of the world wasn't utterly and irrevocably obliterated until Bill Clinton's presidency.

A COMPLETE AND TOTAL REFUTATION

When they took power in 1993, Clinton and his staff fretted about the large deficits they had inherited, as well as the growing gap between rich and poor. So they decided to make their top economic priority reducing the deficit through restrictions on spending and a hike in the top income tax rate, paid by those who earned more than $200,000 a year, from 31 to 39.6 percent. The battle over this plan set up a clear and direct confrontation between supply-side economics and Clinton's New Democrat economics. The Clintonites believed that reducing the deficit would add to future wealth by reducing the debts that future generations inherited. (By 1993, interest on the national debt accounted for 14 percent of the federal budget.)[35] They also believed that deficit reduction might pay economic dividends relatively soon. Reducing the amount of money the government borrowed would free up investment capital for private savings, reduce interest rates, and eventually make business more productive.

The supply-siders were absolutely certain Clinton's plan would fail. According to their view of the world, deficits matter very little. Raising tax rates would discourage work and investment, causing economic growth to shrink, and ultimately causing tax revenues to wither. The most respectable iteration of this view came from Martin Feldstein, a conservative Harvard economist. Feldstein is a legitimate academic who accepts the tenets of mainstream economics, but he is close to the supply-siders in that he has an unusually high estimation of the effects of tax rates on the rich. This viewpoint has made him an influential conduit to Republican politicians: Bush's top two economic advisers, Lawrence Lindsey and Glenn Hubbard, were both Feldstein protégés. And Feldstein's Harvard credentials give his opinions a resonance that extends beyond GOP circles. Therefore, when he repeatedly wrote things such as "there is no possibility that the Clinton plan will produce the deficit reduction that it projects" and that the plan "reflects a fundamentally incorrect view of how taxes affect individual behavior," his view was not dismissed as voodoo economics.[36]

In fact, compared to many conservatives, Feldstein was an optimist. A paper by the conservative Heritage Foundation concluded: "Higher taxes will shrink the tax base and reduce tax revenues." The GOP House whip Newt Gingrich, giving voice to the conservative consensus, predicted that the "three hundred billion in new taxes is going to shrink the economy, put people out of work, lower tax revenues."[37]

It is worth recalling some of the conservative rhetoric of the time to see just how vehemently the supply-siders believed this. The *Wall Street Journal* ran a series of editorials denouncing the tax hike under the headline "The Class Warfare Economy," complete with a graphic of a guillotine. Bartley warned ominously that the tax hike would "cripple" the economy. Lawrence Kudlow, one of the high priests of the supply-side temple, confidently asserted: "There is no question that President Clinton's across-the-board tax increases . . . will throw a wet blanket over the recovery and depress the economy's long-run potential to grow."[38] Indeed, by the time Clinton's plan passed the House of Representatives, the *Journal*'s editorial page stated that the recession had already begun: "We are seeing," the editors opined, "the early signs of the stagflation that we knew so well during the Carter presidency."

Perhaps the hysteria was best captured by *Forbes* magazine, another supply-side outpost. One issue featured a cover story urging readers to move their assets out of the U.S. economy. "We want our clients' money as far away from Bill and Hillary as we can," one investment adviser urged. "The president is a negative for the U.S. market." Two other *Forbes* stories sympathetically profiled wealthy citizens who, fearing Clinton's tax policies, decided to flee the country altogether.[39]

I probably don't need to point out that this was horrible advice. The stock market boomed, and the economy enjoyed its longest expansion in U.S. history. Revenues soared higher than the cheeriest optimists could have predicted. Not only was the deficit cut in half, in keeping with Clinton's goal, but it disappeared altogether, to be replaced by a surplus. This was not merely a product of a stock market bubble, either; productivity, after two decades of stagnation, began growing nearly twice as fast. And despite predictions that soaking the rich would sap their entrepreneurial energies and cause them to report less income, the highest revenue growth came from those same rich who were supposed to be adversely affected. The supply-siders turned out to be spectacularly wrong in every particular.

Did Clinton benefit from the business cycle? Sure he did. While his antideficit policies worked just as they were supposed to —

lower deficits allowed investors to shift their money from unproductive government debt to productive new business technologies — it's safe to say that Clinton wouldn't have fared as well if he had taken office in 1973 rather than 1993. Remember, though, supply-siders don't believe in the business cycle. They believe tax rates determine everything. That's why conservatives didn't say that Clinton's tax hike *might* slow down the economy a bit or that it *probably* wouldn't bring in as much revenue as expected. They insisted that it would *definitely* result in fewer jobs, slower growth, and reduced revenues. This was the necessary consequence of their theory.

FIRST, ADMIT NO WRONG

How, you might ask, did the supply-siders respond to this utter and total humiliation? It's hard to think of a gesture of contrition the supply-siders could have made that would be sufficiently mordant to convey the magnitude of their errors. Mass resignations by supply-siders, complete with signed promises to leave the field of public policy and economics altogether, might have been appropriate. At the very least, one might have expected anguished editorials and conferences at conservative think tanks with titles such as "How Did We Get It So Wrong?" or "Time to Rethink the Premises of Supply-Side Economics." But nothing like this happened. Instead, the supply-siders went on their merry way, their confidence unshaken in the slightest.

At first the conservatives tried arguing that Clinton's expansion did not match the glorious Reagan boom. Yet that explanation didn't quite pass muster — they had predicted disaster, not just a slightly less magnificent boom — and anyway, by the late 1990s, it was demonstrably untrue by any measure. So they came out with a new line: Clinton hadn't really done anything to the economy. The boom actually vindicated . . . Ronald Reagan! "The politician most responsible for laying the groundwork for this prosperous era is not Bill Clinton, but Ronald Reagan," wrote Moore and Kudlow.[40] This line quickly became the new conservative consensus. The Reagan hagiographer Dinesh D'Souza chimed in: "Bill Clinton is reaping a harvest that Ronald Reagan sowed. . . . Clinton has had no economic policy. He hasn't needed one."[41]

In one sense it's impossible to completely disprove this sort of reasoning. You can't prove in a scientific sense that Reagan's policies weren't responsible for the 1990s boom. For that matter, you can't prove that Calvin Coolidge's policies, or control of the magnesium supply, weren't responsible either. All the factors of economic policy are never moving in the same direction at the same time. The monomaniac can always go back and see that the large factor he was sure would play a decisive role later turned out to be less important than some other, smaller counterpressure he failed to consider at the time.* Say a country decides to sell off all its magnesium, and you predict utter ruin will ensue. Instead, the country experiences unprecedented prosperity. You can always look back and decide that some smaller magnesium purchase, or the big magnesium run-up of a decade earlier, was the true decisive factor. The only way to test such theories is to measure what they expected to see going forward.

With the supply-siders, the evidence is clear. Not only did they predict disaster under Clinton's policies, they unambiguously declared an end to Reaganomics and disavowed whatever followed. In

---

* The supply-siders seized on the fact that in 1998 Clinton made a deal in which he cut the capital gains tax in return for higher children's health spending. They portrayed the capital gains tax cut as responsible for the boom. This view has, needless to say, several crippling flaws. First, the boom began several years before the capital gains tax cut. Second, the capital gains tax cut was far smaller than Clinton's income tax hike. And third, Jimmy Carter signed a capital gains tax cut in 1978, yet supply-siders claimed no responsibility for anything the economy did after that — or, indeed, until 1983.

fact, they did this as early as 1990, when Bush raised taxes. They could not have been any more explicit on this point. Here is a 1990 *Journal* editorial:

> The economic ideas expounded in these columns have shared the blame, and sometimes even the credit, for the economy of the 1980s. But now, despite the apparent difficulties of selling its budget agreement, the Bush administration has joined the Democrats in endorsing quite another set of ideas. It appears that the economy of the 1990s is likely to belong to someone else. Good luck.[42]

Yet, in the middle of the 1990s boom, after disowning the economy and insistently predicting tax-induced ruin, the supply-siders decided to reclaim the economy as their own. Not once did any of them attempt to explain, or even mention anywhere, their prophesies of doom. The only loose thread in the It's-Still-Reagan's-Economy gambit was how to explain what happened when the economy finally slowed down again toward the end of Clinton's final term. You can probably guess the answer: *that's* when they decided it was Clinton's economy. When growth began slowing in December 2000, Kudlow complained: "The Clinton policies of rising tax burdens, high interest rates, and re-regulation are responsible for the sinking stock market and the slumping economy."[43] Soon the Clinton Recession was upon us, a mere seven years after Clinton had enacted the heart of the economic policy agenda.

THE END OF THE 1990S boom was occasion to hand the supply-siders yet another repudiation. Toward the end of Clinton's term and into the beginning of Bush's, conservatives argued that emerging budget surpluses ought to be devoted toward tax cuts. Moderates and liberals demurred, insisting that the surpluses could well be temporary. The supply-siders, however, insisted that this was all wrong. Not only did they argue that the projected surpluses would materialize for sure, they argued that they would be much larger than anticipated. The conservative press was filled with columns angrily insisting that dogmatic government budget forecasters, wedded to out-of-date Keynesian models, were underestimating the surplus. Only the supply-siders appreciated the true dynamism of the economy and the endless abundance of revenues that would result.

Here is a small sample of the commentary they produced. Stephen Moore, May 15, 2000:

> Economist Lawrence Kudlow has been the nation's most accurate fiscal prognosticator of the last decade, and he estimates tax surpluses will be twice as large as the official forecast.

Lawrence Kudlow, August 31, 2000:

> Using historical growth trends, budget surpluses over the next decade could easily rise to $7 trillion, 50 percent above the CBO [Congressional Budget Office] estimates.

And after Bush cut taxes, they continued to predict rising surpluses. Here's Kudlow, May 30, 2001:

> What's more, faster economic growth and more profitable productivity returns will generate higher tax revenues at the new lower tax-rate levels. Future budget surpluses will rise, not fall.[44]

Martin Feldstein reappeared as well, showing no signs of humility from his insistence, eight years earlier, that there was "no possibility" that Clinton's tax hike would reduce the deficit as much as expected. Feldstein argued again that the government budget forecasts were underestimating the influence of tax rates on high-income earners. Thus, he wrote, "the true cost of reducing the tax rates is likely to be substantially smaller than the costs projected in the official estimates.[45]

Everybody knows what happened next. Revenues did not just drop, they collapsed utterly. The liberals and moderates who had urged caution had fretted that the government would not be able to pay down the debt, but what happened surpassed the pessimists' worst fears. Income tax payments as a share of the economy fell to their lowest level since 1942.[46]

As with the Clinton surpluses, external circumstances certainly played a role. Revenues would have fallen whether or not Bush cut taxes, and it made sense anyway for the government to run a temporary deficit in the face of the 2001 recession. But the point is that, once again, events confounded the supply-side view of the world. Sensible economists qualify their predictions because they understand that outside events can always intervene unexpectedly. The supply-siders do not qualify their predictions because they are monocausalists. Whatever else may come along to buffet the economy — the popping of the tech bubble, the Enron scandal, the war on terror and the war in Iraq — tax cuts ought to overcome it. Again and again this has proven horribly wrong. It is impossible to think of how events could have turned out worse for them, short of God appearing on Earth to denounce the Laffer Curve as an abomination.

It should come as no surprise that the collapse of revenues following their insistent predictions of endless growth did not chasten the conservatives. Their main response was denial. The *Journal's* editorial page has made a habit of putting scare quotes around the word "deficit" — i.e., "President Bush's tax cut is running into trouble in the Senate, with opponents claiming they are worried about 'the deficit'" — as if the whole thing were a liberal myth. Meanwhile, others have seized on any scrap of positive news to vindicate Bush. Moore wrote a 2005 op-ed piece noting that revenues had begun to rise — "George Bush proves Art Laffer right — again" — without mentioning that they remained far below where government forecasters had projected them to be before Bush's tax cut, let alone below the level wild-eyed optimists like Moore had predicted.*[47]

ALL TOLD, the experience of the last fifteen years points to some clear conclusions. Tax rates under 40 percent simply do not have much effect on economic behavior. And this conclusion squares with most people's experience. Even the rich do not base their decisions on tax rates. The incentives to work hard, invest smartly, or invent a new product — social standing, pride in one's accomplishments, the joy of fulfilling one's creative talents — are such that a tax rate of 40 versus 30 percent just doesn't make very much difference. Whatever difference it does make is overwhelmed by the effect on public finance. In the long run, it was probably worth it even for the very rich themselves to pay the higher tax rates imposed by Clinton in order to get the budget deficit under control, since the long-term benefits of deficit reduction helps them as well.

Despite the empirical failure of their theory, the political standing of the supply-siders has never been higher. That may sound like a strange statement. The public tends to associate supply-side economics with the 1980s and assumes that it has all but disappeared now. In fact, the term has mostly disappeared from the public discourse precisely because of the totality of its triumph within the Republican Party.

When supply-side economics surfaced more than thirty years ago, established conservative economists ridiculed it. (The very name comes from a term of derision coined by Nixon and Ford's chief economist, Herb Stein, who believed that an economic model fo-

---

* Possibly the most notable thing about Moore's op-ed piece was that, in its efforts to convey what he saw as the impressive rise in tax revenues, he seemed to be aping the style of e-mail spammers hawking fake Viagra. Consider Moore's use of capital letters ("New York City, which suddenly finds itself more than $3 billion IN SURPLUS") and his vivid descriptions of rising revenue, which included such phrases as "eye-popping," "surged," "exploded like a cap let off a geyser," and "unexpected gush." Come to think of it, "unexpected gush" may not be the result you want from a sex pill.

cused only on the supply of goods to the total exclusion of demand was self-evidently silly.) At the time, "fiscal conservatism" meant prudence and opposition to deficits. Today, when media reports use "fiscal conservative," they're usually referring to supply-siders. They call them fiscal conservatives because the old fiscal conservatism has disappeared from the conservative movement. Supply-side economics has become the fiscal policy of conservatives.

2

THE SUM OF ALL LOBBIES

In recent years, conservative activists and intellectuals have come to suspect that something has corrupted the Republican Party. That something could be seen very clearly in one episode that began late in President Bush's first term. In 2003, the World Trade Organization ruled that an American subsidy for businesses that export goods overseas was illegal. Congress had to repeal the subsidy, worth $5 billion a year, or face retaliatory tariffs aimed at a wide swath of domestic businesses. Congress decided it had no choice but to comply.

The logical thing, given that the government was hemorrhaging revenue and facing an endless torrent of red ink, would have been to simply cancel the illegal subsidy and use the savings to make a small dent in the deficit. This option was apparently never considered. The next most logical thing would have been to take the proceeds from the canceled subsidy and use them for some kind of broad-based tax cut. This would at least have been in keeping with the pro-market sentiments of the GOP: removing a provision in the tax code favoring certain businesses over others would have eliminated a form of government meddling in the marketplace. The export subsidy, after all, was a pure form of what conservatives refer to (with understandable derision) as industrial policy — a government enterprise to pick winners in the business world and give them preferential treatment over other, less favored businesses. Replacing the export subsidy with an across-the-board business tax cut was, from a free market perspective, a no-brainer. Yet Congress quickly rejected this approach as well.

Instead, Congress decided that, since the illegal tax subsidy benefited manufacturers, the proceeds from rescinding it should go to manufacturers as well. The apparent principle at work was that any group of Americans who have their public benefits taken away must be granted a new set of benefits. This principle is not universally applied. When Republicans reduce market-distorting subsidies for, say, poor people, they do not usually insist that the money be diverted into other programs benefiting the poor. Businesses, however, seem to be more effective than welfare mothers in persuading elected conservatives to bend their free market models.

Having decided to replace one form of aid for manufacturers with another, Congress quickly became bogged down in a Jesuitical dispute: What is a manufacturer? Does a movie studio manufacture films? Does a restaurant manufacture dinners? The lobbyists representing all these industries believed the answer was yes, of course. And the members of Congress, hearing their pleas, were inclined to agree.

Eventually, the pretense of aiding manufacturers fell by the wayside, and the repeal of the illegal export subsidy became the occasion for a massive potpourri of business tax breaks. By the summer of 2004, the proceedings had devolved into a bacchanalia of Caligulan proportions. Special tax breaks appeared for importers of Chinese ceiling fans, NASCAR track owners, sonar fish finders, foreign dog race gamblers, and sundry other businesses large and small. The only qualification for special treatment seemed to be the ability to hire a lobbyist. "This is a godsend for lobbyists," one lobbyist said to the *Washington Post*'s Jonathan Weisman. "You wouldn't be a decent tax lobbyist if you didn't have tons of stuff in [this bill]."[1]

If you were a really topnotch tax lobbyist, like Ken Kies, there was almost no limit to what you could have in the bill. Kies, a pudgy, baby-faced man with soft, wavy hair and wide round glasses, had by this point made himself into the best — which is to say, the most lucrative — tax lawyer in town. He had done this through two and a half decades of relentlessly trading on the political contacts he made from moving back and forth between Capitol Hill and K Street. In the late 1990s, Kies was hauling in around $1 million in annual salary as a lobbyist. He had to represent some fairly odious characters, but his political contacts and bland, buttoned-down demeanor gave his arguments the necessary patina of legitimacy.[2]

Now, in the summer of 2004, he was in his glory. It was the perfect atmosphere for a lobbyist — no request was too outlandish to turn down. To be Ken Kies at a time like this was like having a license to print money. Representing a host of clients, Kies won tens of billions of dollars in special provisions and personally made off with $8.69 million in fees from that one corporate tax bill.[3] And Kies was just one lobbyist among many.

The practice of larding legislation with special interest lucre has, of course, a lengthy pedigree in American politics. Yet this particular episode stands out for several reasons. First, the sheer scale of the gluttony overwhelmed everything else. This was not merely a dollop of pork to grease the skids for some reputable purpose. The pork was the whole point of the thing. As an anonymous lobbyist confessed, the process had "risen to a new level of sleaze."[4] Second, the distinction between public and private interests did not merely blur, it disappeared altogether. The Republican leadership actually delegated the task of rounding up votes to a coalition of lobbyists.[5]

But perhaps the most notable thing about the episode is that almost nobody felt the need to present a public policy rationale for it. The closest anybody came was the House Ways and Means Committee chairman, Bill Thomas, who gamely insisted that "everybody deserves one day every 20 years" to win favorable treatment in Washington.[6] The bill did not reflect a triumph of any ideology, even conservative ideology. Supply-siders believe in cutting marginal tax rates for individuals and corporations. But they do *not* believe that the government should set tax rates according to which businesses have better lobbyists in Washington. Economists across the political spectrum agree that letting the government pick winners and losers distorts the free market, causing capital and labor to follow the dictates of Washington rather than the invisible hand. So conservative intellectuals had almost nothing to say about the corporate tax bill, and those who did mention it — Robert Novak, the former Bush economic adviser Glenn Hubbard, the *Journal*'s editorial page — condemned it.

What this in turn suggests is that the radical turn of the Republican Party cannot be understood solely as an ideological phenomenon. One of the paradoxes of the Bush years is that, while the president and his allies are staunch conservatives, their economics is not pure conservatism. The policy mix is nothing that a Friedrich Hayek or a Milton Friedman would recognize as his own. Nor is it the kind of moderate Republicanism of an Eisenhower or a Nixon. The new brand of conservatism reflects not just the advent of the supply-siders but also the rise and ideological transformation of the business lobby. Over the last thirty-five years — the same period of time that has seen the ascent of the supply-siders — American business has grown both vastly more politically powerful and vastly more rapacious in the way it wields that power. The rise of the business lobby has distorted — and, finally, corrupted — the Republican Party and the conservative movement.

A BRIEF HISTORY OF BUSINESS IN WASHINGTON

The closest historical precedent for the atmosphere that pervades the capital today is the Washington of the late nineteenth century. During the Gilded Age, the culture of the Robber Barons defined the political system. There was very little sense of embarrassment about buying political influence. The politicians of the era, known by some as "the spoilsmen," assumed that their role was to accommodate the demands of businessmen and that they deserved to share in the bounty they created.

Around the beginning of the twentieth century, this political system organized around patronage and unfettered support for business gave way to a new set of assumptions. The politicians in the Progressive Era believed that the national interest did not always coincide with the interests of business owners, that parties in power could not simply dispense lucre to their supporters without some compelling public interest justification, and that elected officials should be guided by the advice of disinterested experts.

Inevitably, many of the reforms the Progressives set in place were met by fierce opposition from corporations. Yet eventually much of the business community accepted them, and the ethos of accommodation between business and government that blossomed during World War II continued in the years that followed. With the advanced economies of Europe and Japan in shambles, American corporations enjoyed a secure and unchallenged position in the global economy. Most corporations accepted progressive taxation, unions, and reasonable regulation. Their munificence was undergirded by the postwar boom, which allowed businesses to pay their workers higher wages and to support the New Deal edifice while still enjoying steady profits.

Their obliging stance also reflected the prevailing corporate culture. As John Judis notes in *The Paradox of American Democracy,* businessmen saw themselves as responsible for the good of the country as a whole, not just their immediate bottom line. It seems not to have occurred to corporate America to enter the political arena to fight for a bigger piece of the pie. In 1961, just fifty corporations retained Washington lobbyists; these were mainly firms that sold products directly to the federal government. Business went about its business and did not see the need to dominate Washington.

This history runs against the mythology of the left, in which American business is seen as a constant, thoroughly evil, and near-omnipotent force. But this was far from true during the postwar years. Almost all of Lyndon Johnson's Great Society legislation passed without significant business opposition. Theodore Levitt wrote in the *Harvard Business Review* during Johnson's administration that "the American business community has finally and with unexpected suddenness embraced the idea of the interventionist state."[7] In 1970, 57 percent of Fortune 500 executives agreed that Washington should "step up regulatory activities."[8]

THE SEEDS OF the business backlash were sown in the late 1960s and early 1970s, though at the time no one could have imagined it. Decades of prosperity had instilled a broad sense that the economy was a solved problem and that society could aspire to things greater than mere material accumulation. Out of this sentiment grew a new politics, personified by Ralph Nader, that emphasized the failure of corporations to safeguard the environment and consumer safety. In a brief time, these movements became astonishingly popular. Hundreds of thousands of Americans joined environmental organizations; twenty million people participated in the first Earth Day, in 1970. Polls showed that Ralph Nader, who crusaded against unsafe cars and countless other products, was the most admired man in America.[9]

This upsurge in liberal sentiment produced a flood of legislation. Within a few years Washington created the Environmental Protection Agency, the Occupational Safety and Health Administration, the Consumer Product Safety Commission, the Clean Air and Water acts, and numerous other liberal reforms. Before this legislative onslaught business lay prostrate. Hardly any industries lobbied to alter the Clean Air Act in 1970, for instance. They were ready for uniform federal standards and, as one corporate representative put it, "tired of being cast as the heavy." The Democratic senator Ed Muskie, replying to complaints that his proposed automobile emissions standards were not technologically feasible, replied, "The deadline is based not, I repeat, on economic and technical feasibility, but on considerations of public health." Muskie, in turn, was soon denounced by a Naderite group for insufficient vigilance to the environmental cause. In the political dynamics of the time, little price was to be paid for offending industry, but a great price to be paid for offending the many Nader-affiliated research and lobbying groups popping up throughout the capital.

Business's view of liberal reform went quickly from willing accommodation to genuine terror.[10] What bothered corporations far more than the atmosphere in Washington was the broader cultural hostility that seemed to accompany it. All at once, American society seemed to turn against corporate America. The percentage of Americans who believed "business tries to strike a fair balance between profits and the interest of the public" plummeted from 70 percent in 1968 to 33 percent in 1970.[11] Part of this drop reflected the Nader-inspired horror stories of corporate malfeasance then proliferating in the media. It also reflected the influence of the counterculture, which rejected the business world as a bastion of conformity and selfishness. Businessmen complained that graduates of elite universities no longer deigned to work for them. Articles in the business press began expressing panic over the future of capitalism.

The immediate response came from conservative intellectuals, who saw business as a wayward ally with vast, unrealized potential. In a 1971 memo to the Chamber of Commerce, the corporate lawyer and future Supreme Court justice Lewis Powell urged business to fund a massive offensive against the left. "The painfully sad truth," he wrote, "is that business . . . often have responded — if at all — by appeasement, ineptitude and ignoring the problem . . . The time has come — indeed, it is long overdue — for the wisdom, ingenuity and resources of American business to be marshalled [*sic*] against those who would destroy it." Corporations had grown accustomed to seeing themselves as guardians of the broader national interest, not ideological combatants seeking to maximize their own share. Traditionally they had directed their public involvement toward institutions like the Committee for Economic Development or the Brookings Institution, which steered a center course between capital and labor. Conservatives now insisted that business must abandon this noblesse oblige.[12] As Irving Kristol wrote, "Corporate philanthropy should not be, and cannot be, disinterested."[13] In part as a result of these exhortations, corporations began funding a vast apparatus of foundations, think tanks, pressure groups, and media to advance views congenial to their bottom line.

While these memos carried some influence, what really changed the disposition of business was an economic downturn. While conservatives began calling for business to do battle with its enemies in 1970 and 1971, few heeded the call until 1973. The year is significant because it represents the point at which the long postwar expansion ended. Corporate profits declined by a third between the mid-1960s and the mid-1970s. The growing economic strength of Japan, Germany, and other emerging industrial powers threatened manufacturers, which could no longer pass on higher labor costs to the consumer. One expression of business's new vulnerability came in its dealings with organized labor. In 1965, 42 percent of companies immediately complied when their workers petitioned to unionize. In 1973, only 16 percent did so. Businesses did whatever they could to resist organized labor, and over the next decade, unions' complaints over unfair trade practices skyrocketed.[14] The most important result was the creation of a powerful business lobby. Initially, the impetus was purely defensive. Liberals swept the 1974, post-Watergate elections. "We had to prevent business from being rolled up and put in the trash can by that Congress," one lobbyist explained.[15] Massive resources went into the effort. At a series of meetings in 1974 and 1975, writes David Vogel in *Fluctuating Fortunes*, several CEOs "urged their colleagues to intensify their own political activity." Over the following decade lobbyists flocked into Washington, grouping themselves downtown on K Street, not far from the White House. Between 1968 and 1979, the number of corporations with public affairs representatives in the capital increased fivefold. From 1974 to 1980, the U.S. Chamber of Commerce doubled its membership and tripled its budget.[16]

More important than sheer growth, however, was that the whole purpose of the business lobby changed. Before, businesses focused their pleadings on narrow concerns, often putting them in conflict with other businesses. Starting in the mid-1970s, corporate lobbying developed what can only be called a class consciousness. As Edsall wrote in his 1984 book, *The New Politics of Inequality*, "The dominant theme in the political strategy of business became a shared interest in the defeat of such bills as consumer protection and labor law reform, and in the enactment of favorable tax, regulatory, and antitrust legislation."[17]

Business's newfound power stunned the left. Over the succeeding years, liberals suffered a rapid series of defeats on labor and consumer reform legislation that all sides had expected to pass into law. The losing streak continued even after Jimmy Carter won the presidency, giving Democrats control of Washington. Even then, business's victories were mostly defensive. Then Ronald Reagan took office in 1981. At that point, the political system opened itself up to the blandishments of corporations in a way that had not been seen since the 1920s. The prestige of business was suddenly rehabilitated. Chief executives like Lee Iacocca, Peter Ueberroth, and Donald Trump published best-selling books and won enormous popular followings. Reagan urged a major tax cut for business and high-earning individuals, and the two parties engaged in a furious bidding war over who could cut corporate taxes the deepest the fastest. Reagan filled his administration with allies or representatives of business and dramatically scaled back the growth of regulations.

And yet, for reasons we'll see in the next chapter, corporate power in Washington was still not fully realized. At the beginning of Bill Clinton's presidency, K Street was larger than ever in its physical size and scope, but its ideological and operational unity had deteriorated. Many businessmen noted that Clinton was not terribly liberal by the standards of the time — he favored expanded free trade and deficit reduction — and considered him the sort of Democrat they could live with.

But that moment in the early 1990s turned out to be a mere pause at the foot of an ascent just as steep as the one that occurred during the 1970s. And the episode that set off this next revolution in the role of business in government was Clinton's efforts to remake the health care system. At the time, health care reform seemed an unlikely candidate to spark a business backlash. Everybody assumed some kind of major health reform would pass. Solid majorities of the public said they favored overhauling health care in general and liked the Clinton plan in particular. Business not only reconciled itself to reform but for the most part actively favored it, since skyrocketing health care costs were, after all, eating away at profit margins. At the outset of Clinton's first term, the giants of the business lobby — the Chamber of Commerce, the Business Roundtable, and the National Association of Manufacturers — all favored universal health care.

In due time, however, business turned sharply against this reform — but not because its interests were under attack. It did so because conservatives demanded it. Republicans, for both partisan and ideological reasons, wanted to kill health care reform and were enraged at business's conciliatory posture. The conservative activist Grover Norquist began convening a weekly meeting of business lobbyists opposed to health care (mostly representing small businesses, which for the most part did not insure their workers and did not want to start) along with conservative groups like the National Rifle Association and right-leaning pundits. These strategy sessions produced, among other things, a concerted effort to pressure business lobbies to withdraw their support for reform. The conservatives denounced groups like the Chamber of Commerce as a sellout to big government and disseminated their attacks through talk radio, taped television spots, and *Wall Street Journal* editorials. Congressional Republicans boycotted a Chamber awards ceremony and threatened to ignore Chamber lobbying on other issues. Under this pressure, the Chamber reversed itself, and corporate support for health care reform collapsed.[18]

A BRISK WALK DOWN K STREET

The curious, and seemingly backward, spectacle of elected officials lobbying lobbyists, a novelty in the early '90s, has since become a regular feature of American politics, and it reflects the new cast that business lobbying has taken. For decades, including the 1970s and 1980s, corporate lobbyists sought support from both Democrats and Republicans. Indeed, winning over liberal Democrats, who had the least natural sympathy for the pleadings of business leaders, was the biggest trick, so the most prominent lobbyists in Washington — men like Lloyd Cutler and Tommy Boggs — had impeccable credentials building the New Deal. There was nothing pure or even honest about this arrangement. It spawned the widely shared and not entirely incorrect sense that both parties were in hock to the same set of interests. Yet, as sleazy as that culture was, what has replaced it is far more dangerous.

When Republicans won control of Congress in 1994, in part as a result of having defeated health care reform, they set about to reshape K Street as a partisan Republican force. Conservatives called the undertaking the K Street Project. It involved, in part, pressuring business lobbies to stop spreading their donations between both parties and instead donate exclusively to the GOP. They also demanded that lobbying firms hire only Republicans for top positions and use their political muscle to support the Republican position. In return, Republicans gave these lobbyists extraordinary deference in shaping legislation. Republicans demanded total loyalty from K Street and offered total loyalty in return. The business lobby and the GOP would no longer be separate parties with overlapping interests but partners in an ironclad alliance.

As the enforcer of this campaign the Republicans appointed majority whip, and later majority leader, Tom DeLay, who — even in the perfervid atmosphere of "the Republican Revolution" — stood out for his ruthlessness and partisan zeal. DeLay kept a book detailing how much major corporations had donated to each party and divided them into "friendly" and "unfriendly" columns. He made a practice of calling lobbyists into his office, opening the book, and showing them where they stood. "If you want to play in our revolution," he famously declared, "you have to live by our rules."[19]

The broad outlines of the K Street Project are publicly known, but its day-to-day workings genuinely go on behind closed doors. Lobbyists do not hold press conferences, are not subject to Freedom of Information requests, are not given anything like the journalistic scrutiny politicians are, and generally have a strong incentive not to publicize their political dealings. Yet every once in a while a few details surface and give some of the flavor of its inner workings.

In 2003, staffers working for Michael Oxley, the chairman of the House Financial Services Committee, told lobbyists for the mutual fund industry that the committee would call off its investigation of their practices if its Washington office would fire its Democratic-affiliated chief lobbyist and replace her with a Republican.[20] The following year, Republicans warned the Motion Picture Industry Association not to hire a Democrat for its top lobbying position. When it did, they vowed revenge — the industry's "ability to work with the House and Senate is greatly reduced," vowed Grover Norquist — and exacted it later that year, killing a profitable export subsidy in the otherwise bloated corporate tax bill of 2004.[21]

As part of this broad effort to discipline K Street, Republicans have demanded that business lobbies unite behind whatever collective decision the party makes, despite any qualms they may harbor. Historically, businesses tended to be narrow and parochial in their demands, sitting out fights that didn't concern them and sometimes making demands that pitted them against other business interests. During the 1970s, business lobbies first began uniting behind a shared agenda. The K Street Project set about to accelerate, systemize, and enforce the trend. Republicans have created large business coalitions to lobby Congress and the public for nearly every major initiative they have proposed. A 2001 memo by a Republican lobbyist, imploring his colleagues to join a coalition behind the energy bill, gives a sense of how these coalitions operate. The memo, obtained by the *Washington Post's* Michael Grunwald, explained:

> To join the coalition, you must agree to support the Bush energy proposal in its entirety and not to lobby for changes to the bill. Should the bill change, you must support the changes in the legislation or drop out of the coalition. If you are caught attempting to lobby behind the back of the White House, you will be expelled from the coalition. I have been advised that this White House "will have a long memory."[22]

These revelations may suggest that the elected officials have the whip hand, with lobbyists reduced to passive cheerleading. Nothing could be further from the truth. The essence of the new relationship is that, in return for its undivided political loyalty, K Street receives influence of a sort that would have been unthinkable a generation ago. Again, most of the relations between lobbyists and elected officials are submerged from public view, but examples bob up above the surface with enough regularity to offer a general picture. After taking control of Congress, Republicans began letting lobbyists write legislation for them — a practice initially considered scandalous but, as time has passed, is now met with either acceptance or resignation.

The Bush administration has routinely — so routinely it no longer makes news — appointed lobbyists to oversee their former employers. Harvey Pitt, Bush's first choice to head the Securities and Exchange Commission, had made his name defending the accounting industry, Ivan Boesky, and anybody else seeking more lenient treatment of financial malfeasance. Pitt took the helm of the SEC and promised a "kinder, gentler" agency where "we aren't going to play gotcha."[23] William Geary Myers III, a lobbyist for cattle grazers seeking to preserve federal subsidies, received an appointment to the Interior Department. Mark Weinberger, the Bush treasury official charged with regulating tax shelters, is a former lobbyist for purveyors of tax shelters. Soon after taking office he declared, "I want to change the 'us' versus 'them' mentality — the 'us' being government, the 'them' being business."[24]

That is a fitting summation of modern Republicanism. It has become increasingly difficult to distinguish between business and government, with the former regularly taking on the duties of the latter. In 2001, Enron interviewed several candidates to head the Federal Energy Regulatory Commission, and Bush ultimately appointed two who met with their approval. Enron's chairman Ken Lay met with the holdover FERC chairman and instructed him that he could keep his job only if he reversed his opposition to energy deregulation. The next year, two of Bush's appointees to a commission regulating lead poisoning revealed that they were first approached not by the administration but by the lead industry itself.[25] The pattern is not merely "influence," it is the wholesale delegation of the tasks of governing.

This merger of the functions of business and government in contemporary Washington is treated as a matter of course. It would simply never occur to Republicans to question the fidelity of somebody who had gone to work for a private interest. If anything, working for K Street is further evidence of one's ideological bona fides. Andrew M. Shore, chief of staff of the House Republican Conference, was asked by the *Washington Post* in 2005 about former aides to Tom DeLay who had gone into lobbying work. He said, "People who have worked for Mr. DeLay become, like other senior Republican staffers, members in good standing of a club and are accepted back by many members [of Congress] and staffers. The idea is that we are a team. What's good for one is good for all; anything to cultivate that team mentality is seen in a positive light."[26]

For many years DeLay symbolized the nexus of money and power in Washington. He was an obvious target, with a snarling personality, a colorful nickname ("the Hammer"), and a propensity for stating his intentions baldly. The system that emerged around him was not a product of his personality, though, but rather the basic evolution of the Republican Party. The hallmark of any institution is that it can go on relatively unchanged when its leader departs. In that sense, the blending roles of lawmaker and lobbyist was best personified by DeLay's successor, Roy Blunt.

Blunt was elected to the House in 1996, after Republicans had already taken control of Congress. Unlike DeLay, he did not burn with anger at his enemies. He saw the K Street Project less as a crusade to destroy the vestiges of the old Democratic establishment and more as a business opportunity. He joined the GOP leadership almost immediately and shrewdly established his own political action committee, the Rely On Your Beliefs fund. (Lest his beliefs alone prove insufficient, ROYB raised hundreds of thousands of dollars and dispensed them to grateful members of the Republican rank and file, who in turn supported Blunt and his rapid rise.)

Unlike other politicians, Blunt was never corrupted by K Street after his arrival in Washington for one simple reason: it surrounded him from the very outset. His second wife and two of his children were lobbyists. In 2003, while Blunt and his future wife were still dating, he slipped a provision benefiting Philip Morris, her employer, into a Homeland Security bill, a move so brazen that even fellow Republicans excised it for fear of negative publicity.[27]

This incident exemplified the difference between Blunt and the Republican revolutionaries who preceded him. Activities they felt compelled to hide he carried out openly and unashamedly. Mike Rogers, a Republican congressmen elected four years after Blunt, gushed to the Capitol Hill newspaper *Roll Call* about the way Blunt had systemized the integration of K Street into the Republican decision-making apparatus. Lobbyists, he explained, "are really an extension of the whip team. Through Roy's leadership, we've been able to take this to the next level."[28]

INFLUENCE PEDDLING AND CORRUPTION

The evidence of the GOP's enmeshment with its business supporters is so overwhelming that few conservatives deny it outright. Instead, they offer two basic defenses. The first is that Republicans behaved no differently than Democrats. But the contrast between the chummy bipartisan sleaze that suffused the old Democratic Washington, and has returned in milder form in the new one, and the highly partisan sleaze that characterizes Republican Washington is enormous. It's not just a difference in degree but a difference in kind. Democrats accept the prevailing political culture by which lobbyists would cultivate ties with both sides. They do not expect total loyalty, nor do they grant it. The depredations produced by the K Street Project — government treating lobbyists as full partners, not merely interests with a seat at the table — are unique Republican innovations.

More to the point, Democrats have frequently found themselves working at cross-purposes with K Street. This is because the nature of the two parties is fundamentally different. The Democrats' economic base consists not only of business but also labor, environmentalists, and consumer groups. In Congress, most Democrats do the bidding of their home district employers, and there are pro-business Democrats on the right as well as pro-labor Democrats on the left. The party's center of balance is caught squarely between these currents. It's impossible for the Democratic Party to be completely captive to its funding base because its base disagrees with itself so frequently. Nearly all of Bill Clinton's domestic agenda alienated large segments of his party's base. His push for free trade alienated labor unions, and his push for higher upper-bracket taxes and health care reform displeased corporate lobbyists, and his support for welfare reform infuriated liberal activists of all sorts.

The GOP, on the other hand, faces minimal divisions within its economic base. Yes, social conservatives do not always agree with economic conservatives, but the social conservatives focus almost exclusively on social issues and so do not usually weigh in with much force on economic issues. In the economic realm, Republicans enjoy no significant labor, consumer, or environmental support. Their economic base is uniformly corporate. And while businesses can disagree over certain issues — most notably foreign trade — they all want to pay as little in taxes, face the least amount of government regulation, and enjoy the most generous subsidies that they possibly can.

Even at the height of their political power, Democrats never sought, let alone won, the sort of alliance with K Street that Republicans enjoy today. A slight odor of disrepute hung over the profession of influence-peddling. Clark Clifford, a veteran of the Truman White House who won a place as Washington's most prominent lawyer, felt the need to deny that he was an influence peddler at all — "I do not consider that this firm will have any influence in Washington . . . If you want influence you should consider going elsewhere," he boasted about lecturing every client.[29] (Of course, Clifford *was* trading on his influence, but the point is that his reticence shows that such behavior was looked down on and had to be both denied and kept within reasonable bounds.)

Among the Republicans who succeeded the old Democratic establishment, the lobbying profession had nothing to apologize for. A few years ago, a former Gingrich spokesman, Tony Blankley, writing in the conservative *Washington Times,* issued an impassioned defense of DeLay and his lobbying ties. "In a thousand ways that are hard to publicly spot," he wrote, "the K Street effort helped all Republicans win elections, pass legislation they believed in and generally govern the country."[30] The very idea that there ought to be a stigma attached to using public service as a way to burnish one's marketability as an access peddler is foreign to the Republican majority. DeLay alone, according to John Judis, has placed twenty-nine former staffers into key lobbying positions.[31] Such behavior is expected, even encouraged. To hold a prestigious position in government without eventually cashing your access in on K Street would simply be foolish, like slaving away through medical school without ever practicing medicine. Republicans actually called DeLay's office "the DeLay School," a training ground for lobbyists.

*

THE GOP'S SECOND main defense against the charge of corruption is that business support for Republicans merely reflects shared ideological goals. Most businesses want less taxation and regulation, and so, according to this argument, the support of the business lobby doesn't really alter the behavior of Republicans at all. It merely rewards them for following their natural philosophical instincts.

This defense has a certain germ of truth, since a large segment of the Republican economic agenda dovetails neatly with the interests of business. Most of the tax cuts enacted under Bush — the pork-laden 2004 corporate tax bill to the contrary — uphold conservative ideology while offering enormous benefits to the rich and powerful. His administration's efforts to weaken the enforcement of securities laws or environmental regulations fit the same mold: they reflect a free market model while they also please well-organized lobbies. These cases, then, tell us little about whether the contemporary GOP is driven by K Street or its philosophy.

The way to distinguish between genuine free marketers and mere lackeys of business is when the interests of the two diverge. Here the evidence is unambiguous and the defense falls apart. In almost every instance where free market conservatism collides with K Street, the contemporary GOP has sided with K Street. Indeed, the great bulk of Bush's economic achievements have fallen into this category.

The list of Republican accommodations to business interests that lacked any plausible free market rationale is, alas, lengthy. In 2002, Bush signed a bill lavishing $180 billion of crop payments on farms. Agricultural subsidies are possibly the least justifiable government program in existence, for they lack any moral or economic rationale. Despite the romantic myths surrounding hardscrabble farmers, families in agriculture enjoy higher incomes than average nonfarm families. There's no more need to give special protections to family farms than there is to the family-owned restaurant or gas station. Moreover, crop supports raise the price of food, which particularly hurts poor Americans. And protecting the agricultural sector impoverishes Third World countries, whose farmers are priced out of American markets. Economists from left to right were pleased when, in 1996, President Clinton (in conjunction with the Republican Congress) signed the Freedom to Farm Act, which phased out agricultural subsidies.

In contrast, the 2003 farm bill has no justification whatsoever save as a straight payoff. The height of the grotesquerie came when rural Democrats in the Senate sought to limit payments to no more than $275,000 per family per year. Conservatives in Congress reacted hysterically.[32] "This is nothing less than war on southern farmers," thundered Arkansas's Senator Tim Hutchinson. "Do you know what this farm bill says to the South? 'Hold still, little catfish. All I'm going to do is just gut you,'" complained Georgia's Senator Zell Miller,[33] a nominal Democrat then in the process of shifting his allegiance to the GOP.* The Republican leadership duly did away with the payment cap.

That same year, Bush enacted tariffs on steel after heavy lobbying by the steel industry. (After steel-consuming industries saw their costs rise and organized a counterlobby, the administration subsequently backed down.) The administration has also slapped restrictions on imported lumber, shrimp, textiles, and other goods at the behest of domestic manufacturers. Even the small free trade agreement with Central America, called Cafta, was so littered with special protections for pharmaceuticals, sugar, and other goods that its net effect was more to restrict free trade than expand it. All this came after the White House, in response to pleas from the airlines,

---

* In the course of endorsing the first Bush tax cut, Miller asserted, "If we don't send this overpayment of taxes back to those who paid it, most of it will just be frittered away." Apparently handing out payments to wealthy farmers did not constitute frittering away money.

awarded $10 billion in loan guarantees and $5 billion in cash payments to the airline industry. The former labor secretary Robert Reich called it "the worst kind of industrial policy."[34]

The examples continue. In 2003, Bush and the Republican Congress enacted a bill extending Medicare coverage to prescription drugs, representing the largest expansion of entitlements in nearly forty years. Yet the ostensible purpose of the bill — helping retirees pay for their medicine — was almost incidental to its political momentum. Republicans stuffed the bill with hundreds of billions of dollars of subsidies to health insurance companies, the prescription drug industry, and other supplicants. All told, sundry grants to businesses accounted for around half the cost of the legislation.

Thomas Scully, Bush's appointee to run the Medicare program, told business lobbyists they had gotten "way beyond their wildest requests" and "should be having a giant ticker-tape parade."[35] A ticker-tape parade may have come across as unseemly, but grateful pharmaceutical makers did hire Scully as a lobbyist shortly after the bill was enacted. Scully shrewdly maximized his leverage by negotiating with his future employers even as he helped craft the bill that shoveled billions of dollars their way.[36]

One small but telling measure of the distinction between the Republican style and that which preceded it is the old-fashioned practice of pork barrel spending. Classic pork comes in the form of something called "earmarks," which means projects that circumvent the normal procedures for doling out federal cash. (Regular spending projects go through a federal agency and have their effectiveness subject to study and review. Earmarks don't.) The use of earmarks exploded roughly tenfold over the dozen years after Republicans took control of Congress.*

---

* In 2005, when DeLay was asked about cutting wasteful spending, he replied that there was no waste to cut. "After 11 years of Republican majority, we've pared it down pretty good," he insisted.

By the time Bush signed an energy bill in 2005, the thin veneer of public purpose behind it had been stripped away almost entirely. It was neither a deregulation bill nor an effort to shift production to certain industries deemed more environmentally sound. It simply consisted of a massive wish list of subsidies for just about every segment of the energy industry. A single sentence, published in the *Washington Post* in 2003, tells you all you need to know: "The assembled lobbyists — representing farm, corn, soybean, wind, geothermal, coal, oil and gas interests that benefit from provisions in the 1,100-page bill — gave [the GOP senator and energy bill champion Pete] Domenici a standing ovation, and he thanked them for helping to push the legislation to the brink of passage, according to one person who was present."[37] One analyst called the energy bill "the sum of all lobbies."[38]

That phrase — "the sum of all lobbies" — applies just as well to the whole contemporary Republican domestic agenda. And here is the really striking thing about Bush's economic policies. Other than tax cuts, they enjoy no support whatsoever from any ideological quarter. Policy analysts of liberal, conservative, and moderate persuasion alike have uniformly denounced his Medicare expansion, his energy bill, his tariffs, his farm subsidies, and the like. Conservatives hate them because they represent inefficient meddling with the free market. Liberals hate them because they commandeer public resources for the benefit of the rich. And centrists hate them for both reasons.

Essentially nobody except their direct beneficiaries, and the politicians whose loyalty they reward, supports these measures. They are lacking in any serious intellectual rationale. They exist only because they benefit rich and politically powerful constituencies. And ultimately this is the one variable that can explain Republican economic policies in the Bush era. If you summed up the accumulated desires of the business lobby, you would get a government that taxes very little — especially on business and the affluent — and spends a great deal of money, especially on corporate subsidies and pork. It would favor free trade agreements, which enjoy the support of large corporations, but it would also carve out numerous protections for vulnerable industries. You would get, in other words, something that looks exactly like George W. Bush's economic program.

A BETRAYAL OF CONSERVATISM OR ITS NATURAL OUTGROWTH?

So the peculiar mix of policies that has emerged during the Bush presidency — tax cuts for the rich, plus spending hikes for the powerful — has no basis in genuine conservatism. It is less a philosophy than a form of corruption. And conservatives readily concede that the Republican Party has turned its back on limited government principles. It's therefore natural to conclude that Bush has simply betrayed conservatism, and therefore that conservative intellectuals and activists bear none of the blame for the iniquities perpetrated by Republicans in office. That, certainly, is the defense put forward by conservative activists, who in the wake of the 2006 election debacle rushed to denounce Bush and the GOP Congress as ideological apostates.

This, however, lets the right off the hook too easily. If modern conservatives (that is, those who venerate tax cuts) look closely at the big government conservatism of the GOP, they will see a reflection, however gross and misshapen, of their own philosophy. First, there is the veneration of the businessman and the rich. The supply-siders taught the right that economic growth hinges above all else on satisfying the desire of the affluent to grow even more affluent, and they heaped scorn on the traditional liberal concern for equity. Second, there is the dismissal of budget deficits as a trifling detail. Conservative opinion outlets have a stable of epithets — "green eyeshades," "austerity," "Rubinomics" — that they hurl with robotic consistency at anybody in public life who suggests that red ink might, in some circumstances, matter more than tax cuts.

Thus the broad thrust of conservative ideology winds up pushing in the same general direction as K Street. There is a powerful lobby to reduce taxes on, or directly subsidize, the rich. There is not much of a lobby to reduce the deficit. Naturally, politicians bathed in an ideology geared around placating the rich and shrugging at deficits would find these demands congenial.

It is also telling to look more closely at the conservative opposition to Bush's expansion of government. Conservative opinion outlets have consistently condemned Republican spending hikes or tariffs. Yet those condemnations are inevitably restrained, often carrying an air of resignation about them. Consider one utterly typical example — a 2004 *Wall Street Journal* editorial called "GOP Spending Spree," expressing dissatisfaction with a pork-laden spending bill. After ticking off the bill's many flaws, the editorial concluded: "We're not holding our breath for a change of heart, but President Bush can help shore up his conservative base and appeal to many moderate voters by exercising his very first veto here."[39]

Or take *National Review*'s editorial endorsing Bush's reelection. The massive increase in spending that Bush had presided over is dealt with in glancing fashion. "On campaign finance, on education, on immigration, and above all on spending he has disappointed us, sometimes deeply. In a second term we will urge him to do better — and urge congressional Republicans to insist on it," the editorial scolded before going on to conclude, "For conservatives, however, backing Bush's reelection should be an easy decision."[40]

There is a "boys will be boys" tone here, like a father halfheartedly reprimanding his son for getting into a schoolyard scrap. Perhaps you think this is because the conservative intelligentsia are mere partisan shills for the GOP. But, as we'll see in the next chapter, this is not the case. When Republican politicians deviate even slightly from anti-tax orthodoxy, conservative activists and opinion leaders denounce them in the most vituperative terms — sounding more like wives who have discovered that their husbands have cheated on them.

Republicans who hold elected office have no doubt drawn from this contrast the inevitable conclusion that conservative activists tacitly accept big government conservatism. As long as they devote maximum political capital to reducing the top tax rate, Republican politicians have almost unlimited freedom with their base to capitulate to the demands of K Street.

WHO NEEDS EXPERT OPINION?

There is also another, more roundabout way in which conservative ideology has nurtured the Republican Party's corruption: it has undermined the principle of a neutral and technocratic government.

Many of us take for granted the ideal, if not always the reality, of a government that attempts to protect the broad public interest and seeks expert advice to help solve complex public policy questions. In fact, these ideals are specifically the legacy of the Progressives, a reform movement that arose more than a century ago, and they took hold only after protracted ideological conflict.

The Progressives abhorred political movements organized around narrow class interests. They saw the federal government as a disinterested arbiter that could rise above class conflict. And they created a new set of rules and institutions designed to curtail the old machines. They instituted civil service reform so that federal employees would be hired on the basis of their qualifications rather than partisan loyalties. And they established vast new government agencies staffed by sundry experts, a trend that continued as Washington expanded and modernized throughout the century. This was particularly noticeable in the economic realm. Agencies like the Federal Reserve (1913), the Council of Economic Advisors (1946), and the Office of Management and Budget (1974) all sprang up as a balance against raw political calculation. They were supplemented by outside institutions like Brookings and the National Bureau for Economic Research, which steered a middle ground between the interests of business and labor.

These institutions had always drawn bitter criticism from both the far right (which saw them as a quasi-socialist coastal elite) and the far left (which considered them a captive of corporate self-interest). These complaints carried little political weight until the 1970s, when the technocracy, which had abetted the burgeoning welfare state, came under sustained assault from the neoconservatives. The most prominent one was Irving Kristol, and he came to his populist position in a roundabout and surprising fashion. In 1965, Kristol helped found a journal called the *Public Interest* in order to promote scholarly solutions to problems of the political economy. Kristol was then a liberal, as were his fellow editors Nathan Glazer, Patrick Moynihan, and Daniel Bell, and the *Public Interest* crowd began with an optimistic view about the possibilities of social science research informing the welfare state. The mid-1960s, though, coincided with the liberal overreach associated with the Great Society, and the *Public Interest* decried the lack of sound research underlying the swaths of new programs emanating from Washington.

Kristol grew increasingly strident in his attacks on liberalism and bureaucracy. Moynihan and Bell remained skeptical liberals, but Kristol and Glazer came to be identified as "neoconservatives." In a rightist echo of his Marxist past, Kristol theorized that the government had been hijacked by a "new class." He defined this "new class" to include scientists, teachers, scholars, intellectuals, and — most important — "those who created and populate the new regulatory agencies" as well as "the upper levels of the government bureaucracy."[41]

Over time, this neoconservative critique metastasized into a general skepticism about the very possibility of neutral expertise and became a cherished part of the conservative creed. In one 1979 essay Robert Bartley lamented, "When business finds it has problems in the regulatory or public arena, its instinctive response is to seek out 'the experts.' Predictably enough, the experts — in public relations, advertising, law, etc. — have the skills of the New Class, and are thus the people most likely to share its outlooks, interests, and agendas."[42]

The conservative skepticism toward experts — or, as they would put it, "the experts" — has reached its full flowering during the Bush presidency. The Bush administration has gotten the most attention for ignoring the reports of its own experts on occupying Iraq, weapons of mass destruction, and environmental science. Its general penchant for distrusting wonks has been most pervasive in the economic sphere.

Bruce Bartlett, a conservative columnist and an economist for the Reagan administration, noted with dismay that the Bush administration has reversed the normal flow of ideas and analysis. In most administrations, experts in federal agencies draft plans and try to sell them to the White House. In the Bush administration, the White House generates all the ideas, and the agencies' only role is to promote them. Not surprisingly, important economic policymaking positions at the Treasury Department have simply been left vacant for years. The Council of Economic Advisors, long headquartered next to the White House, was moved several blocks away — "exiled to the Washington equivalent of Siberia," as a pair of scholars from the conservative American Enterprise Institute complained.[43] When the administration hired Stephen Friedman to head the National Economic Council and John Snow to run the Treasury Department in 2002, it openly put out the word that the two were being brought in not to help formulate policy but simply to sell it.

"There is no precedent in any modern White House for what is going on in this one: a complete lack of a policy apparatus," wrote John DiIulio, a moderately conservative professor at Penn tapped by Bush in 2001 to head his Faith-Based Initiative. DiIulio continued in a letter to the journalist Ron Suskind:

> I heard many, many staff discussions but not three meaningful, substantive policy discussions. There were no actual policy white papers on domestic issues. There were, truth be told, only a couple of people in the West Wing who worried at all about policy substance and analysis, and they were even more overworked than the stereotypical nonstop, twenty-hour-a-day White House staff. Every modern presidency moves on the fly, but on social policy and related issues, the lack of even basic policy knowledge, and the only casual interest in knowing more, was somewhat breathtaking: discussions by fairly senior people who meant Medicaid but were talking Medicare; near-instant shifts from discussing any actual policy pros and cons to discussing political communications, media strategy, et cetera. Even quite junior staff would sometimes hear quite senior staff poohpooh any need to dig deeper for pertinent information on a given issue.[44]

The new conservative spoilsmen regard the old progressive ideal of dispassionate experts guiding policy as elitist hogwash. This is why, for instance, they have so unashamedly expanded the use of pork barrel spending. Normal spending is supposed to be carried out through federal agencies, which try to allocate programs on the basis of need and effectiveness. Pork barrel spending circumvents this process altogether, allowing congressmen to allocate money directly without study or review. Joe Knollenberg, a Republican on the Appropriations Committee, which sits at the epicenter of the pork explosion, summed up the new ethos: "We say that we know better than federal officials and bureaucrats . . . where to spend money."[45]

This disdain for expertise creates a power vacuum in matters of policy, and into this void has flowed a stream of lobbyists. It has been a golden age for K Street. During the first five years of the Bush presidency, the number of registered lobbyists in Washington more than doubled. The starting salaries of political aides moving to K Street rose more than 50 percent, and the average fees charged by lobbyists approximately doubled, according to Jeffrey Birnbaum of the *Washington Post*.

Just as the technocracy was meant in part to displace the political machines of the Gilded Age, K Street has displaced the technocracy and taken on the same functions the machines once carried out. It provides funding for the party's campaigns, funnels lucre to its supporters, and offers patronage jobs for its cadres.

One of the consistent tasks of the Republican agenda over the last decade has been to nurture the K Street machine. Every new subsidy directed to the business lobby creates a new sector of the economy dependent in some way on its relationship with Washington. The Medicare bill is a classic example. Here is how Robert E. Moffitt, a policy analyst at the conservative Heritage Foundation, put it in an interview with the *Boston Globe:* "The Medicare system has now become a vast arena of special interest politics. It has been transformed from a system where we were providing health care for seniors into a system where there is a massive redistribution of income among health care providers."[46] The various tariffs, the corporate tax bill, the pork barrel spending, and the like all have the same effect. The beneficiaries understand that their interests are best served if they return a portion of their largesse in the form of donations and contribute to the spreading patronage network by employing Republicans in their Washington offices.

The new machine bosses, like the bosses of the Gilded Age, do have the delightful virtue of occasional candor. In 2002, David Pace of the Associated Press conducted a remarkable study of how federal spending shifted during GOP control of Congress. In 1995, the last year of Democratic control, the federal government spent an average of $35 million more in Democratic House districts than in

Republican districts. (This isn't surprising, since Democrats represent most of the poor districts that benefit from Medicaid, food stamps, and the like.) By 2001, the government was spending an average of $612 million more in *Republican* districts. Dick Armey, the former House majority leader, justified this massive transfer of wealth: "To the victor go the spoils."[47]

THE REVOLVING DOOR

O, the spoils to be reaped by those enterprising souls unburdened by conscience! The mathematical logic behind the explosive growth of K Street is inescapable. Large political contributions are measured in the tens or hundreds of thousands. Large tax cuts or expenditures are measured in the tens or hundreds of billions. The disparity between the scale of the money that flows into the political system and the scale of the money that flows out is simply enormous. If the government is controlled by a party unashamed at the prospect of doling out favors to its contributors, then the opportunities for arbitrage — for converting hundred-thousand-dollar contributions into billion-dollar tax breaks — are nearly endless.

Today's spoilsmen also see politics as a way to amass great wealth. But they are not pure mercenaries. The striking thing about the contemporary version is how seamlessly they have been able to blend personal gain with fealty to the conservative movement and Republican Party.

Jack Abramoff offers the quintessential case. His career path is fairly typical. He began, like Karl Rove, Ralph Reed, and other Republican icons, with the College Republicans, then went to work as a low-level party activist. He built personal relationships with other Republicans, got his law degree, and had his big break when the 1994 elections created a huge demand for Republican lobbyists.

Abramoff openly proclaimed his attachment to the GOP and its goals. "Tom [DeLay]'s goal is specific — to keep the Republicans in power and advance the conservative movement," he said. "I have Tom's goal precisely."[48] Indeed, Abramoff did his bit for the party. When he recruited clients, he instructed them to donate tens of thousands of dollars to the Republican Party and affiliated conservative groups, and he arranged lavish overseas trips for GOP members of Congress and their staff.

Abramoff's downfall in 2005 came about almost entirely by chance. The *Alexandria Town Talk*, a tiny newspaper in Louisiana, found that Indian tribes had paid tens of millions of dollars in fees to Abramoff and his partner, Michael Scanlon. A Senate investigative committee, outraged at the notion that the tribes were being bilked, cracked open Abramoff's finances and correspondence, and what oozed out did not flatter him. Abramoff wrote messages deriding his clients as "monkeys" and "troglodytes" and yearned, "I'd love us to get our mitts on that moolah!!"[49] His tawdriness bordered on the comical. At one point, he found himself seeking admission to the prestigious Cosmos Club and beseeched a friend who headed the conservative group Toward Tradition to polish his credentials:

> Problem for me is that most prospective members have received awards and I have received none. I was wondering if you thought it possible that I could put that I have received an award from Toward Tradition with a sufficiently academic title, perhaps something like Scholar of Talmudic Studies? . . . Indeed, it would be even better if it were possible that I received these in years past, if you know what I mean.[50]

In his personal indecency and the sheer scale of his greed — Abramoff and his partners took in $66 million from Indian casinos over three years — Abramoff stood apart.[52] On the other hand, there was something entirely typical about his place in the social and political structure of Washington. He was able to do good for his party by doing well for himself. This feature is the defining characteristic of the spoilsmen, as a small sampling of the type makes clear:

- One hesitates to define Ed Gillespie's formal job because at any given moment it is likely to change. Gillespie started his career in the 1980s as a Republican staffer on Capitol Hill, then moved to the Republican National Committee during the 1990s. In 1997, he quit his post to work as a lobbyist, but his influence in Republican politics continued to rise. Gillespie joined a committee of lobbyists who met weekly with top Republican officials to coordinate message, policy, and the K Street project. He was so highly regarded in this role that he was eventually invited into the Bush campaign's inner circle in 2000. That summer, he served as program chairman for the Republican National Convention and as one of the campaign's chief surrogates for disseminating hostile stories about Al Gore in the media.

  After briefly serving on Bush's transition team — where he was able to help place a colleague from his lobbying firm in the administration — Gillespie returned to his private practice. In so doing, his influence with Bush only increased. Now one of Washington's richest lobbyists, Gillespie was hired by the steel industry to help persuade Bush to adopt tariffs, which he did. He also organized corporate coalitions, featuring lobbying clients such as Enron and Microsoft, to raise money for public relations campaigns supporting initiatives like Bush's education reforms and the energy bill.[52]

  Over time, the pace of change in his C.V. has accelerated. In 2003, Bush tapped Gillespie to head the RNC, which he did through the 2004 campaign, this time suspending his lobbying work. Afterward, he returned to K Street but was tapped in 2005 to run Bush's efforts to promote his next Supreme Court nomination. (Gillespie managed to work out of the White House in this capacity while still lobbying for his corporate clients.) He retains his hybrid lobbyist-activist role today.

- Steven Griles was a lobbyist for oil, coal, and gas before Bush appointed him in 2001 to the second-ranking position in the Interior Department. His lobbying firm agreed to pay him $284,000 a year for four years as a buyout after he joined the public sector.

  It is actually legal to receive a salary from private interests while working in government as long as you recuse yourself from any decisions affecting your former firm. Griles, alas, made a regular practice of meeting with and making decisions affecting his former clients. When the Environmental Protection Agency threatened to take action that would harm a former client, he wrote a memo urging the agency to stop. He held a dinner party for the head of his former lobbying firm and other Interior officials and directed a $1.6 million government contract to a former client.

  In 2005 Griles left the department. Surprisingly, he did not return to his former lobbying firm. Unsurprisingly, he landed at a different lobbying firm, this one representing energy interests.[53]

- By the time Billy Tauzin retired from Congress in 2004, there was no question but that he would head to K Street. The only mystery involved exactly which business interest he would join — he had served so many so faithfully. As chairman of the House Energy and Commerce Committee, which has jurisdiction over a massive swath of the economy, he had done so much for so many. When, in the late 1990s, the SEC chairman, Arthur Levitt, tried to prevent accounting firms from soliciting consulting work from the same corporations they audited, Tauzin bullied Levitt into backing down. When a moderate Republican sought to enact stricter fuel efficiency standards, Tauzin went to bat for the oil companies. And he buried a bipartisan initiative to slow down media consolidation, delighting the broadcast lobby, which also happened to employ two of his children.[54]

  Ultimately, the most valuable payout that Tauzin had his hand in was the prescription drug bill, which featured measures worth hundreds of billions of dollars to the pharmaceutical industry. He began negotiating for the presidency of the Pharmaceutical Research and Manufacturers of America either while he was drafting the bill (according to his critics) or shortly thereafter (according to himself). Tauzin's compensation as president of the association was a reported $2 million a year, a princely sum for a former congressman but a pittance next to the vast fortune he had helped steer toward the industry.[55]

- Joe Barton, the chairman of the House Energy and Commerce Committee, hailed the energy bill as "well-crafted policy based on the free market."[56] How, one might wonder, could anybody regard this great mass of government subsidies as a triumph of the free market? The answer probably has something to do with Barton's own circumstances, where the distinction between government and private enterprise has grown increasingly blurry. As the *Wall Street Journal*'s Brody Mullins reported in 2005, Barton has turned his office into a veritable outpost of a Houston firm called Reliant Energy, which has donated some $35,000 to Barton's campaigns. Barton has placed a pair of former Reliant executives on his staff, and Reliant has hired away two Barton staffers as lobbyists. (Barton's spokesman defended the arrangement with an archetypal attack on the New Class: "Some think people with actual experience should be barred from helping make policy in their field of knowledge . . . that Congress should get all its policy advice from activists, bureaucrats and newspapers. That's hokum.")

  Reliant made out particularly well in the energy bill, having "bested industry rivals in lobbying for how the bill would shape the market," as the *Journal* noted. No doubt this did no harm to Barton's personal investment portfolio, which includes some $15,000 worth of Reliant stock.[57] That, however, is a trifling sum next to what awaits Barton should he eventually decide to go into lobbying. One suspects the thought that he just might do so has occurred to Barton as well as his likely future employer.

This is not a Republican rogues gallery but a pretty fair sample of the behavioral norms that prevail among the conservative political class. The most striking thing is that the conservatives in the public sector appear no less devoted to private interests than those directly employed by corporate lobbies. Indeed, there seems to be no sense, as there was in the old Democratic Washington, that when you move from partisan operative or government employee to hired gun you have "sold out" or even changed your basic professional allegiance.

This is certainly, in part, a story of corruption, of people who came to Washington believing in certain conservative ideals but who ultimately tailored their own views to those of the highest bidder. But the really striking corruption is not that of the individuals but of the movement itself. The spoilsmen are all Republicans and conservatives in good standing. They have not really needed to betray their principles because Republican ideology has evolved in such a way that it and the appetites of the business lobby have become one and the same.

3

DRIVING OUT THE HERETICS

In June 2004, Peter Kirsanow, a member of the U.S. Commission on Civil Rights, wrote a column for *National Review Online* urging that Ronald Reagan's bust be added to Mount Rushmore. "Not all great men merit great memorials," he began. "Those with spectacular achievements should surely be honored in ways more distinctive than mere recitations in history books. Statues, parks, and libraries usually suffice, for while many great leaders have momentous achievements, those of only a few are transcendent. Ronald Reagan's achievements were incontrovertibly the latter."[1]

There are a number of problems with the notion of chiseling the fortieth president's visage on Mount Rushmore, the most serious one being geology. The Park Service long ago concluded that Mount Rushmore was too unstable for future drilling. Douglas Blankenship, a geo-mechanics expert in Rapid City, South Dakota, has further explained that there is not enough room to add another presidential head.[2] Kirsanow nonetheless championed the idea, and in his column he waved off the objections with the grand conclusion: "It's doable. If Reagan's optimism taught us anything, it's that."

The remarkable thing about this column was that it was completely unremarkable. Reagan veneration is a distinct subgenre within the conservative media. It exists as a kind of contest of superlatives. Reagan's wisdom can be invoked to overcome any obstacles, even the seemingly insurmountable limits of geology and physics.

In the conservative mind, the Reagan presidency lives on in the golden shimmering past, an ideal that Reagan's successors must always strive to approach but can never fully live up to, like the teachings of Christ. There is indeed something distinctly religious about the expressions that the adoration of Reagan has taken. I have been told that it is fashionable for conservatives to name their children, both boys and girls, Reagan. (Since the mid-1980s, it has shot up the list of popular baby names.)[3] Right-leaning magazines periodically advertise bronze busts of the fortieth president. And rather than leave the commemoration efforts to the free market, conservatives have undertaken a vast national campaign. Renaming Washington National Airport after Reagan in 1998 was merely the first step. Americans for Tax Reform, the activist group headed by the conservative impresario Grover Norquist, has been at work on a campaign to name something after Reagan in every county in the United States. The efforts range from the kitschy (Reagan's hometown of Dixon, Illinois, commissioned a six-foot portrait of the Gipper made of jelly beans, his favorite snack) to the grandiose (an aircraft carrier was christened the U.S.S. *Ronald Reagan* in 2001).[4]

Conservatives invariably invoke Reagan as humble acolytes, seeking to spread his word to the faithful and beyond. The American Enterprise Institute scholar Dinesh D'Souza once wrote: "The right simply needs to approach public policy questions by asking: what would Reagan have done?"[5] He was simply making explicit a widespread assumption on the right. In the conservative press, where Reagan is a living, breathing presence cited almost daily, "What would Reagan do?" is among the most hackneyed phrases. Conservatives speak constantly of "the lessons of Ronald Reagan" or "what Reagan taught us."

Just as the Bible or the Koran can be interpreted to impart wisdom on questions not directly addressed therein, the lessons of Reagan are not necessarily limited to those issues on which he had any kind of public position. In 2000, the *Wall Street Journal* columnist and former Reagan speechwriter Peggy Noonan argued for the proposition that dolphins acting on God's orders rescued the Cuban refugee Elián González. "Mr. Reagan," she wrote, "would not have dismissed the story of the dolphins as Christian kitsch, but seen it as possible evidence of the reasonable assumption that God's creatures have been commanded to rescue one of God's children."[6] A person unfamiliar with the conservative subculture reading this sentence might have assumed that Noonan was belittling Reagan. But of course she was not. Noonan assumed her conservative readers would share her faith that if Reagan believed it, then it must be true.

On those issues that divide conservatives, each side invariably grasps for the mantle of Reaganism. On the matter of, say, opening the market to Chinese imports, supporters will cite Reagan's commitment to free trade, while opponents will expound on his anticommunism. The conservative discord over immigration that floated to the surface in 2006 was a classic example. Reagan never gave the issue more than passing attention. But seventeen years after he left office, feuding conservatives frantically combed the Reagan canon for evidence of his views, which they then produced triumphantly against each other. The GOP strategist Craig Shirley wrote in one op-ed piece: "Reagan argued that it was our government's duty to 'humanely regain control of our borders and thereby preserve the value of one of the most sacred possessions of our people: American citizenship.'" The *Wall Street Journal* struck back with a lengthy editorial, "Reagan on Immigration," quoting letters and radio addresses for hints, some of them quite oblique, pointing to Reagan's sympathy for open borders.[7] In the world of the right, to associate a position with Reagan is to establish its truth axiomatically.

While the Reagan liturgy can be extended to exotic causes such as dolphin miracles, it is most often applied to its most essential and agreed-on themes. Those, to quote a completely typical bit of doggerel published in the *Washington Times,* would be "Mr. Reagan's unwavering commitment to a few core ideas," namely, military strength and lower taxes.[8] In a 2005 editorial, the *Weekly Standard*'s editor, William Kristol, urged, "It's not too soon for the president to start recapturing the Reaganite high ground of tax cuts and economic growth and opportunity."[9] One might have thought that the four major tax cuts Bush had enacted up to that point would have sufficiently claimed the tax-cutting high ground. But since Reagan was utterly unwavering in his devotion to lower taxes, others can only but strive to match him.

If you ask Republicans how it came to be that their party embraced tax cuts as the be-all and end-all of its domestic policy, they will almost certainly invoke Reagan. The former treasury secretary Paul O'Neill recounted in his book that when he expressed reservations over another tax cut in the face of deficits during a Cabinet meeting after the 2002 elections, Dick Cheney responded, "Reagan proved deficits don't matter."[10] Among Republicans, that argument is usually definitive. Ours is not to question Reagan's will, only to carry it out.

CONSERVATIVES IN THE WILDERNESS

Why does the right not merely admire but nearly worship (in the literal sense) Ronald Reagan? A major part of the answer is that, before he came along, the conservative movement was deeply estranged from the leadership of the Republican Party, especially at the presidential level.

After World War II, the mainstream of the GOP made its peace with the new, expanded role for government ushered in by Franklin Roosevelt. Eisenhower accepted the Keynesian view, such an anathema to conservatives just a decade or two before, that recessions were not self-correcting and required government activity. He accepted as well the New Deal's expansions of government like Social Security, labor laws, and unemployment insurance.[11] Conservatives regarded Eisenhower with almost complete hostility. The *National Review*'s founder, William F. Buckley, called his program "undirected by principle, unchained to any coherent idea as to the nature of man and society, uncommitted to any sustained estimate of the nature or potential of the enemy."[12] To the extent that he was "conservative," it was a conservatism wholly alien to that of the modern right: fiscal conservatism, not tax-cutting. Eisenhower, his administrative assistant wrote, "once told the cabinet that if he was able to do nothing as president except balance the budget he would feel that his time in the White House had been well spent."[13]

Things got even worse for conservatives under Richard Nixon — who, as many people now realize, would by contemporary standards rank as a fanatic liberal. It was Nixon who famously declared: "We are all Keynesians now." He dramatically expanded federal regulation of the environment and occupational safety. He signed a progressive tax reform, wiping out tax shelters and other forms of special treatment for owners of capital. (The *New Republic* called it "far and away the most 'anti-rich' tax reform proposal ever imposed by a Republican president.") Nixon also proposed a generous family assistance plan and health care reform, both of which liberal Democrats, astonishingly, killed because they didn't go far enough.[14] Gerald Ford governed in a more conservative fashion, but his con-

VISIT US AT
WWW.USNEWS.COM

BUSINESS REPLY MAIL
FIRST-CLASS MAIL   PERMIT NO. 268   FLAGLER BEACH FL

POSTAGE WILL BE PAID BY ADDRESSEE

US NEWS & WORLD REPORT
SUBSCRIPTION DEPT
PO BOX 421177
PALM COAST FL 32142-7749

Brevity being about a certain

Comment of distinction

whether the cause be a lunheat, when any
not be adequate cause to interfere
precis, ungerprint physiogene and do not
need to decide on over to know etpicule

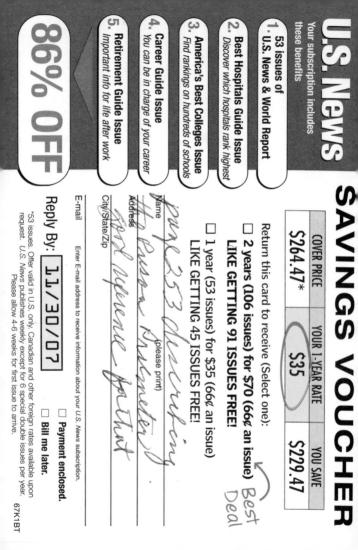

servatism was in the Eisenhower mold — born of opposition to deficits, not rolling back the size of government.

Reagan is the one who delivered conservatives from political exile. In his inaugural address, he broke from decades of bipartisan acceptance of big government when he announced: "Government is not the solution to our problem; government is the problem." He slashed taxes and unapologetically championed businessmen and the pursuit of wealth. He fired the air traffic controllers and railed against "welfare queens." Conservatism, confined to the margins of the national discourse for nearly fifty years before Reagan, has remained at or near the center ever since. No wonder conservatives regard him as a savior.

YET HERE IS the funny thing. The Reagan administration was not, in fact, the epitome of unwavering conservatism. In foreign affairs, Reagan withdrew the marines from Lebanon after a 1983 car bomb attack, and he enraged hawks by signing an arms control treaty with the Soviet Union in 1987. On social policy, he avoided associating himself too closely with the Right-to-Life movement, declined to press for constitutional amendments on issues like school prayer and abortion, and (after the defeat of Robert Bork) appointed moderate Supreme Court justices, Sandra Day O'Connor and Anthony Kennedy. Conservatives at the time frequently savaged the president for his ideological infidelity. In 1982, *Conservative Digest* published an entire issue criticizing Reagan from the right under the headline: "Has Reagan Deserted the Conservatives?"[15] In 1984, when the Heritage Foundation's journal *Policy Review* asked eleven conservative activists and intellectuals to evaluate Reagan's tenure to date, eight gave him negative reviews.[16]

Nowhere was Reagan less faithful to conservative ideals than in the economic realm. It is true, as his adherents remind one another continuously, that he enacted a huge supply-side tax cut in 1981 that unapologetically targeted the highest income levels. Yet he also spent the remaining seven years of his presidency backtracking. Conservatives have written these last seven years almost completely out of their history. On the occasion of Reagan's death, a *Washington Times* editorial summed up his economic record. It cited his tax cuts, then noted: "At great political cost to himself, Mr. Reagan steadfastly, and rightly, insisted on 'staying the course' throughout the deep, Volcker-instigated recession of 1981–82."[17] In fact, the Reagan administration, panicked by rising deficits, signed on to the largest tax increase in American history in 1982 and another major tax hike in 1983.[18]

Reagan's most shocking act of ideological heterodoxy was to embrace tax reform. In the run-up to the 1984 election, a liberal group called Citizens for Tax Justice issued a report showing that, due to loopholes opened by Reagan's 1981 tax cut, 128 out of 250 large and profitable corporations had paid no income tax at all during some, or even all, of the previous three years.[19] The Reagan administration promised to put an end to these inequities, and assigned the Treasury secretary, Don Regan, to design a sweeping overhaul of the tax code. Some of the Reaganites merely wanted to avoid handing the Democrats a weapon in the 1984 elections. Others, though, felt genuine regret at the unfairness of the loopholes. Regan would fill the president with populist ire against the unfairness of the tax code. "The tax system we now have," he told Reagan, according to Cannon, "is designed to make the avoidance of taxes easy for the rich and has the effect of making it almost impossible for people who work for wages and salaries to do the same."[20]

While it did lower the top tax rate, in every other respect the Tax Reform Act that Reagan signed in 1986 was a liberal triumph. It dramatically raised effective tax rates on corporations. It did away with preferential treatment for capital gains and other investment income, embodying the longtime goal of reformers to treat income from wages and income from wealth equally. Overall, Reagan's reform raised the proportion of taxes paid by the rich and reduced the proportion paid by the poor.[21]

The Republican right considered this apostasy, and still does. In 2005, the *National Review*'s Ramesh Ponnuru summed up the contemporary conservative view when he called the 1986 Tax Reform Act "a major setback for conservatives. Congress adopted the liberal definition of tax reform, and broadened the tax base to include things it should not have included. . . . For most of the subsequent two decades, conservatives have been trying to undo the policy damages wrought by those changes."*[22]

If it frustrated ideological conservatives, it infuriated K Street. A major goal of tax reform was to wipe out political preferences in the tax code, so naturally the beneficiaries of those preferences sent their lobbyists out to fight for them tooth and nail. The battle between the reformers and the lobbyists swung back and forth. In their classic account of the battle, "Showdown at Gucci Gulch," the *Wall Street Journal* reporters Alan Murray and Jeffrey Birnbaum captured one moment when the latter had gained the upper hand:

> On April 10, the [Senate Finance] committee adopted a crazy-quilt depreciation system that ostensibly gave more generous write-offs for machinery and equipment that were used in "productive" purposes than those that were not. This dubious distinction was the invention of lobbyists Charles Walker and Ernest Christian and their heavy-industry allies in the Carlton Group that represented major rubber, steel, aluminum, and petroleum producers. The system, in fact, was largely a ruse to mask the committee members' frenzy to aid the industries they were beholden to.[23]

---

* How do conservatives reconcile their veneration of Reagan and their dismay at the Tax Reform Act? Very carefully. Their main technique is to keep discussions of the policy and discussions of Reagan in separate spheres. In the context of a discussion of tax policy, they will denigrate the 1986 Tax Reform Act and glance over their hero's role in signing it. In the context of discussing Reagan's legacy, they will praise the fact that the act reduced marginal tax rates and ignore the other provisions that made it so abhorrent to them.

"Frenzy to aid the industries they were beholden to" is a pretty good description of the tax policy under today's Republican Party. In fact, the tax lobbyist Ernest Christian has formulated a plan, known as "Five Easy Pieces," that the Bush administration and its allies have embraced as their vision of the tax code.[24] Its thrust has been to undo most of the 1986 reforms. Rather than tax investment income and labor income on an equal basis, Bush has tried to wipe out all taxes on capital by eliminating the estate tax and slashing rates on capital gains and dividends. Rather than eliminate tax loopholes, Bush has signed into law countless new ones. And rather than make the tax code more progressive, Bush has made it less so. That's what happens when lobbyists design your tax plan rather than go to war against it.

None of this is to say that Reagan was an economic liberal or even a moderate. He was a staunch conservative *by the standards of his day*. But the definition of what counts as conservative has lurched far to the right over the last two decades. By the standards of the present day, Reagan was relatively moderate. A Republican president today could no more undertake Reagan's tax hikes or reform than a contemporary Democratic president could reinstate Woodrow Wilson's policies of racial segregation. In the broad sweep of things, Reagan ought to be seen as a transition figure, roughly halfway between the moderate Republican Party of Eisenhower and Nixon and the radical party of George W. Bush.

IT MAY SEEM curious that the metamorphosis of the GOP did not fully come to fruition during Reagan's presidency, for the primary elements were all in place during the 1980s. The previous decade had already seen the onset of the supply-siders and the rise of K Street. Given all this, why did Reagan's policies take on what is in retrospect a relatively moderate cast?

The answer is that Reagan's administration was filled with advisers in the traditional Republican mold. While supply-siders deified

Reagan retrospectively, at the time they saw themselves as a small, embattled minority within the administration. In 1981, the columnists Rowland Evans and Robert Novak complained that Reagan "has to fight better than two-thirds of his economic team to save his program."[25] Paul Craig Roberts, an ardent supply-sider in the Treasury Department, later wrote in a memoir: "The advisors with the readiest access to the President were mostly people who saw tax *increases* as the means to a stronger economy."[26]

Those influential advisers included moderates like David Gergen, Richard Darman, James Baker, Ken Duberstein, David Stockman (after he realized that the original goals of Reaganomics had failed), and Howard Baker (late in Reagan's second term), among others. These were men reared in the mores of the Washington establishment. Gergen later told Lou Cannon that the White House staff would often gather around the evening news programs, which they considered "a reality check."[27] (George W. Bush, of course, disdains the mainstream media and once said he thinks the most objective news comes from his subordinates.)[28] Stockman revealed a great deal about the mindset that prevailed among most of these aides when he explained his decision to give a long series of interviews about Reagan's economic plan to the *Washington Post's* William Greider. "My intellectual impulse was to try to penetrate the citadel of establishment opinion makers — and those opinion makers hung out, so to speak, in the pages of the *Washington Post*," he wrote.[29] This sort of mentality would be utterly alien to members of George W. Bush's staff, who regard journalists, other than committed partisans like Rush Limbaugh, as unalterably hostile.

In late 2005, when Bush's popularity was sinking under the weight of his inept response to Hurricane Katrina, the CIA leak scandal, and other failures, moderate Reagan veterans urged Bush to shake up his presidency. Kenneth Duberstein wrote an op-ed piece recalling how Reagan made some small concessions to the opposition (for instance, reversing his past opposition to reparations for Japanese Americans), apologized for the Iran-Contra scandal, "opened the doors of the West Wing to fresh voices," and recommended that Bush follow suit. Gergen echoed Duberstein's counsel.[30] But Fred Barnes, a conservative pundit who unfailingly reflects Bush's sentiments, dismissed them as "establishment mouthpieces,"[31] and of course Bush rejected the advice out of hand.

It is hard to imagine today that there was a time, just two decades earlier, when the Ken Dubersteins and David Gergens of the world held real power in a conservative Republican administration. The moderates surrounding Reagan shared his goals in a broad sense, but their partisanship had limits. They were committed to a broader, cross-party ethos of good government. They did not see themselves as the shock troops of a revolution. They would pursue ideological goals, but if those goals proved unworkable, they would change course. It would never occur to them to tailor large swaths of domestic policy for the sole purpose of funneling largesse to their political supporters.[32]

They are the kinds of men, in other words, who could never be allowed to hold any position of influence in the contemporary Republican Party. The transformation of the party into what it is today could not have happened until the moderate party elites were driven completely out of the corridors of power. Which, in short order, they were.

THE APOSTASY OF GEORGE H. W. BUSH

In the Republican cosmology, there is also a very bad man, an anti-Reagan, who serves as a cautionary tale. That man is George Herbert Walker Bush. When the faithful invoke his name, it is in rueful tones. He departed from the true path and suffered terribly and deservedly as a result. The lesson of his betrayal must never be forgotten.

Bush's crime, of course, was to raise taxes. Though he had won the presidency in 1988 in part due to his promise of "no new taxes," by the second year of his term, the government was facing a massive fiscal crisis. The catch was that Democrats, who controlled Congress, insisted that some of the burden of reducing the deficit be shared by the affluent in the form of tax hikes.

Bush understood that reneging on his pledge would hurt him politically, but he felt he had no choice but to go along. You can see why it made sense to him. After all, Reagan had raised taxes in 1982 and 1983, and he had soaked the rich in 1986, all without fatal consequences. And it was not at all clear that the deal Bush struck in 1990 was bad from a conservative standpoint, at least not a *traditional* conservative standpoint. In return for acceding to a small hike in the top tax bracket, from 28 to 31 percent, Bush won very stringent limits on spending.[33] It was the responsible, establishment Republican thing to do.

Conservatives rose up in open revolt in a reaction that was nothing less than hysterical. House Republicans called the budget deal "the fiscal equivalent of Yalta" — the 1945 meeting at which Roosevelt met with Stalin to map out the postwar world and, conservatives believe, was duped into allowing the Soviet conquest of Eastern Europe.[34] What Bush failed to realize was that the Republican establishment he had known was fast disappearing, and the 1990 budget deal was its final gasp. Just consider three relatively similar efforts to reduce the deficit. In 1982, Reagan's plan to raise taxes and trim spending attracted slightly higher support from Republicans than from Democrats (who, traditionally, had worried less about deficit spending).[35] In 1990, the balance began tipping the other way, with most Republicans voting no, forcing the plan to squeak through with higher levels of Democratic support.[36] By 1993, Republican support for the notion of cutting the deficit through a mix of tax hikes and spending cuts had collapsed entirely. That year, when Bill Clinton declared his intent to chip away at the deficit again, Republicans categorically ruled out any tax hike. Clinton's budget passed without a single GOP vote in either the House or the Senate.[37]

The moment that set off the final banishment of the moderates was Bush's defeat in the 1992 election. Suddenly the catechism was clear. Taxes explained why Reagan had won and why Bush had lost, and this blazingly simple message would now be understood by one and all. As Norquist told the *New Yorker* in 2005, "Bush 41, the dad, he ran as Ronald Reagan '88. The problem was he didn't govern as Reagan. He raised taxes. He betrayed the people who elected him, and he was rejected."[38] This explanation was at best a massive oversimplification. Bush lost in 1992 because of a poor economy, a strong challenger in Bill Clinton, a third-party candidate in Ross Perot who divided his base, and the general exhaustion of the conservative agenda.

The conservatives, though, insisted on interpreting Bush's loss as a betrayal rather than a defeat. And at the heart of that betrayal stood one man: Richard Darman. In many ways, Darman epitomized the centrist Republican establishment that had held sway for most of the postwar years. After studying at Harvard, he came into government as a protégé of Elliot Richardson, the moderate Republican who gained fame for resigning rather than obey Nixon's order to fire the Watergate special prosecutor. Darman then served as assistant secretary of commerce in the Ford administration. James Baker brought him into the Reagan administration, where, as assistant to the president, he gained a reputation as a policy wonk's policy wonk. His status as rising bureaucratic star, and his connection to Baker, caused George Bush to make him budget director in 1989.[39] Since leaving Washington in 1993, he has taught politics at Harvard's Kennedy School of Government and written sonorous op-ed pieces urging bipartisanship and castigating both parties for failing to take the deficit seriously. He would seem to be an unlikely candidate for a symbol of evil and treachery.

But it was Darman who helped engineer the 1990 budget compromise, and hence Darman who bore the brunt of the backlash. A story in *National Review* attacked the budget deal as "Darman's Disaster — Bush's Responsibility." Conservative Republicans in Congress called it "Darmaggedon."[40] When Bush lost his bid for re-election in 1992, Darman was quickly blamed and immediately became an outcast, even a sort of bogeyman. Conservative pundits use the word "Darman" as an insult, signifying a betrayal of the movement's core beliefs. In 2000, John Harwood reported a story for the *Wall Street Journal* noting that Darman, absent from the GOP convention in Philadelphia, had become "the party's untouchable."[41]

It was Bush's loss that inspired the right to deify Reagan. At the outset of the Clinton presidency, with Republican fortunes at their nadir, the conservative David Frum wrote a book called *Dead Right*. In it he lamented, "Post-Bush conservatives look back on the accomplishments of the early Reagan years the way seventh-century Romans must have looked at their aqueducts: to think that we once built all this!"[42] And so they turned with urgency to the task of purifying their party in the Reagan image. Henceforth, every standard-bearer would be scrutinized for his or her fidelity to the teachings of the great leader — which meant, above all, unquestioning devotion to tax cuts.

Bob Dole appeared before the Republic National Committee seeking the 1996 nomination and declared, with his characteristic cynical bluntness: "I'm willing to be another Ronald Reagan if that's what you want."[43] (That is what they wanted.) When Dole dutifully went on to propose a sweeping 15 percent income tax cut, conservatives responded ecstatically. A *Wall Street Journal* editorial lauded his "determination to return the GOP to pro-growth, Reaganite themes."[44] Norquist exulted, "When Bob Dole released his economic plan on August 5 and chose Jack Kemp as his running mate five days later, he opted for Ronald Reagan over Richard Nixon — and guaranteed that this presidential election will be about tax cuts, tax cuts, and tax cuts."[45]

When Dole failed to gain ground, conservatives complained that he had not given the tax cut sufficient emphasis. So he began appearing in front of giant banners advertising his tax cuts and affixing a "15 percent" button to his sport coats at all times, so that any photograph or video image of him would reflect his central campaign issue. Alas, he nonetheless failed to win. One might suspect that the resounding defeat of a high-profile tax-cutter would have provoked a minor crisis of faith among the Reagan acolytes. Not at all. "Mr. Dole's across-the-board tax plan failed to catch on because, unlike Ronald Reagan, he did not have any credibility as a tax-cutter," noted the *Washington Times,* summing up the consensus among the faithful.[46] Once again, defeat could be explained by the candidate's insufficient fealty to Reaganism.

George W. Bush's campaign understood that winning over the conservatives — the new party establishment — would require aligning himself with Reagan against his father. Over the course of 1999, when he sowed the support of the GOP hierarchy, he established his bona fides with a series of interviews where he dropped a series of catchphrases that by and large escaped detection by the mainstream press but were unmistakable to the conservative subculture. In a written answer to a query from the *Weekly Standard*'s editor, Fred Barnes, Bush stated that his favorite Supreme Court justice was Reagan's appointee Antonin Scalia, not his father's appointee Clarence Thomas. Barnes read this as highly significant and also noted that "Bush is not an admirer of his father's other nominee, David Souter."[47] Bush's foreign policy speech from November of that year, conservatives happily pointed out, took place at the Reagan library, not the Bush library, and it mentioned Reagan's name six times, with just one passing reference to his father. "The Texas Republican is sending a message," wrote the conservative columnist Cal Thomas. "A George W. Bush presidency, he signaled, will be Reagan III, not Bush II."[48]

In a December interview with Robert Bartley, the younger Bush endorsed virtually the whole of the conservative litany against his father. Bush told Bartley that his father's broken pledge on taxes "destabilized his base," costing him the election. "I don't think he properly spent the political capital coming out of the Gulf War," he added. Bartley, pleased, noted, "When the governor first assembled his economic team, he told them to notice the absence of Dick Darman." In the interview, Bush fairly apologized for not going further in denouncing his father. "Forget politics; he's a fabulous man, and a great father and a great husband," he explained. "And that's what matters, more than politics or polls or read-my-lips . . . So you've got to understand a little bit about me." (Not so subtle message: Only family loyalty prevents me from repudiating my dad more forcefully.) The *Journal*, impressed, editorialized that Bush's tax cut "moves in the Reagan direction."[49]

And what does 2008 hold? As Norquist says, "The person who runs closest to the model of Ronald Reagan will win."

GROVER NORQUIST AND THE ANTI-TAX IMPERATIVE

Norquist, as the president of the Ronald Reagan Legacy project, is obviously a central figure in the campaign to memorialize the former president. Fittingly, he is also a central figure in the organization of the conservative movement. To define Reaganism, as we have seen, is to define the goals and priorities of the movement and the Republican Party. Because Republicans see the Reagan legacy as a kind of religious text — a source of eternal truth from which all wisdom derives — enormous power is vested in the hands of the clerical elite that translates its meaning for the flock. As Norquist sees it, Reaganism means, above all else, cutting taxes, especially for businesses and wealthy individuals. He has helped to shape the movement and the party into a vast apparatus dedicated almost single-mindedly to that goal.

Norquist, a roundish man with a red-brown beard, established his rabid antistatism from a young age. Raised in an upper-middle-class household in Massachusetts, Norquist's father would frequently remind him of the evils of the welfare state by stealing bites from young Grover's ice cream cone — one bite for sales tax, another bite for income tax, and so on. At Harvard, Norquist was remembered as a brainy but socially maladjusted conservative rebel. After graduation, he joined the College Republicans, where he forged a friendship with his future fellow Republican operative Ralph Reed. Far from taming his radical impulses, Norquist's arrival in Washington only stoked them. He later recalled his horror at seeing the gleaming marble monuments of the capital — "stuff that looks like Albert Speer designed it," he later said — all built with money unfairly stolen from the taxpayers. Norquist would drive around the city late at night singing anarchist anthems:

> The state conceived in blood and hate
> Remains our only foe.
> So circle brothers, circle brothers,
> Victory is nigh!
> Come meet thy fate, destroy the state
> And raise black banners high.[50]

Unlike other ideological radicals, Norquist did not wind up cranking out obscure pamphlets or hoarding handmade bombs in a mountain cabin. Instead, he channeled his energies into the Republican Party. Norquist has described himself, aptly, as a "Market-Leninist." In Leninist fashion, he sees politics as a Manichean struggle between what he calls "our team" and "their team." He does not see power as something that can be shared between the two sides — he famously compared bipartisanship to date rape — or as something that naturally swings back and forth over time. Rather, he deals in dialectical shifts, such as the inevitable death of the World War II generation, a group that Norquist has called "anti-American" for its statist proclivities, or the rise of stock ownership, which conservatives call "the investor class." "You can't have a hate-and-envy class if 80 percent of the public owns stock," he once declared, "That makes it impossible for Democrats to govern. It spells the end of their world."[51] He frequently refers to the conservative struggle, and its inevitable triumph, as "the revolution."

Norquist, like a James Bond villain, has an irrepressible penchant for spelling out his master plans in their full, nefarious detail. He delights in casting his goals in the coarsest and most sinister terms. According to the journalist Nina Easton,* he kept a pet boa constrictor and fed it a series of mice named after the former Democratic whip David Bonior. After the 2004 election, he proposed to the *Washington Post* that Democrats would become content once they accepted their permanent minority status. "Once the minority of House and Senate are comfortable in their minority status, they will have no problem socializing with the Republicans," he noted. "Any farmer will tell you that certain animals run around and are unpleasant, but when they've been fixed, then they are happy and sedate."[52] He once railed against a group of millionaires seeking to preserve the estate tax, which was already scheduled for termination. "They're embarrassing," he said. "They're flopping around like that stupid fish in the boat. It's over, fish! It's done! You're dinner!"[53]

Norquist boasts close links with powerful Republicans, having conferred regularly with Newt Gingrich during his heyday and currently maintaining close ties with Karl Rove and the GOP leadership. He also presides over the Wednesday Group, a weekly meeting often called "the Grand Central Station of the conservative movement." There, the sundry elements of the GOP coalition hash

---

* Who profiled Norquist and four other movement figures in her outstanding book *Gang of Five.*

out the party line. Lobbyists, partisans, activists, and conservative journalists all commingle, with the shared sense that they are all part of what Norquist calls "our team." *Slate's* editor, Jacob Weisberg, once described the vanguard of the conservative movement as the "conintern" — an apparatus, like the old Bolshevik comintern, designed to encourage intellectual accord within the movement.[54] Norquist's meetings are the heart of the conintern. "I spend a lot of time working with the conservative press to make sure that we're all thinking alike and talking alike," Norquist once said.[55] Once hashed out in the Wednesday Group, the party line will soon emanate throughout the conservative media.

Norquist describes the components of the GOP as the "leave us alone coalition" — an assemblage of groups that, however diverse their interests, stand united in their essential desire to be free of interference from the federal government. It's a concept of government very much slanted toward Norquist's own inclinations, which run heavily toward libertarianism.[56] Of course, Norquist's econocentric vision is hardly a natural fit for every element of the GOP coalition. Religious conservatives, for example, do not just want the federal government to leave them alone. They want it to ban abortion, clamp down on gay rights, and in general promote traditional values. Norquist refuses to state his position on legalized abortion and gay rights, but nobody doubts that he personally supports them. He simply insists that religious conservatives share his agenda.

"Southern Baptists will be happy in George Bush's America with lower taxes and less regulation," he told the *New Yorker*. "And everybody will be able to go to the pornographic theater as they see fit."[57] Norquist welcomes pro-choice Republicans and other social moderates and liberals to his meetings. When divisive social issues arise, he deflects them by insisting, "No sex talk, please."[58]

The one issue on which dissent is completely forbidden is, of course, taxes. To that end, Norquist has devised a Taxpayer Protection Pledge — a form that Republican candidates must sign wherein they promise never to raise taxes under any circumstances. Over time, the pledge has become mandatory for GOP office-holders at the national level. The last three Republican presidential candidates and nearly every Republican member of Congress have signed it. Norquist frequently invokes George Bush's 1992 defeat as the ultimate affirmation of the power of the pledge. He notes with pride that since that point, no Republican at the national level has ever voted for a tax hike.[59]

The only significant part of the Republican Party where dissent exists on taxes is at the state level. States, unlike the federal government, are required to balance their budget every year. This means Republican governors, unlike Republican members of Congress, often have to match tax cuts with spending cuts, which tend to be unpopular. Thus Norquist has had to swoop down regularly to quash heretical governors. Staunch conservatives such as Bill Owens of Colorado and Mitch Daniels of Indiana, simply because they have blanched at the prospect of slashing their state's physical infrastructure or leaving the disabled to fend for themselves, have faced Norquist's wrath.

Norquist's most flamboyant suppression of heresy came in, of all places, Alabama. The heretic was Governor Bob Riley, a staunch conservative who as a former member of Congress had supported Bush's tax cuts in 2001. (In that capacity, Riley had received from Americans for Tax Reform a "Hero of the Taxpayer" award, one of Norquist's Leninist touches.) When he came into office in 2003, Riley faced a $675 million deficit. He did not want to slash funding for prisons or schools. Moreover — and here was the really shocking part — he found himself disgusted by the state's antique tax system. Enshrined in the state constitution a century earlier, the Alabama tax code was designed to protect the timber and cotton industries that had dictated it. Timber companies, for instance, owned 71 percent of the state's land but paid a mere 2 percent of the property taxes. The poor, on the other hand, were punished. The poorest one-fifth of Alabamans paid more than 10 percent of their income in state taxes, while the richest 1 percent paid less than 4 percent.[60]

The blunt force of these facts seems to have struck Riley as a revelation. He underwent a sort of Bulworth conversion, furiously denouncing the status quo and vowing to equalize the tax burden by slashing rates on the poor while raising them on the rich. This is what made his defection so galling. It was not just that a Republican governor was recognizing the need for higher revenue. He was explicitly embracing the moral logic of forcing the rich to pay higher tax rates than the poor. Norquist recognized that this sort of heresy threatened the anti-tax movement's grip on the Republican Party. If a reliable figure like Riley could be struck by his social conscience, anybody could. And if Republicans could be persuaded to embrace the logic of "fairness" in the tax code, it was just a matter of time before they applied this concept at the federal level as well.

When Riley put his reform before the voters, therefore, Norquist set out to extinguish it. "It is not good enough to win; it has to be a painful and devastating defeat," he declared. "We're sending a message here. It is like when the king would take his opponent's head and stick it on a pike for everyone to see." National conservative groups mobilized against Riley, and conservative pundits everywhere denounced him. Norquist funneled hundreds of thousands of dollars to the Alabama chapter of the Christian Coalition, which campaigned against the reform. Ultimately, it lost soundly.[61]

NO DISSENT FROM ORTHODOXY

Norquist obviously does not speak for all conservatives, but his vision predominates in Washington. Stephen Moore, then president of an anti-tax lobby called the Club for Growth and currently a

Wall Street Journal editorial writer, explained the state of affairs: "Low taxes are the central linchpin of conservatism. We always say it's possible to disagree about abortion, gay rights, the proper level of Americorps funding or military spending, but we can't disagree about our one unifying message as conservatives."[62]

A conventional wisdom has formed to the effect that Republicans cut taxes in order to please their base. This is true if you define the base as the lobbyists, pundits, intellectuals, and other cadres revolving around Washington in general and Norquist's meetings in particular. But the party *voting* base does not cherish tax cuts to anything like the degree that the party elite does. A *New York Times* poll in early 2003 found that "a majority of the poll's respondents — including 49 percent of Republicans — said reducing the deficit would be more likely to revive the economy than would cutting taxes." Another, taken a few weeks after the 2004 election, showed that 51 percent of Republicans preferred reducing the deficit to cutting taxes.[63]

The most thorough exegesis of how the Republican rank and file thinks about politics comes from an extensive survey conducted in 2005 by the Pew Research Center. Rather than merely poll the electorate, the Pew survey broke the voting population into distinct ideological blocs. The GOP base, Pew found, consists of three groups, accounting among them for a third of the electorate. One of those groups, which the survey termed Enterprisers, holds conservative views on economic and social policy. But Enterprisers only account for 10 percent of all voters. Two other groups help form the Republican base — Social Conservatives, who comprise 13 percent of voters, and Pro-Government Conservatives, who account for 10 percent. Both dissent markedly from conservative economic thinking.[64]

While Enterprisers oppose raising taxes in order to extend government health insurance to all, it is favored by wide margins by Social Conservatives (59 to 37 percent) and Pro-Government Conservatives (63 to 33 percent). Enterprisers overwhelmingly oppose repealing the portion of the Bush tax cuts that benefit the affluent, but the other two groups support it — Pro-Government Conservatives by a thirty-point margin. Republicans, then, follow an economic policy dictated not by their base but by a group that constitutes less than a third of the base. And even that segment cannot match the Republican Party in Washington for sheer zealotry. When asked by Pew if tax cuts mattered more than deficit reduction, Social and Pro-Government Conservatives chose deficit reduction by wide margins. Even Enterprisers chose tax cuts by only a narrow margin (50 to 43 percent).[65] Which is to say, the Republican Party's position on fiscal policy is to the right of even the most conservative 10 percent of the electorate.

The anti-tax movement's triumph does not represent a burbling up of grassroots sentiment within the Republican Party. It is a top-down takeover by an elite ideological vanguard that has successfully redefined Republicanism as conservatism, conservatism as Reaganism, and Reaganism as a relentless and uncompromising opposition to taxes, especially those paid by the rich.

Of course, Norquist and his allies enjoy the enormous advantage of having far more money than other segments of the Republican base. As noted earlier, the Republican agenda has increasingly become synonymous with the accumulated desires of its funding base.

But the disappearance of fiscal moderation among Republican elites owes a great deal to the lack of outlets for its intellectual expression. What newspaper, magazine, columnist, or talk show host exists to give voice to the old Eisenhower Republican ideal of fiscal conservatism? None. The Bush tax cuts* have received editorial endorsement from literally every major conservative opinion outlet. The same handful of supply-siders write — and, presumably,

---

* With the exception of the 2004 corporate tax bill described in chapter 2.

set the editorial line for — the *Washington Times,* the *Wall Street Journal's* editorial page, the *Weekly Standard,* and the *National Review.* Of those publications, which are the primary places conservatives who wish to influence GOP policy-makers publish their work, only the *Standard* ever allows articles skeptical of tax cuts to appear. And even those rare dissents are invariably couched in the most oblique terms. In 2005, for example, the conservative economist Irwin Stelzer published an essay noting the mismatch between the grandiose goals of the Bush foreign policy and the miserly expenditures devoted to fund them. He urged that we instead "devote the necessary resources" to protect the homeland from terrorists, defeat the insurgency in Iraq, and attain energy independence, and he drew a comparison to Franklin Roosevelt, who "enlisted close to half of our annual GDP to rid the world of Hitler & Co."[66] Since the federal government currently spends only about a fifth of the GDP on all its functions, an undertaking even remotely similar to FDR's would require a massive tax increase. Yet even in an essay devoted to the need for more government "resources," Stelzer never mentioned anything about tax increases. Such a sentiment would be completely beyond the pale.

SELLING OUT FOR TAX CUTS

The most startling thing about the anti-tax movement's takeover of the party is the acquiescence of the rest of the conservative coalition. If your primary goal is, say, banning abortion or shrinking the federal budget, you would seem to have little incentive to accept the Norquist definition of the GOP, one that says deviation on social issues or spending programs is acceptable but deviation on taxes is not. Yet the activists representing those other causes have meekly accepted their own subordination.

Take, for instance, the social conservatives. Organizations representing the religious right have loyally rallied their members to support the conservative agenda, often using some deft intellectual gymnastics to justify their support. When business groups were fighting fuel economy standards in 1995, Norquist convinced Phyllis Schlafly's Eagle Forum to oppose them as well, according to the *Washington Post*, "because the mileage goals could be portrayed as threatening such mainstays of the family as the station wagon and the mini-van."[67] A random visit in 2005 to the Christian Coalition's Internet home page found the top two items on its legislative agenda to be "Passing President Bush's Social Security reform" and "Making permanent President Bush's 2001 federal tax cuts." (Neither theme featured prominently in the Sermon on the Mount.)[68]

This loyalty has not been reciprocated. Rather, Republican leaders have persistently declined to expend political capital on behalf of social conservative causes. For the Christian right, a Supreme Court nomination is the culmination of decades worth of struggle, a chance to overturn numerous ungodly rulings — above all, *Roe v. Wade*, which they consider the legalization of mass murder. Yet Bush's Supreme Court nominations, while right of center, refused to commit to overturning socially liberal precedents. The contrast with Bush's commitment to his economic agenda is striking. Almost every major piece of fiscal legislation during Bush's presidency has passed through Congress by a single vote, and usually after ferocious arm-twisting. The strategy was to compromise as little as possible and to deliver the maximal benefits to the base.

By contrast, Bush's first Supreme Court justice, John Roberts, swept through the Senate with 78 votes.[69] He received substantial support from moderates and liberals precisely because he sent out ambiguous signals, suggesting he would respect precedents like *Roe*. The moderate liberal legal analyst Jeffrey Rosen called Roberts's nomination "a peace offering from Bush to Democrats."[70] Bush could have nominated a justice committed to a sweeping conservative overhaul, a justice who might have squeaked through with no votes to spare. Instead, he declined to spend the political capital needed to muscle through an unpopular choice. For his second Supreme Court opening, Bush selected his own counsel, Harriet Myers, an utterly undistinguished choice with a long history of social liberalism. Myers was so outrageously underqualified, and so ideologically suspect, that social conservatives rebelled, and she had to withdraw her candidacy. Even then, rather than push for the most hard-line conservative he could get, Bush nominated Samuel Alito, a mainstream conservative who made it through the Senate by a relatively comfortable 16-vote margin.

Even starker is the contrast between how Bush handled privatizing Social Security and how he dealt with a constitutional amendment to ban gay marriage in the months following his reelection in 2004. Take the marriage amendment first. Here, public opinion was ambiguous. The public by a wide majority opposed gay marriage but split on whether a constitutional amendment was necessary, with some polls showing narrow support, others, narrow opposition. That November, all eleven state ballot measures against gay marriage passed easily, and social conservatives believed a devoted campaign by Bush could produce a constitutional amendment on a matter they cared about deeply.[71] Yet Bush declined to lift a finger, explaining, "Senators have made it clear that, so long as [the 1996 Defense of Marriage Act] is deemed constitutional, nothing will happen. I'd take their admonition seriously."[72]

At the same time, Bush faced even more public skepticism on Social Security privatization, where polls showed massive disapproval of his central goal to reduce guaranteed benefits and replace them with individually controlled investment accounts. Members of Congress had likewise indicated their deep reluctance to act.[73] Rather than throw up his hands, though, Bush barnstormed the country, delivering speech after speech. He kept this up even though learning more about Bush's plans caused voters to turn against it even more strongly. Bush persisted even after fellow Republicans were warning publicly that he had no chance of success, only giving in long after any shred of hope had disappeared. The contrast between Bush's Winston Churchill–like defense of privatization and his Neville Chamberlin–like defense of the gay marriage amendment produced some grumbling among social conservatives but no open rupture.

THE SURRENDER OF the spending hawks is, in some sense, even more complete than that of the social conservatives. Few rank-and-file Republican voters have ever been sold on the notion that tax cuts create enough economic growth to pay for themselves. That's why GOP leaders almost always present tax cuts as a way of forcing spending cuts. A favorite analogy, used by Reagan among others, is "cutting the government's allowance."* George W. Bush spoke endlessly of the need to get surplus tax dollars out of Washington lest they be spent.

Yet the disappearance of the surplus did not keep Washington from spending money. Conservatives have not shied away from admitting the explosion of spending that has occurred under Republican rule. They have shouted it from the rooftops. Conservative think tanks and pundits of all stripes — not to mention dozens of conservative Republican rebels in Congress — have endlessly bemoaned their party's spendthrift ways. Yet not a single one of them has questioned the underlying strategy of cutting taxes in order to restrain government.

Like the social conservatives, the spending hawks have acceded to a division of priorities that relegates them to the bottom rung of their party's concerns. George Herbert Walker Bush's modest tax

---

* It's remarkable how many conservatives take seriously such an obviously witless analogy. Cutting the government's "allowance" does not limit its capacity to spend. The proper analogy would be reducing your child's allowance but giving him unlimited use of your credit card.

hike was grounds for excommunication; his son's expansion of Medicare spending — far larger than the 1990 tax hike — produced only grumbling. While virtually the entire Republican Party has signed on to Norquist's pledge against taxes, no comparable pledge against spending exists.

What makes this acquiescence all the more baffling is that there is an alternative way to restrain federal spending that clearly has proven successful. When Ronald Reagan agreed to tax hikes in 1982 and 1983 and when George Bush did so in 1990, they extracted in return tens of billions of dollars in spending cuts. Indeed, the hated 1990 budget produced nearly half a trillion dollars in reduced spending over five years.[74] Clinton's 1993 budget cut nearly a quarter trillion dollars.[75] In 2005, Republicans in Congress sought to cut around $50 billion in spending — a tenth of what Bush had cut fifteen years earlier — and failed.[76] The recent evidence is overwhelming: "starving the beast" does not work.

The reason that tax-hikers have succeeded at restraining federal spending while tax-cutters have failed is clear enough. Cutting spending is hard because spending programs are popular. Democrats can be persuaded to accept spending cuts in the spirit of bipartisan fiscal responsibility, but they recoil at cutting spending in order to finance tax cuts that mainly benefit the affluent. When Republicans cut taxes, then, they have to insulate themselves from the charge that they are cutting education or Medicaid or Social Security in order to give tax cuts to millionaires. As a result, when they cut taxes, Republicans either avoid spending cuts or they restrict them to small programs, like food stamps for immigrants, which benefit only a tiny minority of voters. Or they feel obliged to raise spending so they can assure the voters they weren't denied their Medicare drug benefits or their crop subsidies in order to cut taxes for the rich.

In 2004, Democrats in Congress proposed a deal that a spending hawk ought to have leapt at. They suggested imposing a rule that any new spending program or any new tax cut could be enacted only by raising taxes or cutting spending elsewhere. This is called a "pay as you go" requirement, and it was one of the central tools that the 1990 budget used to whittle down federal spending. This obscure legislative debate actually offered a perfect test of the GOP's loyalty to controlling the size of government versus its loyalty to tax cuts. Here was an unimpeachably effective tool to keep Congress from launching the spending binges conservatives so disdain. The only price was making tax cuts harder to enact. The Republican reaction to this offer was telling. Conservative pundits denounced it unanimously, and the GOP Congress buried it. As Tom DeLay said at the time, the "pay as you go" requirement was "so contrary to our fundamental beliefs."[77]

The perplexing question is why the spending hawks never question their subservient place in the Republican coalition. After all, their party's reigning ideology inevitably fails to shrink government, and it demonizes an alternative path (make deals with moderate Democrats to raise taxes and cut spending) that has been proven to succeed. But, while they may incessantly bemoan their party's failure to cut spending, they never question the underlying priorities that produce this failure.

A lone exception to this trend proves the rule. In 2006, William Niskanen, the chairman of the libertarian Cato Institute, measured the relationship between changes in tax levels and changes in spending. He found that the premise of the "starve the beast" strategy was wrong. Indeed, it was backwards. Since 1981, tax cuts tended to spur *higher* levels of spending, while tax hikes tended to produce *lower* spending. (In fact, Richard Kogan of the Center on Budget and Policy Priorities had found the same thing in 2002, but Kogan was a liberal and therefore predictably ignored.) The moderate columnists Jonathan Rauch of the *Atlantic* and Sebastian Mallaby of the *Washington Post* excitedly wrote up Niskanen's findings.[78] Surely this would demonstrate to the starve-the-beast conservatives the folly of their ways.

Not surprisingly, no rethinking whatsoever ensued. The best window into the mindset of the right came in *National Review*'s weblog from Jonah Goldberg, one of the conservative movement's more respected writers. Conceding the undeniable implications of Niskanen's research, as cited by Rauch, Goldberg wrote that "conservatives are going to have to respond to Jonathan Rauch's argument in the new *Atlantic*." But no conservatives of any standing responded, and, indeed, the next day *National Review* went on as before, editorializing for more tax cuts. Why did Goldberg himself, then, not rethink his adherence to a discredited dogma? The answer could be found in the same posting, where he wrote: "There are others better qualified to deal with the economic issues. But if tax increases can be demonstrated to shrink government in some significant way, I'm certainly open to them."[79]

This is a fine summation of how most conservatives think. Their main domestic priority is to shrink spending. They favor tax cuts in the belief they will further their goal. They believe this largely because other conservatives — those "better qualified" than themselves — tell them so. Essentially, they have outsourced their thinking to a handful of conservative polemicists who specialize in economics and whom other conservatives regard as experts. The problem is that these "experts" are all supply-siders. Not only are they charlatans, but — more to the point — they don't care very much about spending. To be sure, the supply-siders would *prefer* to keep down spending. (Though, when they have the opportunity to preach their case to liberals, they are happy to argue that tax cuts would produce a gusher of revenue that could fund more generous programs.) The point is that the supply-siders care primarily about keeping tax rates low. Since most conservatives care more about spending, the supply-siders carefully emphasize this result, but the argument is merely instrumental. And yet the anti-spending conservatives do not feel comfortable challenging their liturgy, so the supply-siders end up setting policy for the whole movement.

THE DOOMED REVOLT OF JOHN MCCAIN

There was only one brief moment when Norquist and his allies found their control of the Republican Party threatened. It happened during the 2000 Republican primary, when John McCain challenged George W. Bush for the GOP nomination. The conventional journalistic narrative interpreted the battle in mostly personal terms — McCain as straight-talking war hero standing up to the party establishment. In fact, the deeply ideological character of McCain's insurrection is what gave it its historic importance.

Before his primary run, almost nobody would have figured McCain as a likely candidate to lead an ideological rebellion. While the dwindling base of moderate Republicanism is based in the Northeast, McCain hails from conservative Arizona. He was elected on his promise to uphold the legacy of Barry Goldwater (who preceded Reagan as a conservative icon) and amassed a staunchly conservative and partisan voting record over nearly two decades.

During the 1980s, McCain found himself entangled in the Keating Five Scandal — an episode in which a sleazy savings and loans operator plied congressmen with campaign donations — and this prompted him to embrace campaign finance reform. McCain's enthusiastic championing of limits on campaign donations alienated him from fellow Republicans. As long as his ideological heterodoxy was limited to this one issue, though, it was grudgingly tolerated.

McCain became a full-blown heretic only when he deviated on taxes. Two things seem to have triggered McCain's apostasy. The first was his campaign finance reform crusade. For the first time, he found himself embraced by Democrats, liberals, and establishment journalists and criticized by the conservatives he had long considered his natural allies. The episode apparently set off a broader critique of the GOP. "I think the party to some degree has lost its way," he said in early 2000, "and I think this is because of the influence of big money."[80]

The second thing was the mere fact of his presidential candidacy. For most of his career, McCain devoted his primary attention to military issues. Like most members of Congress (in both parties), he was not an intellectual. He took his cues on votes from party leaders. During his primary campaign, he explained, "I didn't pay nearly the attention to [domestic] issues in the past. I was probably a 'supply-sider' based on the fact that I didn't jump into the issue." Running for president forced McCain to put together a platform, and the process of reconciling different priorities for the first time led him to some unorthodox conclusions. The overriding domestic question of the time was what to do with the budget surplus. Bush, the candidate of the establishment, proposed a large tax cut. McCain suggested devoting most of the surplus to reducing the national debt, thereby shoring up Social Security and Medicare.[81]

McCain's position was overwhelmingly popular among the GOP rank-and-file, as consistently shown by polls in the primary states. In Iowa, 56 percent of Republicans (and 58 percent of Bush voters) preferred McCain's plan of using the surplus for Medicare and Social Security over Bush's plan for tax cuts. In New Hampshire, the margin was slightly larger. In South Carolina, an astonishing three-quarters of Republicans said they preferred McCain's approach to Bush's.[82] So the eventual party backlash against McCain was not because his skepticism toward massive tax cuts was unpopular among Republicans. It was precisely because it was popular. It was bad enough for McCain to rail in general terms against "powerful interests." Now he was exposing the vast gulf between the GOP's voting base and the supply-siders and business lobbyists who dictated its economic policies.

Unbelievably, McCain compounded his sin by declaring his concern that Bush's tax cut would widen the growing gap between rich and poor. It was not completely unheard of for a moderate Republican to dissent meekly on tax cuts on fiscal grounds, but to do so on moral grounds was completely beyond the pale. The conservative *Washington Times* thundered in an editorial: "In other comments that could have come straight out of the Democratic playbook, Mr. McCain over the weekend wailed about the 'growing gap between rich and poor in America' and 'the haves and the have-nots in America.'"[83] Even McCain's friends appeared ashen. Jack Kemp stammered, "John McCain, who's a friend of mine, has done a — has made a big mistake."

When McCain surged to a surprising blowout win in the New Hampshire primary, the establishment reacted with sheer terror. A gloomy *Washington Times* reported: "Conservatives who were on the front lines of the Reagan revolution and who led the ground forces that spearheaded a movement that has largely kept the GOP in conservative hands for two decades, now see their hold on the party slipping away if Mr. McCain succeeds in beating George W. Bush for the nomination."[84] So the GOP establishment leveled a fierce barrage against McCain in South Carolina and elsewhere. The central theme was that he was disloyal to the Republican Party. Norquist's Americans for Tax Reform ran ads morphing McCain's likeness into that of Bill Clinton, but that was not the end of it. Virtually every appendage of the conservative movement hammered away at McCain, from Rush Limbaugh to the Christian Coalition. (McCain did lash out against the leadership of the religious right, but this was a result and not a cause of their attack.)

In the end, the debate between McCain and Bush, like most debates among Republicans, was ultimately settled by who was the more loyal Reaganite. Bush ran television ads proclaiming himself to be "the candidate with a tax cut called 'Reaganesque.'" McCain insisted, over and over, "I'm a proud Reagan conservative,"[85] and cited his pro-life views and career-long support for a strong and active military. To wrest control of the party from the conservative establishment, McCain understood that he had to wrest control of the definition of Reaganism. But in the end, he could not escape the pervasive belief that he had been disloyal to the Republican Party. And the truth is, he was — perhaps not disloyal to what the party once was, but certainly disloyal to what it had become.

McCain went on to vote against Bush's tax cuts in 2001 and 2003 on the grounds of both affordability and fairness.[86] Sometime around 2004, though, he decided he wanted the 2008 Republican presidential nomination. This meant he had to make peace with the party power brokers. Most of the moves he made to this end were symbolic — embracing Bush in public repeatedly, appearing with Jerry Falwell at Liberty University, and the like. Symbolism is, after all, the traditional fare GOP leaders or prospective leaders offer up to the social conservative base.

But the party's economic base can't be so easily mollified. They want substance, not image. So McCain did the one thing he knew he had to do to avoid being ostracized again: he flip-flopped on taxes. First, in 2005, he announced he would support a cloture vote on permanently repealing the estate tax, which he had long championed as the great cause of his hero, Teddy Roosevelt.[87] Then the next year he declared himself in favor of making permanent the Bush tax cuts he had once denounced as a giveaway to the rich.[88] These were the magic words the party's inner circle needed to hear. Once he had renounced his economic apostasy, he could be welcomed back into the party's bosom.

There was one final step for McCain to take in order to demonstrate that his conversion was true and that he would never stray again. He brought on as economic adviser none other than Arthur Laffer. Soon McCain was spouting the supply-side gospel in its purest form. In a 2007 interview with the *National Review,* he declared, "Tax cuts, starting with Kennedy, as we all know, increase revenues." The reconversion was complete.[89] In December 2006, the conservative columnist Robert Novak reported:

> Some 30 invited corporate representatives and other lobbyists gathered at the Phoenix Park Hotel on Capitol Hill Tuesday morning to hear two senior mainstream Republican senators pitch the 2008 presidential campaign of Sen. John McCain. They were selling him to establishment Republicans as the establishment's candidate.[90]

Thus ended the last great attempt to reform the Republican Party from the inside.

4

THE NECESSITY OF DECEIT

On February 27, 2001, George W. Bush appeared before a joint session of Congress and a national television audience to address the direction of his new presidency. It was a pregnant moment in American governance. With a budget surplus projected to top $4 trillion shimmering over the horizon, there was an opportunity not seen in decades to reshape the size and the purpose of the federal government. He had run for office as "a compassionate conservative" who had distanced himself from his party's antigovernment thrust, and here was his chance to sketch out this new center-right vision.

Rhetorically, he did not disappoint. Even a close listener, let alone the casual audience, could scarcely have guessed that Bush stood poised to steer the ship of state on a sharp rightward turn, for his speech sounded like the sort of thing Teddy Kennedy might say. He began his litany of goals by asserting, twice, that "education is my top priority" and promising to triple spending on reading programs. He promised to double "the Medicare budget," "the number of people served at community health care centers," and "the budget for the National Institutes of Health." He promised increased spending on environmental protections, adding new incentives for charitable donations, and keeping sacrosanct the Social Security surplus.[1]

Reviewing the expansive list, Bush declared: "My budget has funded a responsible increase in our ongoing operations. It has funded our nation's important priorities. It has protected Social Security and Medicare. And our surpluses are big enough that there is still money left over." An astute listener would have noticed something curious at this moment. The president had slipped into the past tense — "has funded," "has protected" — even though he was apportioning projected surpluses that may or may not have materialized. Most of the audience probably assumed that Bush was speaking of money he had already spent. He continued with his pledge to retire the national debt — "We owe it to our children and grandchildren," he explained. And in case anybody was at all nervous that he had not gone far enough, he assured the audience that his budget "sets aside almost a trillion dollars over ten years" for contingencies.

So, with all these priorities fulfilled and trillions yet remaining, there was nothing left to do but return that surplus to the taxpayers. "The people of America have been overcharged," he said, "and, on their behalf, I'm here asking for a refund." He came to this conclusion only at the end of his list of priorities and with a seeming reluctance, as if he had no other choice.

Bush portrayed his tax cut this way for a very good reason. Opinion polls showed that the public, by overwhelming margins, preferred using the surplus for things other than tax cuts. A Pew poll conducted a few weeks earlier, for instance, asked people to choose between using the surplus for Social Security and Medicare, other domestic programs, paying off the national debt, or tax cuts. A mere 19 percent chose tax cuts; 77 percent favored other uses.[2] That finding was consistent with most polling. When given a choice of how they would apportion the surplus, only around a fifth of the public choose cutting taxes.

And it's far from clear that even that fifth shared Bush's priorities. In addition to the question of whether to cut taxes, there is always the question of how. At the time of Bush's speech, liberals argued that tax cuts should go to all taxpayers in relatively equal chunks, whereas conservatives insisted that the rich should get the largest sums since they pay the most in the first place. By vast margins, the public sided with the liberal position. A poll from March of that year, for instance, asked respondents to choose between a tax cut in which "the largest share of this tax cut would go to wealthier Americans, who currently pay the most in taxes," and one that "would be aimed more at middle income Americans." The latter won by a crushing margin of 73 to 20 percent. Another poll the next month showed that the public, by nearly as large a margin, preferred "giving larger tax cuts to lower and middle income taxpayers and smaller tax cuts to upper income taxpayers."[3]

The Bush administration was clearly aware that the public did not share its priorities, so the president and his spokesmen persistently minimized the size of the tax cuts and their upward tilt. One internal document, in particular, showed just how keenly aware the administration was of the unpopularity of its stance. After Paul O'Neill was fired as treasury secretary in 2002, he turned over a trove of documents to *Esquire's* Ron Suskind. One of them was a memo that the White House political team had given to O'Neill directing his public advocacy for the tax cuts. It read: "The public prefers spending on things like health care and education over cutting taxes. It's crucial that your remarks make clear that there is no tradeoff here."[4]

Of course there *was* a tradeoff. As was clear to anyone remotely familiar with the situation in 2001, over the long run the government could not meet its present obligations. Cutting taxes would mean reducing funds available for other purposes. Conservatives hoped that locking in tax cuts would force spending reductions that the public would not otherwise accept. The conservative columnist Andrew Sullivan acknowledged this quite bluntly in the *New Republic:*

> Some commentators — at this magazine and elsewhere — get steamed because Bush has obscured this figure or claimed his tax cut will cost less than it actually will, or because he is using Medicare surplus money today that will be needed tomorrow and beyond. Many of these arguments have merit — but they miss the deeper point. The fact that Bush has to obfuscate his real goals of reducing spending with the smoke screen of "compassionate conservatism" shows how uphill the struggle is.
>
> Yes, some of the time he is full of it on his economic policies. But a certain amount of B.S. is necessary for any vaguely successful retrenchment of government power in an insatiable entitlement state.[5]

In other words, as Sullivan's argument makes clear, when the administration instructed O'Neill that the crucial thing was to deny a tradeoff, it meant the crucial thing was to lie.

This business about lying is tricky. Historically, we are not used to thinking of lying as a driving factor in American politics. When it comes to presidents, especially, historians tend to treat rhetoric as a proxy for substance. A reference to Franklin Roosevelt's expansion of government into the realm of economic security is apt to cite his call for "freedom from want, freedom from fear," or some other stirring liberal rhetoric. A discussion of Reagan's efforts to slash taxes and spending will usually note his famous observation that "government is not the solution to our problem; government is the problem." The underlying assumption is that our leaders say more or less what they mean.

There is also a natural — and, in many ways, commendable — skepticism about one-sided accusations of dishonesty. Those who confine their accusations to one side are usually partisans best taken with a grain of salt. Lying and spinning have always been a part of politics, and it is the rare elected official who prevails by offering the voters an objective and unvarnished assessment of his plans. Moreover, since we tend to think of lying as an idiosyncratic personal trait, there's no reason to think that one side has more liars than the other any more than there's reason to think one side has more drunks or adulterers.

Yet, as will become clear, the fact remains that dishonesty has become integral to the Republican economic agenda in a way that it is not to the Democratic economic agenda. The reason is not that Republicans are individually less honest than Democrats. Far from it. It is simply that the GOP, and the conservative movement, have embraced an economic agenda far out of step with the majority of the voting public. Republicans simply can't win office or get their plans enacted into law, without fundamentally misleading the public. Lying has become a systematic necessity.

ANY RATIONALE WILL DO

Economic conservatives have not always had to conceal their intentions from the public so aggressively. After liberalism hit a high-water mark in the mid-1960s, a genuine backlash emerged. Middle- and working-class voters began to believe that Democrats had an unlimited appetite for taxing the middle class and lavishing benefits upon the poor (which, in the minds of many voters, meant poor blacks). In his 1969 manifesto, "The Emerging Republican Majority," Kevin Phillips wrote, "The Democratic Party fell victim to the ideological impetus of a liberalism which had carried it beyond programs taxing the few for the benefit of the many, to programs taxing the many on behalf of the few."[6] This was compounded during the 1970s, when inflation had pushed middle-income earners into ever higher tax brackets without them making any real income gains. In 1978, California's voters surprised pundits by electing to roll back taxes and spending. This "tax revolt" presaged the 1980 election of Ronald Reagan.

But Reagan's election marked the high-water point for the popular conservative backlash. Over the next two decades, both parties responded to most of the complaints that middle-class voters had with economic liberalism. Reagan indexed the tax code for inflation so that rising prices did not automatically lead to higher tax rates. Bill Clinton reformed welfare, the government program that most offended middle-class sensibilities.

By that time, the conservative backlash had already crested. James Stimson, a political scientist at the University of North Carolina, has created a historical measure of public support for energetic government over time. Stimson's master survey shows public support for liberal government peaking around 1960, the year John F. Kennedy won the presidency. Subsequently, liberalism declined precipitously, bottoming out in 1980. Then it began rising again — despite a trough in the mid-1990s, around the time Republicans won control of Congress — and by 2004 had neared its historical peak.[7] During the 1970s and early 1980s, it had been possible to build popular majorities for retrenching the role of government. By the time George W. Bush took office, that majority had disappeared.

IN MARCH OF 2001, a coalition of Washington business lobbyists planned a rally to support the Bush tax cuts. The crucial thing was to convey the impression that the tax cut benefited regular workers. A memo circulated among the groups, and obtained by the *Washington Post*, explained: "The theme involves working Americans. Visually, this will involve a sea of hard hats . . . the Speaker's office was very clear in saying that they do not need people in suits. If people want to participate — AND WE DO NEED BODIES — they must be DRESSED DOWN, appear to be REAL WORKER types, etc."

Hard hats were provided for the lobbyists in attendance, though individuals were encouraged to provide their own proletarian touch. Fred Nichols, the political director for the National Association of Manufacturers, appeared in a rugby shirt and faded blue "Farm Credit" hat.[8]

If the Republicans had truly believed that the public shared their goals, a memo like this would never have existed. There would have been no need to show that "real worker types" supported tax cuts. (Indeed, they would not have made a quasi-Marxist distinction between executives and "real worker types" in the first place.) Businessmen would simply have come forward to proudly announce their support for the tax cuts, explaining that rewarding wealth and success would create a rising tide for one and all. And the real worker types across the country would nod their heads in agreement. But in their bones the conservatives knew that this would never happen.

So, when Bush and his allies came to the task of selling their tax-cut plan, what was required was not mere spin or exaggeration but a giant Potemkin edifice of rhetoric. The administration offered the public three broad rationales for cutting taxes. The first was the need to eliminate "overpayments." The existence of a surplus, Bush said over and over, "means the government has more money than it needs." Or, as his spokesmen sometimes put it: "It is not a budget surplus. It is a tax surplus."[9] Obviously they didn't remotely believe this. If a surplus was a tax surplus, then a deficit would be a tax deficit. But of course when surpluses were replaced by deficits, Bush maintained nothing of the kind.

Indeed, when the fiscal picture darkened, the Republicans flipped all their arguments, just as they had done during the Clinton years. Initially, the tax cuts were needed to reduce government revenues in order to prevent overspending. But after deficits appeared, they claimed tax cuts were needed to stimulate the economy and thereby cause revenues to rise. In 2002, Bush's spokesman Ari Fleischer said,

"The president does believe that cutting taxes is the best way to spur growth and therefore to have a return of bigger surpluses."[10] First tax cuts were a way to eliminate the surplus. Then they were a way to bring it back.

But what if the extra money never materialized? To this frequent objection, the administration never failed to insist that the projections were as good as gold. The White House budget director, Mitch Daniels, asserted, for instance, "Well, we really can't miss. . . . We've been underestimating revenue by as much as $80 billion a year. And we are likely to continue doing that. . . . We've constructed a budget very carefully, on very conservative assumptions, and leaving lots of room for the unforeseen contingencies of the future."[11] This statement was typical. And yet, when deficits did first appear, the administration dismissed them as unknowable. When asked in 2002 about collapsing tax receipts, which budget forecasters believed would create a deficit the following year, Bush replied, "Of course it's all speculative to begin with. I don't know the models that they guessed, but it's guesswork thus far."[12] So projections for ten years down the road were dependable enough to bet the house on, but projections one year down the road were pure guesswork.

AS A SECOND rationale, the administration sold the tax cut as a timely remedy to fight a recession — in the words of one member, "immediate tax relief that would bring a stimulus to our economy."[13] This claim had a veneer of plausibility. Traditional Keynesian economics holds that recessions happen when people and businesses stop spending money. The solution is for the government to encourage spending, either by cutting taxes or by spending the money itself.

Bush's tax cut, however, was not designed for that purpose. Its chief architect, Larry Lindsey, is a supply-sider who has fiercely attacked the core of Keynesian economics. And while he tried to defend the tax cut as a Keynesian response to the recession in 2002, it was clearly a product of supply-side thinking, which is altogether different. Supply-siders scorn the very idea of stimulus. They don't believe that a failure to spend money causes recessions. Instead, they believe that high tax rates discourage entrepreneurship and investing, and therefore lower rates will encourage faster growth. Unlike Keynesians, supply-siders believe tax-cutting is appropriate at all times, not merely when the economy is slowing down.

And while Keynesian theory suggests giving tax cuts to lower- and middle-income workers, who are most likely to spend their bounty, supply-siders prefer tax cuts aimed at high-income workers, who they believe drive economic growth. The differences may sound esoteric, but they're utterly divergent approaches, with completely different effects. A Keynesian would want temporary tax cuts aimed at the middle and bottom, while a supply-sider would prefer permanent tax cuts aimed mostly at the top.* Bush's tax cut was in the supply-side mold. While it claimed to address a short-term problem (the recession), it imposed long-term changes on the tax code, many of which would not take effect for years, after the recession had already ended.

All this is to say that Bush seized upon the pretext of a recession to impose the changes he had always wanted. Indeed, he first unveiled his tax cut with the economy at its peak. (He called it "an insurance policy" against recession, which sounds like spraying a fire hose on a house to make sure it doesn't catch fire.) When deficits appeared, Republicans insisted it would be the height of folly to raise taxes during a recession. Then the recession ended, but deficits remained. No problem. The fact that the economy was growing again proved "the tax cuts have worked," and therefore should be

---

* Some conservatives argued that temporary tax cuts wouldn't work because people wouldn't spend the windfall if they knew it would disappear the next year. But the idea of permanently cutting taxes every time the economy slows down is ludicrous. After enough turns of the business cycle, the government would go bankrupt.

repeated. When, inevitably, the economy slowed down again, it was held up as evidence not that the tax cuts failed but that still more are needed.

Keeping straight the various contradictory rationales was tricky for the party's in-house intellectuals. The occasional slip was to be expected. William Kristol, editor of the *Weekly Standard,* argued simultaneously in 2005 that more tax cuts were needed because the economy was slowing and because the last round of tax cuts succeeded in boosting the economy. Both these arguments appeared not only in the same editorial but *in the same sentence* in the same editorial: "In the face of what will likely be a slowing economy in 2006, and in light of the success of these supply-side tax cuts . . . the administration needs to insist on these cuts, and move as quickly as possible to make the other tax cuts permanent."[14] But if the economy was slowing, how was the last round of tax cuts a success?

BUSH'S THIRD JUSTIFICATION was to portray his tax cuts as a way of making the tax code fairer to the poor. "On principle, those with the greatest need should receive the greatest help," he said in his 2000 acceptance speech. He repeatedly held up the example of a single-mother waitress earning $22,000 a year. "Somebody struggling to get ahead, somebody working the hardest job in America, pays a higher marginal rate than successful folks, Wall Street bankers," the president declared. "And that's not fair. And that's not right."[15] He boasted that, under his plan, the hard-working waitress would "pay no income tax at all." Under his plan, the rich got the biggest tax cuts, both in absolute terms and as a percentage of their federal tax burden. (Bush's tax cuts reduced the federal tax burden of the richest 1 percent of taxpayers by a quarter, while the bottom 95 percent saw its federal tax burden fall by just a tenth.) But the salient point is this: the only reason waitress mothers would pay no tax under his plan was that *they paid no income tax to begin with.*

Contemporary Republicans feel an endemic need to garb their

plans in populist lingo. Bush has perfected the technique, but he did not invent it. In the mid-1990s, conservative proponents of the flat tax persistently implied that it would force the rich to pay a higher share of the tax burden. "Are you free if you're toiling away in factory, plant, or office, forking over more than a third of your earnings while some other guy with ten times your income pays nothing?" wrote the former GOP majority leader Dick Armey in his book championing flat taxes.[16] (In fact, Robert Hall and Alvin Rabushka, the economists who devised the flat tax, once bluntly admitted that their plan "will be a tremendous boon to the economic elite" and "it is an obvious mathematical law that lower taxes on the successful will have to be made up by higher taxes on average people.")[17] Proponents of repealing the estate tax incessantly cited the plight of the family forced to sell off its farm to pay estate taxes, although proponents could not cite a single example of this ever having happened. And for good reason: the estate tax only applies to very high inheritances, is riddled with exceptions and loopholes, and thus applies only to vast sums of inherited wealth.

There are, of course, honest and deeply felt reasons to support the Republican economic agenda. But those reasons invariably bear almost no relation to the reasons offered up in public. The public rationale is a mere cynical contrivance, one that can be discarded, or turned upside down, as the situation requires. So conservatives can defend their policies as a perfectly tailored remedy for a particular set of economic circumstances and, later, as a perfectly tailored remedy for the opposite circumstances. They can present a plan to cut the share of taxes paid by the rich as a plan to soak the rich. All this underscores how little confidence the right has that the public supports its agenda.

WHILE THIS MAY sound like some sort of global indictment of the trustworthiness of the conservatives and the Republican Party, it is nothing of the sort. This is simply what happens when a gap exists between what's for sale and what people want to buy. It's completely natural, though not usually laudable, for those who hold unpopular views to mislead the public about them. And those unpopular views may not necessarily be wrong. My alma mater, the University of Michigan, steadfastly denied for many years that it was running a two-track admissions policy, with lower academic standards for African-American applicants and other under-represented minorities. Only after a successful lawsuit forcing the university to expose its system did the administration admit the plain truth. While the years of dissembling may have been risible, the motive was completely understandable. The public overwhelmingly believed that colleges ought to admit applicants on a color-blind basis, yet the administrators understood that doing so would leave them with very few black and Latino students. What choice did they have? They were, by their way of thinking, defending a powerless minority against the prejudices of the majority.

This is more or less how conservatives feel about their alliance with the rich. They believe very earnestly that what is good for the rich is good for the country. Some do so from their adherence to the tenets of supply-side economics. Probably a greater number simply believe it in their gut. This isn't the sort of sentiment politicians like to advertise, but it slips out every once in a while. Bill Archer, the Republican former head of the Ways and Means Committee and a current tax lobbyist, once declared, "The engine that pulls the train must continue to be fueled." Phil Gramm, the conservative former senator, used to say, "No poor man ever gave me a job."[18] This is a very old conservative sentiment — less Adam Smith than Edmund Burke, and one often verging on outright plutocracy. It has less to do with the Laffer Curve than an almost mystical faith in the centrality and virtue of the upper class. Tony Snow gave this view a particularly blunt expression when, as a columnist and Fox News talking head, he wrote: "Upper classes have always pulled societies forward economically — and their conspicuous prosperity has always aroused the jealousies of the lower classes. The envious set out to strip the rich of their lucre, believing mistakenly that by redistributing income they could make everybody affluent."[19]

The prospect of the electorate's splitting along class lines, with the grubby masses voting to divvy up the assets of the rich, strikes an elemental fear in the hearts of the right. There is an old quote, whose provenance has never been conclusively established, that gives voice to this fear: "A democracy cannot exist as a permanent form of government. It can only exist until a majority of voters discover that they can vote themselves largess out of the public treasury." Conservatives from Ronald Reagan (while stumping for Barry Goldwater) to P. J. O'Rourke have cited it. The obvious corollary is that democracy can only be preserved by preventing voters from discovering their ability to redistribute money to themselves.

The impulse arising from this fear is fundamentally anti-democratic. You can see this sentiment in an exchange between Grover Norquist and a member of the Log Cabin Republicans, a GOP group that supports gay rights, witnessed by the *New Yorker's* John Cassidy: "She pressed Norquist again on what he thought of targeting gays, adding, 'It's bad, right?' At last, he answered her. 'Yes, it's bad,' he said. 'Democracies are dangerous. Look what happens in California, where they pick on the richest ten per cent.'"[20] Or consider this 2001 *Wall Street Journal* op-ed piece by Bill Archer, in which he fretted about the prospect of fewer voters paying income taxes. "Politicians may find it easier and easier to raise tax rates that apply only to a minority of middle- and upper-income earners, in order to finance new government spending primarily benefiting lower-income individuals," he wrote. "The result will be class warfare at its worst and a sort of tyranny of the majority."[21] "Tyranny of the majority" is, of course, merely a derogatory term for democracy.

LIBERALISM AND WEALTH: A HISTORY

In principle, it is healthy to have some skepticism about the majoritarian principle. As Norquist notes, democratic majorities can be abusive, and having some checks on their baser impulses is appropriate. There are legal protections in place, for instance, that keep majorities from trampling on gay rights or imposing prayer in the public schools. Economic minorities, however, enjoy no similar protections. There is no law keeping 99 percent of the country from voting to impose a 100 percent tax on the wealth of the richest 1 percent and dividing it among themselves. No doubt that defenselessness contributes to the conservative fear of egalitarianism. History is replete with examples of political movements on the left whose efforts to rally the working class in defense of its own interest degenerated into demagoguery, violence, or tyranny. Even the lesser dangers of confiscatory or punitive taxation ought to give us pause before we full-throatedly embrace economic populism.

But in the context of the world we inhabit, this fear is wildly misplaced. The notion of punishing the rich is alien to the modern liberal agenda. The main philosophical basis for progressive taxation has always been that the rich benefited from the stable economic environment provided by the government, a stability for which they could more easily afford to pay than could the poor. When the income tax was first imposed, its advocates made clear they saw it as a moderate measure that would ultimately benefit the rich along with the country as a whole. "The Democratic Party, if it is anything, is the friend of the capitalist and the poor man alike," argued Benton McMillan, the most prominent champion of the income tax. "We would put in lockup the law-breaking anarchist and then we would tax the capitalist. This is no assault upon wealth."[22] In the United States, unlike in Europe, socialism has never penetrated the mainstream left. Liberalism remains connected to its roots in classical liberalism, and Marxism has always been a foreign creed.

Liberal support for progressive taxation has always balanced considerations of equality and economic growth. In the mid-1970s, a moment when liberal prestige was at its already waning height, the Brookings economist and former Johnson adviser Arthur Okun summed up progressive thinking in a short book, *Equality and Efficiency: The Big Tradeoff*.[23] He argued that measures to impose equality usually came at some cost to economic growth. The key was to navigate between the two goals without going too far in either direction — a world where the poor starved, on the one hand, and one where the rich were so heavily taxed that the economy stagnated, on the other. The leveling impulse of the mainstream left has always been tame. Even at his most populist moment, Bill Clinton cast his upper-bracket tax hike not as punishment but as a correction for the rising inequality and regressive tax shift of the Reagan era: "I will ask the economic elite, who made the most money and paid less in taxes, to pay their fair share."[24]

Needless to say, today's upper classes are hardly trembling in fear that proletarian mobs will snatch the last scraps of their wealth. It's true that the federal tax system is moderately progressive. According to calculations by Citizens for Tax Justice — a liberal research group whose calculations are accepted by economists of all ideological stripes — workers in the middle of the income scale pay about 16 percent of their income in federal taxes, whereas those in the top 1 percent pay about 25 percent. But that's offset in part by state and local taxes, which hit the poor and middle class much harder. Taking into account *all* taxes, the top 1 percent pay a third of their income in taxes, and the middle fifth pay 27.5 percent of their income. This is a very modestly progressive system.[25]

The meagerness of the leveling effect can only be understood in light of an underlying economy that has grown dramatically more unequal over the last three decades. Since the late 1970s, wages for workers in the middle have barely kept pace with inflation, yet incomes at the very top have skyrocketed. Republicans are not to blame for the underlying economic changes that have caused this inequality. Nonetheless, it is an important fact to consider when deciding what levels of tax each class ought to pay.

And here is where the right's fear of the mob devolves into a kind of hysteria. Conservatives have, bizarrely, seized on the growing share of income held by the rich as evidence that the rich are being punished. The *Wall Street Journal* published a series of editorials noting that the upper crust has been paying a higher share of federal taxes over the last two or three decades. In 1979, the highest-earning 0.1 percent of taxpayers — that is, those who earn more than 999 out of every 1,000 taxpayers — paid just over 5 percent of the federal tax take. The total has nearly doubled over the last twenty-five years. The *Journal's* editors see this trend as evidence of rampant Jacobism. One recent editorial concluded that "the overall tax burden grew more progressive from 1979 to 1999" and insisted that any higher taxes on the rich would be unfair since the put-upon economic elite "already bear an outsized share of the American tax burden."[26]

This line of argument has been a consistent theme on the right in general and on the *Journal's* editorial page in particular. In 2002, for instance, a *Journal* editorial noted: "The top 1 percent of tax filers are also paying a much higher share than they used to. . . . There's a word for this kind of tax system. It's called progressive, not to mention confiscatory." Again, in 2003, the *Journal* editorialized that another study showed "the [tax] share of the lowest quintile was 1.6 percent, while the share of the highest quintile was 60.2 percent. Karl Marx, call your office."

It is true that the very richest have been paying a higher share of the federal tax burden. *But that is entirely because they have earned a larger share of the income.* In 1979, the highest-earning 0.1 percent took home about 3 percent of the national income and paid about 5 percent of the taxes. In 1999, they earned about 10 percent of the national income and paid about 11 percent of the taxes. What this means is that while the share of income held by the richest one-thousandth tripled, their share of the tax burden only doubled. Why the discrepancy? Because the average tax rate faced by that group *dropped* from 32 to 23 percent.[27] The reason they're paying more taxes is that their slice of the income pie has grown faster than their tax rate has fallen. The rich are earning a larger and larger share of the income base and paying a lower and lower tax rate on that base. If you have even a passing familiarity with Marx, you probably know that this is not what he had in mind.

But in conservative rhetoric, the specter of the guillotine often lurks behind any opposition to cutting taxes for the rich. Conservatives cast themselves as the defenders of the tattered banner of free enterprise, holding off the socialist hordes. In reality, mainstream liberals and Democrats accept the underlying changes that have caused the growing inequality and are merely trying to keep in place mildly ameliorative countermeasures. What conservatives are actually fighting for is breathtakingly radical. They argue that they are trying to keep the very rich from paying a larger share of the tax burden. Usually this argument comes from politicians insulated from political consequence. Senator Frank H. Murkowski of Alaska, then slated for retirement, told the *Washington Post* in 2001: "The burden is too great on a small portion of the population." Phil Gramm of Texas, another retiring senator, added, "We are approaching the point when society is becoming unstable."[28]

Remember, though, that the entire reason the very rich are paying a higher share of the tax burden is that they are earning a higher share of the national income. The implication of the conservative argument, then, is that we must cut taxes for the rich as their share of the national income grows. As the economy becomes less equal, we must also make the tax code less equal to keep too large a share of the tax burden from falling on a small group, and they argue this *as a matter of social justice.*

WHAT "CLASS WARFARE"?

The conservative fixation with liberalism's alleged envy and hatred for the rich presumes that the left is obsessed with economic distribution while the right is indifferent. The same presumption underlies most reporting on these matters. Sentences like the following, plucked from a 2001 *Washington Post* story — "the richest Americans would receive the largest dollar benefit from Bush's tax cut — if only because they pay the largest share of income taxes"[29] — are typical. The suggestion is that the rich only get dollars back in proportion to what they put in, and the implication is that the upward slant of Republican tax cuts are a mere accidental byproduct.

This is, however, totally untrue. Bush's tax cuts have not merely pared down tax rates in a proportional way up and down the income ladder. They have sharply cut the proportion of taxes paid by those at the top and therefore raised the proportion paid by those elsewhere. There is nothing indiscriminate about it. Let me briefly explain why. You can look at the federal tax code as a kind of layer cake. At the bottom is the payroll tax, used to finance Social Security and Medicare. This tax is a flat rate and covers wage income only up to around $100,000 a year, with all income above that level exempt. This is the most regressive tax imposed by Washington. Above the payroll tax sits the income tax. The income tax is more progressive, exempting low-wage workers and making high earners pay a higher rate. On top of that are taxes on capital gains and dividends. These taxes are even more concentrated at the top, since they affect only those who receive lots of income from accumulated wealth. The most progressive tax of all is the estate tax, the bulk of which is paid by a tiny handful of fabulously wealthy heirs.

Compare that layer cake to President Bush's policies. The tax at the bottom, the payroll tax, he has not touched at all. The tax just above that, the income tax, he sliced by around a tenth. The taxes just above that, on capital gains and dividends, he cut in half. And the tax at the very top, the estate tax, he abolished altogether (though he has not mustered enough votes to abolish it permanently). Bush's opposition to any given tax is exactly proportional to the degree that it affects the rich. And in this he is merely keeping faith with conservative and Republican thought over the last few decades, which has agitated fiercely against the most progressive taxes and left alone the most regressive ones.

This policy holds as well on the spending side. Since Republicans took over Congress in 1995, their regular (and usually unsuccessful) attempts to cut spending programs tend to concentrate on those that redistribute income from rich to poor. They have set out to cut Medicare and Medicaid, privatize Social Security, and reduce food stamps and other poverty programs. They have ignored, or (in most cases) increased, programs that don't redistribute income downward and that have strong business constituents, like defense spending, highways, and myriad corporate subsidies. Republicans directed the IRS to devote fewer resources to catching rich tax cheats and more to catching poor Earned Income Tax Credit cheats. It strains all credulity to suggest that this persistent tilt is a mere coincidence.

Now, as I've noted, there is more at work here than conservative greed and subservience to the rich. Conservatives truly believe that penalizing the rich and aiding the poor is economically destructive. (Though it must be said that having lots of money makes such theories more appealing.) Nonetheless, it's undeniably true that the contemporary Republican agenda is shot through with class implications. Upward redistribution of income is the central theme of the conservative and Republican economic program, the one thing that ties together nearly every strand. As the GOP has taken control of the domestic economic agenda, class has become the central dynamic of domestic policy.

IN THIS CONTEXT, the conservative revulsion against class rhetoric must be seen not merely as an overwrought fear but as a deliberate ploy. Advocates of any unpopular belief have a natural tendency to smother political discourse by defining opposing views as beyond the pale. Left-wing social activists and campus radicals habitually respond to disagreement by calling it racist or sexist. The buzzword of choice among conservatives when discussing economics is "class warfare." Subcultures tend to create jargon whose meaning cannot be understood by those outside it. Like many such terms, "class warfare" does not denote to conservatives what it would seem to denote to most people. One has to study the use and context of the term to grasp its meaning.

It does not refer to pitched street battles between workers and management, which in any event would be an odd thing to worry about in contemporary America. Instead, conservatives define it as — to use Bush's words — "trying to pit one group of people against another." So relentlessly have they harped on this phrase that objective news media have adopted it ("Democrats are sharply divided over whether class warfare works anymore" — the *New York Times*),[30] and mainstream Democrats have felt compelled to renounce it.

Only a fool would take at face value the exquisite sensitivity about dividing the country. Republicans make a regular practice of dividing the country along cultural lines. Bush in 2004 endlessly repeated his opponent's supposed claim that "the heart and soul of America can be found in Hollywood," contrasting that with his own professed belief that the heart and soul of America could be found in West Virginia or Iowa or whichever usually rural and white campaign stop he happened to be speaking at.[31] Dan Quayle famously attacked the "cultural elite." Clearly, "dividing America" is not the true objection.

Nor, even, are attacks on the rich, provided it is conservatives who are launching them. The fiercest rhetoric against the rich in American politics actually comes from the right. ("We don't know what Washington, D.C., mansion you live in, Senator," snarled one Republican congressman toward Democrat Mary Landrieu.)[32] The *Journal's* editorial page attacked pro–estate tax millionaires as the "fat-cat cavalry."[33] In 2004, the GOP launched an extended attack on John Kerry for being rich. The party produced a game called Kerryopoly, in which a player "can land on properties like Nantucket, worth $9.18 million, Beacon Hill, worth $6.9 million, or Idaho, worth $4.9 million." A television ad from a Republican group mockingly listed his assets. The narrator, his voice dripping with disgust, intoned: "Designer shirt: $250. Forty-two-foot luxury yacht: $1 million. Four lavish mansions and a beachfront estate: over $30 million." A spokesman for the Republican National Committee sounded deeply resentful when he noted, "Most Americans can't afford yachts, private planes, $1,000 haircuts or homes in Nantucket."[34]

So "class warfare" turns out not to mean dividing the country or attacking the rich. Rather, it is a term for any analysis that points out the different impact some policies have on various income groups. "Class warfare" can mean raw populist attacks, but by no means is it limited to them. *National Review* once attacked the Republican senator Charles Grassley for "obsess[ing] over federal debt reduction, and what he calls 'tax equity' (read: class warfare)."[35] This is a telling construction. The conservative magazine was instructing its readers that any concern about the fair distribution of the tax burden should be viewed as class warfare. They believe this holds true of even the most scholarly and dispassionate analysis.

The thing that most sets conservative minds to worrying about class warfare is the practice of calculating how different tax policies affect various income levels. "In practice, the use of tax distribution tables in tax policy is hard to separate from the promotion of class warfare," insisted the Republican chairman of the Joint Economic Committee.[36]

In the course of denouncing class warfare, conservatives almost invariably insist that it "doesn't work in America" or some similar iteration. Conservatives chant this in an almost ritualistic way, as if repeating it often enough will make it so. But surely few of them believe it. (As no less a true believer than Newt Gingrich once griped, "If you go anywhere in America and say to people, 'If we have to raise taxes, would you rather raise them on the rich?' they always say yes.")[37] Their frantic efforts to drive any class analysis from the public debate suggest that they believe very much that it does work. They believe that their economic agenda can prevail only if they conceal it from the voters.

It is easy to see accusations of dishonesty and hidden agendas as a mere partisan spat. Yes, spin pervades every element of the political discourse. Both sides carefully craft labels and slogans ("pro-choice," "pro-life") to frame issues in the way that suits them and conceals the weaknesses of their case. I would argue that the contemporary economic right is in a different category. The hidden agenda is not ancillary to the main agenda — the hidden agenda *is* the agenda. Conservatives' distrust of populism has turned into a distrust of democracy, a belief that they can prevail only by trampling the processes that are meant to do the people's will. The question we will now turn to is: How have they been so successful?

PART II

THE CORRUPTION OF
AMERICAN POLITICS

5

MEDIA: THE DOG THAT DIDN'T WATCH

In hindsight, it is clear that the 2000 presidential election was a momentous turning point in American politics. But at the time very few Americans, at least outside the conservative movement, had any inkling of the enormity of the decision before them. The choice between George W. Bush and Al Gore was widely seen as an affair of marginal consequence, an amusing sideshow. Never in recent memory had seriousness been so unfashionable.

Nowhere was the atmosphere of levity and transience shown more clearly than in the mainstream media. The political dispatches of the time seem as myopic and distant as something written in August 1914, when diplomats repaired to their country homes, expecting a short, splendid war. Kurt Andersen, writing in *Slate*, observed, "Politics don't and really can't matter all that much in this country right now. There are rough, large consensuses on all the big issues — economics, social welfare, civil rights, women's rights, war and peace, even abortion."[1] The liberal *New York Times* columnist Frank Rich summed up the ethos when he complained,

"We're stranded with two establishment, tightly scripted, often robotic candidates who are about as different from one another as J. Crew and Banana Republic. . . . The substantive disputes between the men are, in truth, minimal in a prosperous post-cold-war era when both parties aspire to Rockefeller Republicanism."[2] It was commonly said that the contest between Bush and Gore was "a Seinfeld election" — an election about nothing.

Consider a short essay written from the GOP convention in August 2000 by Joe Klein, the *New Yorker's* chief political observer.[3] Klein, a determined centrist writing for a prestigious liberal magazine and a commentator for *Meet the Press,* the most highly regarded Sunday-morning political talk show, reflected all the prevailing assumptions the news media held at the time. Precisely for that reason it is an anthropologically fascinating document and worth dissecting at some length.

Klein began by describing a staid foreign policy panel held at the convention. The most highly esteemed forms of magazine journalism use scenes such as this to illustrate broader conclusions, and Klein leapt directly from this observation to conclude:

> The panel was reassuring on several counts. For one thing, it was too dull to be anything but real. Furthermore, unlike many Republican policy forums in recent years, it wasn't at all angry. But, most important, it revealed an essential truth about the current Bush project. This is not a new Republican party but a souped-up version of a previous one: the very proper, mostly eastern-establishment party of the Eisenhower era; the party that existed before the Nixon-Reagan-Gingrich sunbelt rebels used racial fears to crack open the solid Democratic south; the Party that Martin Luther King, Sr., belonged to, for lack of a better option. It was Senator Prescott Bush's party, and it might have been President George H. W. Bush's natural home, too, if all those voodoo economists and gun lovers and abortion haters hadn't been riding so high in the prop wash of the Reagan revolution.

Klein finished with his assertion that Bush's Republican Party was "still fairly conservative, but calmer and more concerned with tidiness than the Democrats are."

We shouldn't be too hard on Klein. While his article has proven to be utterly wrong, it was the most common kind of wrongness, shared and repeated endlessly by the most influential journalistic minds. A discerning reader might have noticed at the time Klein's odd belief that the "voodoo economists" — that is, supply-siders — had been driven from power when in fact they supported the Texas governor in lockstep and accounted for every one of his economic advisers. But the rest was pure conventional wisdom, assertions that did not have to be supported with any evidence because they were so widely shared. Bush, it was held, represented a new, moderate kind of Republicanism. From this everything else followed: Gore's attacks on Bush's program were silly and overwrought; the election meant little (a premise from which some two and a half million left-liberals concluded that it was as good a year as any to cast a protest vote for Ralph Nader); and, finally, the candidates were properly judged not on their insignificant ideological differences but on aesthetics — i.e., the superior calmness and tidiness of the GOP ticket.

So when we ask why it is that the right has successfully pushed to the fore deeply unpopular economic policies, part of the answer must lie in the failure of the news media to do its job properly. Political parties in a democracy are not supposed to be able to carry out an agenda by hiding it from the public. And, since most voters have neither the interest nor the expertise to follow the intricacies of Washington policy debates, the primary mechanism to prevent this is the press. That mechanism has begun to break down.

MEDIA PREJUDICE

Blaming the media is, of course, the easiest crutch of the frustrated partisan. We should therefore be clear about our parameters. It is certainly not the case that the media have systematically favored Republicans over Democrats. While decades of conservative complaint have made most reporters and editors ultra-skittish about perceived liberal bias, it is also true that most elite journalists vote Democratic and approach the liberal side of most issues with more familiarity and understanding. Surveys of journalists show that they tend, naturally, to share the belief systems of educated professionals. Compared with the public as a whole, they are more secular, more likely to support gay rights, believe in evolution,[4] and so on.

The same surveys also show, however, that journalists hold somewhat right-of-center views on economic questions. While they oppose supply-side economics, they are far more likely than the voting public to support free trade and to believe that Social Security and Medicare must be pared back. The ideology of the media, then, is not uniform liberalism but the moderate liberalism of the elite, tilting sharply leftward on values and slightly rightward on fiscal issues.

Not surprisingly, then, reporters and mainstream pundits tend to define moderates as politicians who share their socially liberal, fiscally conservative proclivities. Republicans who win the cherished moderate label are usually figures like Christine Todd Whitman, the staunchly anti-tax former New Jersey Republican governor who frequently dissented from her party's social conservatism. (Even Steve Forbes, a rabid supply-sider and Jude Wanniski acolyte, was not infrequently described as a moderate because he had once supported abortion rights.) Conversely, a Republican such as Gary Bauer, a social conservative activist who opposes Social Security privatization and favors a higher minimum wage, has *never* been described as a moderate in any major publication, despite his dissenting from his party's pro-business orthodoxy.

When the GOP congressman John Boehner ascended to the role of House majority leader in 2006, the *Washington Post* described him thus: "A Catholic, Boehner has a strongly conservative voting record but is more of a chamber-of-commerce Republican than a religious conservative."[5] This sentence contains all the prevailing assumptions of the elite media. Boehner's religiosity is held up as evidence of his conservatism, but his alliance with the business lobby is not. Indeed, his pro-business stance is evidence of a mainstream sensibility.

These same prejudices make the media suspicious of populist themes. Neutral reporters habitually use the phrase "class warfare" to describe the Democratic opposition to shifting the burden of the tax code downward, and even more frequently use "demagoguery" to describe any resistance to changes in Medicare or Social Security. On the latter issue, especially, the media have thrown themselves squarely in the Republican corner, which became perfectly clear in the fight over privatizing Social Security. Conservatives have long opposed Social Security on principle. (The 1936 GOP nominee, Alf Landon, called it a "cruel hoax";[6] Barry Goldwater suggested it "should be abolished.") In the 1980s, conservatives recognized the impossibility of abolishing the program altogether and turned instead to the idea of transforming it into a system of personal accounts, whereby each retiree would invest toward his own public pension.

Serious liberal policy analysts interpreted this as a plan to phase the system out completely. For a long time, conservatives did not feel the need to keep this desire secret. Peter Ferrara, who designed the first privatization plan for the Heritage Foundation and tirelessly championed the cause, explained in a 2005 interview with Knight-Ridder: "A lot of conservatives thought Social Security was an unjustified invasion into the private sector. But they weren't getting anywhere, because that was all negative politics. . . . The idea of personal accounts would work because that's positive politics."[7] Ferrara and Michael Tanner of the libertarian Cato Institute wrote a 1998 manifesto, "A New Deal for Social Security," in which they straightforwardly conceded their preference to abolish the program altogether. "[I]n an ideal world," they wrote, "each of us would be free to make our own decisions over how to provide for our retirement — how much and when to save."[8] Cato's Project on Social Security Privatization supplied the staff for Bush's 2001 commission, which recommended privatization,[9] as well as the top two point men for Bush's 2005 privatization campaign, Andrew Biggs and Charles Blahous.*

Yet reporters and mainstream pundits have consistently treated the suggestion that privatizing Social Security would unravel the program's core function as some kind of unhinged conspiracy theory. "Gore knows that Bush isn't really out to 'destroy' Social Security," asserted *Newsweek*'s Howard Fineman in 2000. When, in 2005, a guest on *Meet the Press* noted that conservatives see privatization as a first step toward dismantling the program,[10] Tim Russert responded incredulously, "So you're suggesting that private personal accounts are a secret plan to get rid of Social Security?"†

The conundrum for Democrats is that, as we saw earlier, class is the Achilles' heel of the Republican agenda. Indeed, there are few

---

* Ferrara later broke with Cato on the grounds that the latter was too militant in its opposition to the program. "Cato wants to get rid of the entire Social Security system, and I don't," he complained.

† Of course, Social Security privatization fell flat in 2005. The lesson here is that the disposition of the media matters, but it doesn't guarantee anything. Privatizing Social Security was not only overwhelmingly unpopular, its unpopular aspects (lower guaranteed benefit checks) were readily visible. Tax cuts that benefit a tiny proportion of the voting population, on the other hand, impose costs (higher debt, less opportunity for more popular alternate uses for the same money) that are hard for average voters to detect. The privatization debacle showed the limit of pushing unpopular policies with exposed costs.

GOP economic policies that can't be criticized for redistributing wealth upward. As a result, Democrats who point out the obvious criticism are almost forced into making the very sort of arguments the news media regard most suspiciously.

THE PROUDLY IGNORANT

The establishmentarian instincts of the media are reinforced by a general lack of interest in policy. You might imagine Washington reporters or pundits as policy mavens, spending their days poring over obscure budget tables and their nights in long, earnest discussions of tax reform over drinks. The truth is that the political press corps closely follows political maneuverings and mostly ignores policies. Having spent a great deal of time in the company of newspaper reporters, I can attest that they consider policy, especially economic policy, mind-numbing minutiae beyond their purview. During the 2000 election, for instance, Ted Koppel, the former host of *Nightline,* was asked on *Larry King Live* about the dispute between Gore and Bush over what proportion of the Texas governor's tax cut benefited the very rich. "Were you impressed with this fuzzy, top 1 percent, 1.3 trillion, 1.9 trillion bit?" asked King. Koppel replied, "You know, honestly, it turns my brains to mush. I can't pretend for a minute that I'm really able to follow the argument of the debates. Parts of it, yes. Parts of it, I haven't a clue what they're talking about."[11] This is revealing because, far from being a schlocky talking head, Koppel was (and remains) a symbol of highbrow television journalism. Even among that lofty set, it was and is fashionable to hold yourself above petty squabbles over numbers.

Reporters and pundits can be aggressively judgmental on lifestyle issues, personal character, and questions of pure politics, such as which candidates are winning and which are losing. On economics they simply throw up their hands. As Grover Norquist once put it, "The *New York Times* understands sex. It doesn't understand money."[12] Among the elite media, disdain for policy debates is actually a point of pride. One of the reasons the right has had such an easy time concealing its unpopular positions from the public, then, is that the political media have neither the capacity nor the desire to stop them.

Another episode from the 2000 campaign offers a sense of how easy it can be to smuggle an unpopular economic policy past an unsuspecting public. At the time, Bush had what by all rights should have been a massive political liability. A 2000 *Washington Post* poll found that eight in ten voters who worried about health care issues favored a Patients' Bill of Rights that allowed lawsuits against health maintenance organizations that improperly denied coverage. Gore favored this; Bush opposed it.* The Patients' Bill of Rights that had advanced the furthest in Congress, and had become synonymous in Washington with HMO reform, was sponsored by John Dingell, a Democrat, and Charlie Norwood, a Republican.

In the third presidential debate, the very first questioner asked about the issue. Gore noted, "A national law that is pending on this, the Dingell-Norwood bill, a bipartisan bill, is one that I support and that the governor [Bush] does not." In his reply, Bush shot back, "Actually, Mr. Vice President, it's not true. I do support a national patients' bill of rights. As a matter of fact, I brought Republicans and Democrats together to do just that in the state of Texas, to get a patients' bill of rights through."[13] Bush's reply was doubly misleading. First, he implied that he supported the Dingell-Norwood bill, which he did not. (Bush did support legislation on the issue, but he supported a version that nearly every advocate of HMO reform believed would *weaken* the relevant laws.) Second, he claimed to have shepherded through a patients' bill of rights in Texas when

---

* One can argue that the call for Patients' Bill of Rights was overblown, or possibly even a bad idea, but my point rests on the popularity of the issue rather than its importance.

in fact *the law passed over his objection.* Of course, the average viewer had no capacity to sift through the evidence. He merely heard Bush say that Gore was lying when he said his opponent opposed the bipartisan bill and that Bush had championed such a measure in Texas.

After Bush's response, Gore attempted to interject, "We have a direct disagreement on this." Jim Lehrer, the PBS news anchor and debate host, tried to stop Gore and said impatiently, "Before we go on to another question in the health area, would you agree that you two agree on a national patients' bill of rights?" This was incredible. Not only was Lehrer interjecting himself into the debate to make Bush's point for him, he was saying something clearly untrue. Gore immediately replied, "Absolutely not." He explained the difference between Dingell-Norwood and what he described as the toothless alternative favored by Bush, concluding, "I specifically would like to know whether Governor Bush will support the Dingell-Norwood bill, which is the main one pending."

Lehrer, growing even more impatient, once again stepped in. "Governor Bush, you may answer that if you'd like. But also, I'd like to know how you see the differences between the two of you, and we need to move on." Bush dutifully answered, "Well, the difference is, is that I can get it done." Lehrer tried to move on to another question, but Gore interjected, "What about the Dingell-Norwood bill?" Lehrer interrupted Gore's interruption, letting Bush explain more about his "leadership style."

The consensus reaction to this episode among the punditry was that Al Gore had once again displayed the arrogance and bad manners that made him so tiresome. Gore's repeated invocation of "Dingell-Norwood," in particular, became an instant punchline. The following Sunday, on the ABC News talk show *This Week,* Sam Donaldson launched into a tongue-in-cheek riff on the whole thing: "We thought, as a public service, we'd just show you who Dingell and Norwood are," at which point ABC flashed pictures of the two members of Congress while Donaldson ticked off biographical trivia about them without saying a word about their bill or noting that Bush opposed it.[14]

All this was too much for George Stephanopoulos, the former Clinton adviser who was then holding down the liberal seat on the discussion panel. "The important point there," he insisted, "is that George Bush didn't answer the question about the Dingell/Norwood bill." No, no, insisted his fellow panelist Cokie Roberts, the doyenne of respectable conventional wisdom. "Actually, I don't think that is the important point here." "Why not?" asked Stephanopoulos. "Because that's not what comes across when you're watching the debate," Roberts explained. "What comes across when you're watching the debate is this guy from Washington doing Washington-speak." The notion that the very point of a public affairs program is to explain what this Washington-speak means does not seem to have occurred to Roberts or Donaldson.*

A BROKEN SYSTEM

Yet for all its submerged class snobbery and anti-intellectualism disguised as cool detachment, the ultimate failure of the Washington media lies less with the personal failings of its elite members than its structural inadequacy. During the postwar consensus years, both parties hewed relatively close to the midpoint of popular opinion and therefore had no need to flagrantly misrepresent their positions. Those conditions were the basis for the journalistic prac-

---

* The hilarious postscript to this sorry episode occurred the following year. Bush browbeat Norwood into denouncing his own bill, arguing that Republicans had to stick together and deny victory to the Democrats. As a result, the bipartisan coalition for the bill, which until that point had appeared unstoppable, fell apart, and the bill died. Thus a saga that began with Bush promising to bring the parties together and to "get something done" ended with Bush tearing the parties apart and preventing something from getting done.

tices and assumptions that evolved over the years. In a world where those conditions no longer hold true — where one of the parties methodically conceals its domestic program — those practices and assumptions no longer work. The event that proved the old practices were broken beyond repair was Bush's 2000 presidential campaign.

From the beginning, "compassionate conservatism" was an artifice designed to mask Bush's conservatism from an electorate that did not want a sharp rightward turn. When he spoke with the conservative media, Bush was fairly blunt about his intentions. "The Republican Party must put a compassionate face on a conservative philosophy," he once said.[15] In a 1999 interview, *National Review* asked Bush if he believed that the media harbored a bias against conservatives. He replied, "Yes, I do think they are biased against conservative thought. And the reason is that they think conservative thinkers are not compassionate people. And that's one of the reasons I've attached a moniker to the philosophy that I espouse, because I want people to hear a different message."[16]

The subterfuge worked perfectly. Bush's compassionate conservatism, and its supposed break from the rightward tilt of the congressional party, was the dominant theme of the coverage of his campaign. News accounts agreed that Bush would, as *USA Today* put it, "govern from the center, rejecting the shrill conservative absolutism that turned off swing voters after Republicans won control of Congress in 1994."[17] A 2000 study by the Pew Research Center found that media reports had widely described Bush as "a different kind of Republican — 'a compassionate conservative,' a reformer, bipartisan." An analysis by the journalism professor Jane Hall in the *Columbia Journalism Review* later that year found the same result.[18]

How did the political media get it so wrong? One reason was its obliviousness to any sense of scale. Bush spoke at great length of his passion for measures such as increased spending on education and a new charitable tax deduction. The political press made a great deal out of all this. A dispatch from *Time* in August 1999 typified the coverage:

> At a church in Indianapolis, Ind., Bush laid out a detailed list of proposals — complete with a promise of $8 billion in new federal spending — aimed at expanding the role of charities, churches and community groups in helping the poor. A Republican's pledging to increase federal spending for the poor is novel in its own right. But the speech was less remarkable for its topic — supporting faith-based institutions is in vogue with candidates from both parties — than for how Bush used it to neutralize his critics on both the left and the right. By pursuing a liberal end with conservative means, Bush placed himself and his guiding philosophy of "compassionate conservatism" smack in the center of the political spectrum.[19]

In the context of the federal budget, of course, $8 billion is almost trivial. In comparison with the more than $2 trillion in tax cuts Bush would propose, it came to a mere rounding error. Yet the press, prompted by Bush and his advisers, built these small wisps of substance into a great edifice of ideology.*

Bush also took brilliant advantage of the way journalists crave scoops of any kind even at the expense of truth. The unveiling of the Bush tax cut stood out for its devious ingenuity. The Bush campaign had been advertising its approach to tax cuts as a dramatic break from the old GOP practice of giving the rich the biggest breaks. To quote *Time* once again:

> Though Bush won't unveil his plan until the fall, team member Martin Anderson, who helped craft Ronald Reagan's tax cuts in 1981,

---

* The use of symbolism of imagery to create a misleading impression is hardly new to the Bush administration. Presidents like Bill Clinton and Ronald Reagan made a regular practice of using televised imagery or token concessions to hone their public image. But Bush pushed it so much further that a difference in degree became a difference in kind; he used symbolic measures to create a political identity false in its very essence, not just around the margins.

told TIME last week that Bush's plan "is going to be significantly different from what the Republicans are doing now." Of course, the Texas Governor wants to cut taxes for the middle and upper classes, but sources tell TIME his plan will feature a series of proposals aimed at lowering the tax burden on families earning between $12,500 and $30,000 a year. . . . A tax plan that helps low-income Americans goes deep into Democratic territory and sounds like the perfect policy component to fit Bush's centrist rhetoric.[20]

Laudatory coverage like this kept up for months on end, through the summer of 1999 and into the fall. As the end of the year approached, someone in Bush's camp no doubt realized that at some point they would have to release the actual plan. It was bound to be a somewhat problematic moment. In point of fact, Bush's tax plan was no less regressive than previous Republican plans — it gave an even higher percentage of its benefits to the top 1 percent than the Republican plan vetoed by Clinton in 1999, and it did virtually nothing for families earning under $20,000 a year. So, in December, they hit on the solution of preempting the release of the plan by showing it a day early to a handful of major newspaper reporters. There was one catch: those reporters could not share its details with any outside analysts — such as, say, economists who could run numbers disproving its core claims. Astonishingly, reputable newspapers agreed to this arrangement.

The result was a triumph of propaganda. The *Washington Post* breathlessly reported that Bush's plan would "focus its deepest reductions on the working poor and middle class" and would thus "mark a clear departure from more traditional conservative GOP tax policy."[21] The *Wall Street Journal* noted that Bush was "seeking to steer more benefits to working-poor taxpayers."[22] When the plan was publicly released the next day and tax experts found that it bore little resemblance to what the Bush campaign described, the tenor of the coverage shifted slightly. But the residue of the first, mistaken impression remained, especially in the broadcast news reports. ("In a speech in Iowa, Governor Bush unveiled a tax cut plan that targets the working poor as well as the country's rich," reported CNN.[23] "Governor Bush today offered us the centerpiece of his economic plan of more than $1 trillion [in] tax cuts, targeting especially middle- and lower-income families," echoed NBC.)[24] Even when subsequent newspaper reports corrected the initial errors, the broader theme — that Bush had occupied the political center — remained intact.

What the Bush campaign realized, or perhaps merely stumbled on, was that major political figures can make their own news. The act of George W. Bush releasing his economic program is a news event, and the political media will cover it whether or not Bush gives them a complete picture. The initial coverage, made under deadline pressure, is the more likely to swallow the official spin than whatever comes after. But this initial coverage is also the most important. Even on the rare occasions the press decides to run follow-up articles debunking Bush's claims, those articles are almost never as prominent for the simple reason that "Bush Unveils Plan" is considered an inherently more newsworthy story than "Bush Fudges Details of Plan."

Bush's State of the Union addresses have become an annual opportunity to exploit this particular media limitation. When Bush released his first budget as president in 2001, the administration emphasized higher spending on education, which polls showed to be a top public priority. The news coverage echoed the theme. (A *New York Times* front-page headline announced: "First Bush Budget Proposes to Raise Aid for Education.")[25] It later came out that the 11.5 percent hike in education spending touted by the White House was phony, with the real number being half as large. In 2003, Bush made headlines by calling for $3 billion to fight the global spread of AIDS. He later shortchanged that figure by $1 billion and fought Democrats in Congress to keep the total below his promised sum.[26] In both these cases — as well as in similar instances — the less flattering truth was buried in budget-speak, well off the front pages.

BE FAIR AND BALANCED

But the news media's greatest single weakness was its terror of appearing to take sides in a partisan dispute. A century ago, most newspapers were the organs of political parties, but gradually, and especially after World War II, an ethos of objectivity took hold. Objectivity has since become the holy grail of modern journalism, and appropriately so. But objectivity in political reporting has come to be defined as political neutrality. Probably the most common cliché that journalists use about the topic of bias is: "If we're hearing it from both sides we must be doing something right." This is especially true of economic issues, where the almost total lack of expertise of political journalists renders them largely unable to sort fact from fiction. In practice, "balance" is seen in the form of balancing statements from both parties, regardless of whether the dispute is between differing opinions or matters of verifiable fact.

Jim Lehrer explained the prevalent ethos when he was asked how he treats official statements that are "blatantly untrue."[27] The respected newsman replied:

I don't deal in terms like "blatantly untrue." That's for other people to decide when something's "blatantly untrue." There's always a germ of truth in just about everything . . . My part of journalism is to present what various people say about it the best we can find out [by] reporting and let others — meaning commentators, readers, viewers, bloggers or whatever . . . I'm not in the judgment part of journalism. I'm in the reporting part of journalism.*

It's often said that we're entitled to our own opinions but not to our own facts. The practical reality, though, is that in politics you are entitled to your own facts so long as you can marshal your fellow partisans to insist on them in unison. This has turned out to be a crucial innovation for the modern conservative economic agenda.

Like many innovations, this one was born of necessity. When Republicans took control of Congress in 1995, they wanted sizable tax cuts but also a balanced budget. The combination forced them to impose deep cuts in the federal budget. Inevitably this forced them to cut some $270 billion out of the Medicare budget over a five-year span in order to finance a tax cut of roughly equal size. This left the Republicans to defend a desperately unpopular position. A *New York Times*/CBS poll from that year, for instance, showed that only 27 percent of the public was willing to cut Medicare in order to balance the budget, with 67 percent opposed. And balancing the budget was a far more popular goal than cutting taxes, with huge majorities of the public, including Republicans, preferring a balanced budget over tax cuts if given a choice.[28] Other polls yielded similar findings.

Congressional Republicans commissioned surveys and convened focus groups to determine how they could make their plans more palatable to the public. A pollster named Linda DiVall tested various phrases in conjunction with Medicare. People responded most positively to phrases like "protect," "preserve," and "improve,"

---

* Rob Corddry of the *Daily Show* memorably spoofed this ethos when he declared to his host, Jon Stewart, "I don't have opinions. I'm a reporter, Jon. My job is to spend half the time repeating what one side says and half the time repeating the other. Little thing called objectivity. Might want to look it up someday." Stewart replied, "Doesn't objectivity mean objectively weighing the evidence and calling out what's credible and what isn't credible?" To which Corddry shot back: "Well, well, well, sounds like someone wants the media to act as a *filter*. . . . Listen, buddy. Not my job to stand as a filter between the people talking to me and the people listening to me."

the last of which they associated with prescription drug coverage or other benefit expansions. The phrase conjuring the strongest negative associations was "cut." This was a fairly significant obstacle, given that their central goal was in fact to cut Medicare. Given such overwhelming public opposition, most parties would have simply relented. The Republicans decided instead to banish the word "cut." The new line was that they merely wanted to "reduce the rate of growth." They insisted that their budget would still allow Medicare spending to rise from $4,800 to $6,700 per recipient, hence there would be no cut.[29] But the logic was absurd. Any program has to spend higher dollar figures merely to keep pace with rising costs. Since health care costs were rising especially fast, Medicare needed to let spending rise to $8,000 per recipient in order to keep the same level of service. Spending less would mean cutting back on the services offered. (And of course Republicans recognized this when it came to the programs they supported. They rightly accused President Carter of "cutting" the defense budget even though Carter spent higher dollar figures on defense every year he held office.)

Yet Republicans threw themselves with almost fanatical devotion into the task of banishing the disfavored lingo. Since everyone had always used "cut" to describe the process of reducing spending, the Republicans first had to train themselves in the newspeak. The *Washington Post* reported that the Republican budget chairman, John Kasich, at a meeting of fellow partisans, put a hat on the table and announced that anybody using "cut" had to hand over a dollar. (Kasich himself was subsequently the first violator, proving just how difficult it is to ignore the obvious reality.) Then they took after the media, insisting that any use of "cut" to describe the Republican plan to cut Medicare spending was a vicious lie. In numerous meetings, GOP leaders browbeat news and print reporters and their editors. The chairman of the Republican National Committee vowed to give "unshirted hell" to any scribe daring to use the offending term.[30]

Incredibly, it worked. News outlets all but purged the word from their vocabularies. When they did use it, it was usually confined to scare quotes — Clinton "slammed Republicans over the Medicare 'cuts,'" the *New York Times* reported in a typical passage.[31] More often, journalists dutifully described Republican plans to "slow the rate of growth." (Also from the *Times,* "The [Republican] proposal would slow the rate of growth in Medicaid and Medicare over seven years.")[32] This language reverberated throughout the media. Not only did reporters adopt the Republican lingo, they interpreted any deviation from it by Democrats as political opportunism. The *Los Angeles Times:* "[Clinton's] rejection of GOP proposals to reduce the rate of growth in Medicare and Medicaid brought the most immediate political gains with senior citizens."[33] The *Washington Post:* "Clinton called for greater civility and cooperation in the balanced budget debate even as he authorized ads that attacked Republicans as callously neglecting old people with their plans to slow the rate of growth in the Medicare program."[34] And on and on and on — until a fiction had become an irrevocable fact.

HE SAID, SHE SAID

A nadir of sorts may have been reached during the 2000 presidential campaign. One of the central debates between the two candidates focused on what proportion of Bush's tax cut would accrue to the highest-earning 1 percent of taxpayers. Answering the question did involve a tiny bit of subjectivity, but not very much. There are a few broadly accepted methods of calculating how a change in tax rates affects people at different income levels. The Treasury Department used these methods for years on end, under both Republican and Democratic presidents, until Bush put a stop to it. Those calculations, performed by outside economists using the same methods, found that Bush's tax cut would give about 40 percent of its benefits to the top 1 percent.

At first Bush denied it, phrasing his denials in a way to suggest that Gore was a liar. ("The man's practicing fuzzy math again.")[35] Eventually, in October 2000, the Bush campaign released its own figures, calculated by GOP staffers on Capitol Hill, which claimed that only about 20 percent of its tax cut would go to the top 1 percent.[36] What could have accounted for such a vast discrepancy? The answer is that the Republicans excluded most of the upper-bracket tax cuts as well as the repeal of the estate tax, both of which were phased in after a few years' delay. In other words, they got the number by excluding the portions of the tax cut that did the most to benefit the rich. It was a patently phony effort, whose only possible purpose was to muddy the waters.

That's exactly what happened. News accounts of this dispute reported on Gore's claims and Bush's counterinsults but rarely attempted to adjudicate the truth. When they did, the result was a studied neutrality that amounted to falsity. The *New York Times* reported: "The richest 1 percent of taxpayers would get between 22 percent and 45 percent of the tax benefits, depending on how the calculations are done."[37] A *Newsweek* voter guide asserted: "Gore says that 42 percent of the benefits go to the richest one percent; Bush says the figure is only 21 percent . . . the truth lies in between; just where, nobody knows."[38]

This sort of dynamic has repeated itself over and over throughout the Bush presidency. In 2004, for instance, Bush's campaign claimed repeatedly that raising the top tax rate would force 900,000 small business owners to pay higher taxes. The claim was ludicrous. The Tax Policy Center pointed out that the 900,000 figure mostly comprised individuals who receive parts of their income from outside sources, such as speaking fees or dividends from stock in small corporations. (Bush and Vice President Cheney qualified as "small business owners" under this definition.)[39] For the most part, however, the truth was treated as a matter of normal controversy between the parties. A typical CNN segment, for instance, showed Bush making the "900,000 small business owners" claim and then reported: "On a conference call today, Kerry adviser Roger Altman disputed the president's remarks about the economy and Senator Kerry's tax record and accused Bush of being out of touch with working families." After this, the host moved on to the next topic.[40]

Even when the most prestigious newspapers took the time to dig into the truth of the matter, they simply presented the rebuttal as the Democratic view. The *New York Times*, for instance, devoted a paragraph to Bush's claim, then another paragraph to Kerry's reply:

> Mr. Kerry's campaign said Mr. Bush was distorting the definition of small-business owners by including taxpayers like some doctors, lawyers, corporate chief executives and others who earn income as members of a partnership. Only a tiny fraction of small-business owners earn enough to be in the top income tax bracket, leaving nearly all of them untouched by Mr. Kerry's plan to roll back the Bush tax cuts for people earning more than $200,000 a year, Mr. Kerry's campaign said.[41]

This was about as thorough and responsible as journalistic treatment of the matter got. Still, rather than flatly stating that the 900,000 number did not describe "small business owners" in any way, shape, or form, it simply presented Kerry's view as a rebuttal, introduced as something "Mr. Kerry's campaign said" rather than with an "in fact" or some similarly blunt construction. Hardly anybody in the public knew which side was telling the truth, and hardly anybody in the media cared.

6

HOW WASHINGTON IMAGINES CHARACTER

If the whole of the American people who voted for president in 2004 were condensed into a single person, she would be Shirley Irwin of Dunbar, West Virginia. An October profile in the *Baltimore Sun* explained Irwin's thinking:

> Irwin, a 64-year-old lifelong Democrat, says things have been "terrible" during the nearly four years that Bush has been in the White House. She's scared that he's "ruined" Medicare and would do the same to Social Security, the programs she depends on to get by. Irwin believes Bush planned to invade Iraq from the moment he took office and says he bungled the war there. But she can't bear to vote for Sen. John Kerry, whom she calls a dishonest waffler whose ideas are no better than Bush's. "I don't like Bush either, but if I've got to choose between the two, count me for Bush," Irwin said. "With Kerry, one minute he would vote for something and the next minute he would change his mind."[1]

This sentiment proved to be the dominant theme of the election. It is almost impossible to exaggerate the degree to which the image of Kerry as an unprincipled flip-flopper had penetrated the public consciousness. "Voters routinely describe Kerry as wishy-washy, as a flip-flopper and as a candidate they are not sure they can trust, almost as if they are reading from Bush campaign ad scripts," reported the *Washington Post*.[2] Wisecracks to this effect reverberated throughout the popular culture, from the *Tonight Show* to the announcing team on *Monday Night Football*.

Far from being a joke, the mass distrust of Kerry's personal character had the most profound influence. On almost every specific issue, voters rejected President Bush's record and favored Kerry's approach. Yet the personal disdain they held for Kerry loomed larger. A *New York Times* poll that same month found:

> A majority of voters said that they disapproved of the way Mr. Bush had managed the economy and the war in Iraq, and — echoing a refrain of Mr. Kerry's — that his tax cuts had favored the wealthy. Voters said that Mr. Kerry would do a better job of preserving Social Security, creating jobs and ending the war in Iraq. But a majority of Americans continue to see Mr. Kerry as an untrustworthy politician who will say what he thinks people want to hear.[3]

A *Los Angeles Times* poll asked voters whether they cared more about "character and strength of leadership or how a candidate stands on the issues." Kerry voters said issues by a margin of more than two to one. Bush voters chose character by a margin of nearly three to one.[4] Character — or, at least, the perception of character — truly was destiny.

The funny thing is that a nearly identical dynamic shaped the presidential race four years earlier. George W. Bush's campaign called Al Gore a "serial exaggerator" and pointedly declared that Americans "don't want flip-floppers as president of the United States."[5] News outlets repeated the accusation more or less as fact — "Mr. Gore has a bit of a reputation for flip-flopping and corner-cutting on issues like abortion and trade," reported the *New York Times*.[6]

Personal revulsion against Gore heavily influenced the outcome of the election. An October *Newsweek* poll found that voters clearly preferred Gore over Bush on most issues, namely foreign policy, "helping seniors pay for prescription drugs," health care, "the economy and jobs," Social Security, and abortion. Bush held the edge on only "national defense" and "upholding moral values." (And the latter could be interpreted as more of a character evaluation than an issue position, especially given Bush's repeated promises during the campaign to "uphold the honor and dignity of the Oval Office.") Yet the same poll showed voters far more likely to deem Bush "honest and ethical" and "says what he believes, not just what people want to hear."[7]

The result was typical. A Fox News poll that year showed the public by wide margins preferred Bush over Gore "as a business partner" or if they were "fighting next to you in your foxhole if you had to defend your life."[8] (This result was somewhat amusing, given that Bush as a younger man had run a series of business ventures into the ground and declined to serve in Vietnam.) So once again, whatever political advantage accrued to the Democratic candidate by his substantially more popular policies was all but wiped out by the Republican candidate's more popular personal character.

Funnier still, a similar dynamic could be found once more in the previous two campaigns. During his two presidential runs, Bill Clinton was widely seen as a sleazy and untrustworthy individual, and this theme featured prominently in his opponents' campaigns. "As the case of military service makes most clear, these differing positions are, in fact, more than mere flip-flops," charged Vice President Dan Quayle in 1992. "They reflect a fundamental element of Governor Clinton's character."[9] President George H. W. Bush told voters that Clinton would "turn the White House into a Waffle House," and even visited a Waffle House to drive the point home.[10] A *Time* magazine cover featured a photo negative image of the candidate with the headline: "Why Voters Don't Trust Bill Clinton."[11]

The image of Clinton as dissembler seeped into the popular culture. Garry Trudeau depicted Clinton as a waffle in his *Doonesbury* cartoon. A Maryland truck driver drew media attention when, in the course of confessing that he had driven longer without rest than allowed by regulations, said, "I don't want to pull a Clinton here. Truth is, I have broken them sometimes."[12]

In 1996, the Republican nominee, Bob Dole, also made character a central theme of his candidacy. He emphasized his small-town roots and military service and adopted the slogan "A better man for a better America." A *Los Angeles Times* poll found that some 40 percent of the public considered Dole ethically superior to Clinton, more than double the number who saw Clinton as ethically superior.[13] Of course Dole lost, as did Bush in 1992, but the underlying dynamic was the same as that in 2000 and 2004: the Democratic candidate held the political high ground on policy while the Republican candidate held the high ground on personal character. The only difference is that the Republicans' advantage on character was enough to overcome their deficit on issues in 2000 and 2004, but not in 1992 and 1996.

This pattern suggests two possible interpretations. The first is that, for four straight presidential elections, Republicans have put forth principled, decent, and upstanding men while the Democrats have nominated a succession of cads. But unless there's something inherently immoral about Democrats and inherently virtuous about Republicans — a notion belied by Mark Foley, Duke Cunningham, and countless others — sheer statistical chance suggests this is unlikely. So let us instead consider the alternate possibility: The character of Republican presidential nominees has not been consistently superior to that of Democratic nominees. Rather, it is seen that way because Republicans have done a superior job of influencing Americans' personal impressions of their elected leaders.

THE MAN, NOT THE PLAN

If you look at the character flaws imputed to Clinton, Gore, and Kerry, you will notice something peculiar. While the particulars vary from campaign to campaign, the overall bill of indictments is strikingly similar in all three cases. From 1992 through 2004, variations on two basic themes recur.

The first is personal dishonesty as a metaphor for ideological slipperiness. Republicans labeled Clinton, Gore, and Kerry as flip-floppers, though Clinton was more frequently given the synonymous term "waffler," while the charge against Gore tended to put more emphasis on lying. This is of course a shrewd response to the adoption by Clinton and his successors of the New Democrat theme. The main Democratic presidential strategy since 1992 has been to jettison the party's unpopular positions and seize the ideological center. Invariably, this leaves Democrats defending more nuanced views. In 2003, for instance, Kerry favored war with Iraq only if it could be done with an international coalition while Bush favored it unreservedly. Democrats since Clinton have come to support free trade bills that contain provisions for environmental and labor protections and oppose bills that do not. Since this places them in support of some free trade bills and in opposition to others, they can easily be called flip-floppers on free trade. And so on.

Republicans have learned to portray their support for simpler positions that don't require cognitive dissonance as a reflection of sturdier character. These conservatives are men who know what they think, and they do not trim their sails. The implicit message to voters is that even if they agree with the Democratic candidate on more issues, they should support the Republican because they can be sure he will not change his mind. Sometimes this message is made explicit: President Bush declared while accepting his reelection nomination in 2004, and repeatedly on the stump afterward: "Even when we don't agree, at least you know what I believe and where I stand." This is the consummate statement of the candidate using his personal approval to compensate for his unpopular views.

The second recurring theme is anti-intellectualism, which — since intellectuals are often seen as weak — can be synonymous with attacks on manliness. In 1828, supporters of Andrew Jackson portrayed the election as a choice between "John Quincy Adams who can write/And Andrew Jackson who can fight."[14] In *Anti-Intellectualism in American Life,* Richard Hofstadter observed: "The association of intellectuality and style with effeminacy . . . reappeared in the 1952 campaign," when Adlai Stevenson was savaged for his "fruity" voice, which sounded like "a genteel spinster who can never forget that she got an A in elocution at Miss Smith's Finishing School," in the words of one conservative newspaper.[15]

These sorts of themes have dominated modern Republican election rhetoric. At the 1984 GOP convention, Jeane Kirkpatrick famously denounced the "San Francisco Democrats," and in 1988 George Bush attacked the hapless Michael Dukakis as the candidate of the "Harvard boutique."[16] And while Clinton's southern dialect and folksy speaking style made these attacks less effective, they were hardly less prominent. Conservatives savaged Clinton as a blow-dried, flip-flopping draft-dodger — Marilyn Quayle called him a "blow-dried Jimmy Carter in a younger, hipper package."[17] George H. W. Bush — the prep school–educated scion of a wealthy northeastern political dynasty — in 1992 made prominent use of anti-intellectual rhetoric. As he said of Clinton:

> He and a number of his advisers studied them at Oxford in the 1960s . . . they prefer the false certitude of social engineering fashioned by a new economic elite of the so-called best and brightest. The best and the brightest are right out here in middle America where you know what's going on. From Santa Monica to

Cambridge, my opponents are cranking up their models, ready to test them on you.[18]

The anti-intellectual tone reached a fever pitch in 2000. *National Review*'s editor, Rich Lowry, called Gore a "pointy-head intellectual," and pundits widely mocked him as "the smartest boy in the class" — a phrase they used as an insult.[19] Commentators took note of Gore's debate makeup, which made him look like a "drag queen," as the conservative actor and writer Ben Stein observed.[20] Early in the 2004 campaign, a Republican operative confided to the *New York Times* that he called John Edwards "the Breck Girl."[21] (The nickname stuck and was subsequently repeated more than a hundred times in various media.) The attacks on Kerry ran along the same lines. The liberal writer Naomi Wolf noted bitterly, "Listen to what the Republicans are hitting Kerry with: Indecisive. Effete. French. They are all but calling this tall, accomplished war hero gay."[22]

Anti-intellectualism can often make for a winning political strategy. But it is particularly attractive for a candidate saddled with a less popular platform and who wants to avoid detailed discussion of the issues. During one famous exchange during a 2000 presidential debate, Gore unleashed a fact-laden attack on Bush's Medicare plan. Bush shot back, "I'm beginning to think not only did he invent the Internet, but he invented the calculator."[23] In one fell swoop he dismissed Gore's substantive claims and turned the vice president's familiarity with statistics into evidence of untrustworthiness.

The recurrence of the same character-based attacks shows how little these impressions have to do with the innate qualities of the accused candidates. Slickness and flip-flopping are certainly not totally absent in the recent Democratic nominees, yet there's little to suggest that Clinton, Gore, and Kerry are particularly unmanly or prone to flip-flopping. These are templates that Republicans have had to adopt out of necessity. Their quadrennial use says more about the straits the GOP finds itself in than it does about anything intrinsic to the Democratic nominees' character.

THE RETURN OF THE OLD ORDER

The character-based politics taken up by Republicans today echoes the politics practiced by both parties more than a hundred years ago. In the nineteenth and early twentieth centuries, party politics was very much like a sport in American life. Yankee and Red Sox fans today are divided mainly by inherited fealty rather than a sharply divergent view of how baseball should be played. Likewise, political passions were deeply held but — especially in the era between Abraham Lincoln and Woodrow Wilson — were more closely related to tribal or regional loyalties than to ideological convictions. Extolling the character of one's own party leaders, and savaging that of the other's, was all part of the fun. The Whigs in 1840 put forth their nominee, William Henry Harrison, as "the Log Cabin and Hard Cider" candidate — that is, a man of humble origins and simple tastes. Republicans in 1884 savaged the Democratic nominee, Grover Cleveland, for his out-of-wedlock child with the mocking slogan "Ma, ma, where's my pa?" while the Democrats assailed his opponent, James Blaine, as the "Continental liar from the state of Maine."[24] The character fights of yore were conducted with the weapons of the era — the pamphlet and the partisan newspaper.

This game was revolutionized by the emergence of the professional, nonpartisan press. Thus emerged an arbiter of presidential character that lay outside the hands of the parties. Of course, character is a hard thing for an outsider to judge, so reporters came to rely heavily on small and often symbolic moments to define the character of the candidates. For instance, in 1967 the Republican presidential hopeful George Romney said he had been "brain-washed" by American generals; in 1972 the Democrat Ed Muskie appeared to shed a tear in the course of defending his wife against criticism; in 1992 President George Bush checked his watch during a debate. The political media imbued all these events with deep significance, proving, respectively, that Romney was unstable, Muskie unmanly, and Bush out of touch. The political media as a regular practice seize on incidents like this, and they move as a pack toward a unanimous judgment. It was almost impossible to predict which episodes would escape attention altogether and which would mushroom into character-defining moments. Randomness was the hallmark of the process.

This system was relentlessly stupid and brutally unfair to the individuals involved, but it had the singular virtue of partisan neutrality. So long as Democrats and Republicans alike were equally prone to admitting they had "committed adultery in [their] heart" (Jimmy Carter, 1976) or reading from a cue card that spelled "potatoe" (Dan Quayle, 1992),[25] they were equally likely to be exposed in the media as harboring some deep and possibly disqualifying character flaw.

THE TRANSFORMATION FROM the old world to the new took place during Clinton's presidency. When Clinton first ran for office, his supporters tried to craft a log cabin narrative (Clinton as "the Man from Hope") while his opponents created a counternarrative, describing a man who avoided military service and insisted he "did not inhale" when he tried marijuana. The latter narrative, not altogether unfairly, won out. Yet the assault on Clinton's character took on a scale unseen in modern times as a response to the popularity of Clinton's agenda. The new Democratic president had neutralized many of his party's traditional liabilities — crime, welfare, middle-class taxes — and focused his agenda on those areas where conservative Republicans lacked popular appeal. Highlighting (or, in some cases, manufacturing) Clinton's character flaws was a way to counter the appeal of his agenda. In a 1994 interview with ABC News, the conservative talk show host Rush Limbaugh all but admitted as much:

> Because everybody says — or a lot of the critics said, "We've got to get on to other issues." And I think Whitewater is about health care. Whitewater's about Bosnia. Whitewater is about crime and — and welfare reform. And I'll tell you why. Character — the issue of character was put on hold during the 1992 campaign. Nobody cared about it because so many people were upset with the economic situation, they wanted a change. And it's now coming home to roost.
>
> Most people think that health care's a good idea, but they haven't read the plan. They're taking the president's word for it. Now I think if the president's word is what we're going to rely on for his policies — this is a — a debate in the arena of ideas and this is the man setting the agenda. And if people are going to base their support for the plan on whether or not they can take his word, I think it's fair to examine whether or not he keeps his word.[26]

In fact, it was not Clinton but his opponents who wanted public opinion on health care reform to hinge on the president's personal trustworthiness. The plan to defeat Clinton's policies by weakening his personal image worked perfectly. In 1994, for instance, a *Wall Street Journal* poll found that every element of the Clinton health plan commanded majority support. Only when it was identified as "the Clinton plan" did respondents turn against it.[27]

The Clinton presidency turned into a near-endless stream of scandals, many of which (Whitewater, the firing of the White House travel office) ultimately came up with nothing incriminating. The constant flow of scandal news was driven by the rise of conservative investigative outlets and like-minded pundits, who created an echo chamber of salacious accusations. Even wholly unsubstantiated charges — that Clinton had raped a woman named Juanita

Broderick, that departing Clintonites in 2000 vandalized the White House — found their way into the mainstream news.

In many ways, outlets like Limbaugh's program or the *American Spectator* represented a throwback of sorts. Like the party-controlled newspapers or pamphlets, they dealt in salacious and often fantastic accusations, and they inculcated in their readers a Manichean view of the world. The difference is that the contemporary version coincides with a nonpartisan press that has built up a reservoir of public trust. Media outlets functionally affiliated with the Republican Party have been able to create news that makes its way into the nonpartisan media. It is a kind of machine that manufactures images of character.

THE REPUBLICAN CHARACTER MACHINE

The Republicans' seminal insight was that the random process by which small events came to wield great symbolic insight into the character of presidential candidates didn't *have* to be random. It was possible to prime the pump, in a way. This innovation first made itself felt during the 2000 campaign. It is difficult to remember now, but heading into his presidential campaign, Al Gore had a reputation for earnestness and probity. To the extent that he had any public persona, it was as a dull policy wonk — an image that itself had certain positive connotations, especially in contrast to Clinton's rogue charm. Republicans set about quite deliberately to alter that image. In May 1999, the *New York Times* reported on this effort:

> After years of battling with President Clinton, House Republicans are shifting their sights to Vice President Al Gore and using ridicule as their weapon of choice. The office of the House majority leader, Representative Dick Armey of Texas, has become an unofficial clearinghouse of anti-Gore press releases and activity, with Mr. Armey mocking Mr. Gore over his pronouncements on air travel, the Internet and traffic congestion. . . .

For years Congress ran multiple investigations of Mr. Clinton. But with Mr. Gore, Republicans are betting that well-timed ridicule can be more devastating than any inquiry. In essence, they are trying to do to him what Democrats tried to do to former Vice President Dan Quayle: make him the foil for comedians on late-night television.[28]

In the ensuing months, the case against Gore was refined from his general ridiculousness to a specific tendency to lie, and the cast of the accusation took on a less lighthearted and more sinister tone. The task of fanning the flames passed from the House GOP into the hands of the Republican National Committee chairman, Ed Gillespie, who regularly distributed what he called "candygrams" or "stink bombs" — attacks on various Gore statements that would seep into the media and feed the perception that the vice president was a compulsive liar.[29]

By October 2000, those forays had settled so deeply into the mainstream narrative that the *Times* itself was now repeating them as settled fact: "While many politicians are prone to spice up a story here and there, Republicans and Democrats say Mr. Gore's shading of the truth has become so frequent that some politicians are no longer dismissing it as sloppy oratory from a candidate under the glare of television cameras."[30] The paper of record reported: "Whatever the reason, the vice president's tangled recollections have begun to draw attention because there are so many examples."* The reason there were "so many examples," of course, was that Republi-

---

* The examples were almost laughably weak. For instance, the article cited Gore's statement that he had visited a Florida classroom so overcrowded that a student was forced to stand without a desk. This was true, but after Gore cited it, the embarrassed principal hastily procured a desk. Thus when Gore cited the student the next day, it was no longer true, and therefore a "lie." Gore also "lied" when asserting that he had visited a 1998 disaster cite in Texas with FEMA's director, James Lee Witt. In fact, Gore had visited other disaster sites with Witt, but in that particular instance he visited with Witt's assistant. Furthermore he "falsely" claimed that as a baby his mother had serenaded him with the song "Look for the Union label" as a lullaby, which was not true, but which Gore insisted was a joke. And so on.

cans had spent a year and a half disseminating anything that appeared to impugn Gore's honesty, however tenuous. But by this point the *Times* had become a participant in the very phenomenon it had described a year and a half earlier. (Not that the *Times* was alone — virtually the whole of the campaign press had endorsed this line.) It was no longer a partisan campaign. It was simply the truth.

THE REPUBLICAN CHARACTER machine runs on quantity, not quality. The critical thing is not to generate particularly telling incidents that define the candidates' character but to generate as many incidents as possible. To get a sense of how the game works, consider one incident from the 2004 election. On October 11, 2003, John Kerry visited a famous Philadelphia cheesesteak joint. Alas, he committed what is considered an enormous gaffe when he asked for Swiss cheese on his sandwich rather than Cheez Whiz, in keeping with local custom. This was the sort of incident that seemed to confirm the image of Kerry as estranged from working-class habits — a man who "looks French," as Republicans put it. The following day's *Philadelphia Inquirer* reported on the incident, and that day Fox News picked up the story.[31] "Massachusetts Democratic Senator and presidential candidate John Kerry, who's often needled by conservatives who say he looks and acts French, made, as you can see there, the obligatory stop in Philadelphia yesterday at the famous Pat's King of Steaks," reported Brit Hume later that day. "The distinguished senator ordered a cheesesteak with Swiss cheese. Told that Swiss cheese was unavailable, the senator settled for Cheez Whiz, which, like the cheesesteak, is a uniquely American concoction."

From there the tale spread throughout the national media. "For Kerry, a Boston Brahmin, [the cheesesteak incident] is something of a sore spot," reported the *Washington Post* the following day. "As he seeks to lose his reputation for $75 Salon Christophe haircuts, Turnbull & Asser shirts and long fingernails to play classical guitar, he has been seen riding a motorcycle and doing other regular-guy things."[32] That same day, MSNBC'S pundit Mike Barnicle, CNN's pundit Tucker Carlson, the *Boston Globe's* gossip column, and CNN's political reporter John King again reported the tale of Kerry and the cheesesteak. All told, the incident was recounted more than a hundred times in various media.

Even that was not quite the end of it. The following summer, George W. Bush visited the same restaurant and later told a crowd of Boeing workers in a Philadelphia suburb: "This is the thirty-second time I've been to your state of Pennsylvania, and, you all know the reason why, don't you? It's because I like my cheesesteaks Whiz Wit'"[33] (the preferred lingo). This prompted CNN, the *New York Times,* and numerous other outlets to recount Kerry's cheesesteak gaffe yet again.

One might suppose that the same sort of thing could have happened to Bush if he, rather than Kerry, had been unfortunate enough to flout local culinary custom in Philadelphia or elsewhere. But we know that this is not the case because Bush did in fact repeat Kerry's error. Kathleen E. Carey, a reporter with the *Daily Times* of Delaware County, Pennsylvania, called the proprietor of the cheesesteak establishment and discovered something genuinely newsworthy, at least according to the established standard. Bush, she learned, eschewed Cheez Whiz as well and asked to have his hoagie garnished with American cheese![34] Not only did the president flout local custom, he unashamedly misled the public. Yet this incident garnered a mere three mentions in the media, none from the national campaign press.

Now, one could object that Bush's cheesesteak gaffe received less attention than Kerry's because it flew in the face of well-worn clichés. Kerry had already established a reputation as an out-of-touch patrician while Bush had not. So, the argument would go, evidence of Bush's behaving like a pampered aristocrat is inherently less newsworthy than Kerry's doing the same, just as Al Gore's misspelling a word would spark less media furor than Dan Quayle's doing so. The best response to this objection would be to find an example of a similar incident involving Bush that would seem to confirm the character flaws his critics see in him. In fact there was just such an incident, and by chance it also involved a sandwich.

In November 2000, *Newsweek* reported the following episode from Bush's campaign plane:

> Aboard Bush's plane, [John] McCain's chief strategist, John Weaver, had — without thinking — pulled a peanut-butter-and-jelly sandwich off the snack cart and eaten it. Bush came aboard the plane and asked the flight attendant for his PB&J. She had to tell him it was gone. "It's gone?" Bush said, disbelieving and suddenly angry. "Who ate my peanut-butter-and-jelly sandwich?" After a minute Weaver impishly raised his hand. "I did," he said. "Fine," said Bush. "Don't eat any more of his food," McCain cracked, sotto voce. A few people chuckled, and Bush returned to his seat to pout.[35]

This would seem to be at least as telling a detail as Kerry's sandwich encounter — Bush comes across as a spoiled, petulant man-child. Yet no other media organizations picked up on the story.

Republicans, to be sure, can face the same sort of trivial personality stories that can plague Democrats. Reporters are perfectly capable of blowing up small or meaningless episodes into negative press for Bush or any other Republican. (In the fall of 2000, to take just one example, the *New York Times* published a ludicrous front-page story claiming that a Bush campaign ad subliminally juxtaposed Democrats with the word "rats.")[36] The difference is that only the Republicans have a machine in place. Any episode or detail that seems to reflect poorly on the character of a Democratic candidate will be nurtured and recirculated, and many of them will cohere over time into a broader narrative. When the equivalent thing happens to a Republican candidate, it often sinks without a trace.

It may seem odd that the news media would embrace such a

one-sided portrait, especially given the reluctance of reporters to insert themselves into partisan disputes. The GOP's practice of running character-based presidential campaigns has one additional advantage: the news media is naturally more sympathetic. As we noted in the last chapter, Washington reporters and talking heads know and care very little about the details of policy, except for some social issues. The mainstream press prefers to interpret politics along characterological lines. Jack Germond, one of the most respected members of the Washington press corps and a pundit on *The McLaughlin Group,* summed up the prevailing ethos in his memoir, *Fat Man Fed Up.* "In the end, it is far wiser to focus attention on the kind of people who are running than which one seems to have the best plan for providing drug coverage to old folks . . . ," he wrote. "The only hope for better politics lies in the possibility of better people who can command the public's attention and win on the force of their personalities and the qualities of their service."[37]

Political reporters tend to reward candidates who campaign on the basis of their personalities rather than their platforms. Not surprisingly, the presidential candidate who by all accounts (Republicans, Democrats, and many reporters themselves) received the most laudatory press coverage was John McCain in 2000. McCain's campaign was, in fact, an ideological crusade of enormous consequence (as discussed earlier), but most press coverage concentrated on his history as a prisoner of war and shoot-from-the-hip personal style.

Likewise, reporters often scorn campaigns rooted in issues and lacking in personal narrative. A *Washington Post* story on the candidacy of Steve Forbes represented this assumption stretched to its most absurd conclusion. The story's headline — "Forbes Reveals Little But His Ideas" — reflected the basic premise: a candidate's ideas are a trifling matter. "Forbes's book expounds on dismantling the Internal Revenue Service and instituting a flat tax," reported the amazed writer. "But his column rarely mentions his family and the book index doesn't list his father, wife, or children."[38] The article continued in this vein, portraying Forbes's desire to run for president on the basis of what he would do as president as the product of a bizarre personality disorder.

And so the helpless neutrality that the media displays on policy disputes gives way to an aggressive judgmental streak on matters of character. The *Wall Street Journal* news story calling Kerry "a politician with a troublesome reputation for trying to have it both ways" is no aberration.[39] The *New York Times* can assert in a news story: "Mr. Gore has a bit of a reputation for flip-flopping and corner-cutting on issues like abortion and trade," or "Mr. Bush sometimes came across as cocky, lightweight and over-rehearsed." The popular culture moves along the same currents as the press. Impressions of the character of presidents and would-be presidents form quickly and, once entrenched, are nearly impossible to dislodge. (Unless there is an event of colossal cultural import, such as the September 11 attacks.) Few Americans consider themselves experts on the platforms of a candidate, but most feel confident rendering instant judgment on his inner being.

EPISTEMOLOGICALLY SPEAKING, of course, this is completely backward. It is said that character is what we do when nobody is looking. But our impressions of the character of public figures are formed mainly from what they do when everybody is looking. We try to evaluate character based on how the candidate acts onstage, orders lunch in a restaurant filled with reporters, or clears brush. These moments are not windows to a soul, they are an audition. How such people act in private — when they are not trying to project an image of sound character to the country — is beyond our knowing. We are looking through the glass darkly.

For that reason, our definition of character is inescapably bound to partisan whim. Defining presidential character is the art — not the science — of using small details as a stand-in for large traits.

But which small details? And, for that matter, which large traits? In May 2001, David Brooks wrote in an editorial for the *Weekly Standard:* "Even in his demeanor, Bush seems to understand that he has assumed a serious responsibility. He insists on jackets and ties in the Oval Office. He insists that meetings start on time. In short, he acts like a man who expects that everyone around him will behave responsibly."[40]*

The theme of Bush's serious demeanor as metaphor for his seriousness about governance dominated the conservative press early in his first term. But is an insistence on business attire and punctuality really an obviously admirable quality? On the one hand, it could be a sign of responsibility and seriousness. On the other, it could be seen as an example of control-freak behavior, a disturbing sign of a mind preoccupied with formalities and not concerned with results. Drawing conclusions about character from such details is hopelessly subjective.

And even if we can agree on which candidates have which character traits, ranking one trait over another is no easy task. Take, for example, Mark Helprin, a novelist and frequent contributor to the *Wall Street Journal* op-ed page. Helprin was famous for writing war novels, often featuring gritty, Gary Cooper–esque soldiers as his protagonists. In 1996, Republicans nominated in Bob Dole a candidate whose image, at least in its idealized form, closely matched these characters. So Helprin came aboard the Dole campaign as a speechwriter and wrote movingly of the candidate's World War II military service; it became the central metaphor for the candidate to explain his personal moral superiority over Clinton. In his well-

---

* *U.S. News & World Report* has noted that, according to one White House insider, Bush "can't get enough of fart jokes" and is "also known to cut a few for laughs, especially when greeting new young aides" (Paul Bedard, "Washington Whispers," *U.S. News & World Report,* August 20, 2006). This would seem to undercut the theory of Bush as ultradignified executive.

received acceptance speech, written by Helprin, Dole alluded over and over again to his military record:

> The triumph of this nation lies not in its material wealth but in courage, sacrifice and honor. We tend to forget this when our leaders forget it, and we tend to remember it when they remember it.
>
> It is demeaning to the nation that within the Clinton Administration [is] a corps of the elite who never grew up, never did anything real, never sacrificed, never suffered and never learned . . .
>
> To those who believe that I am too combative, I say, if I am combative, it is for love of country. It is to uphold a standard that I was born and bred to defend. And to those who believe that I live and breathe compromise, I say that in politics, honorable compromise is no sin. It's what protects us from absolutism and intolerance. But one must never compromise in regard to God, and family, and honor, and duty and country.
>
> The principle of unity has been with us in all our successes. The 10th Mountain Division, which I served in Italy, and the black troops of the 92d Division who fought nearby, were the proof for me, once again, of the truth I'm here trying to convey.[41]

It was all very moving and poetic. Oddly enough, nearly four years later, conservative Republicans found themselves fending off a primary challenge from John McCain, who had an even more heroic war history. If one's conduct in uniform offers the clearest view of their character, as Helprin's paeans to Dole repeatedly suggested, then McCain would be even more admirable. (And McCain's chief opponent, George W. Bush, would be somewhat reprehensible for his choice to avoid serving in Vietnam.)

But Helprin didn't support McCain. Indeed, at a crucial moment during the primaries he savaged him in a *Journal* column titled, portentously, "The Uses of Honor." The column began:

> If John McCain wins the Republican nomination, he will have done so not by persuading the Republican Party but by overcoming it

with the help of outsiders and by feverishly endorsing the accusations of its enemies. . . .

These are betrayals, plain and simple, and betrayals by any definition are acts that are hard to square with honor.[42]

But what about McCain's courage in Vietnam? Helprin saw this as a point against him, raging: "It is not honorable to trade upon one's honor, to offer it as a token, to mention it in every other breath." (An odd complaint from the speechwriter who had Dole do this very thing.) Four years earlier, Helprin defined honor as physical courage in the service of one's country. But, faced with an ideological adversary who had those qualities in abundance, he simply found a new definition of honor. "Nor is it honorable," he continued, "for Sen. McCain to turn upon his own party for the imperfections he alleges." Stripped of the poetry, Helprin's point was that loyalty to the Republican Party represented the highest form of honor.

No doubt this is what Helprin, and most partisans of both sides, truly believe. Furthermore, it is what they ought *to* believe. It is well and good to admire a candidate for his military heroism, his lack of extramarital affairs, or his neat attire. Valuing those traits more than the direction in which a candidate wants to take the country, though, would be an act of moral idiocy.

Writers and other pundits who cast their support for their party's standard-bearer in such personal terms are really propagandists. This is not to say they don't believe their own words. Probably they do. Given the human capacity for self-deception, it can't be that hard to convince yourself that the things that make a leader good and right just happen to be the very qualities you see in your party's candidate at any given time. Still, they are propagandists. The reasons they give for their political loyalties are not the real ones, whether they realize it or not. If the reasons they offer ceased to be true — if their party nominated a war-avoider, an adulterer, or a chronically tardy slob — they would find other reasons to tout his superior personal virtue.

WRITING THE BOOK ON CHARACTER

Character propaganda of this sort can be found in both parties. Yet because the Republican Party has grown so reliant on winning the character issue at the presidential level, it has the dominant share.

One window into the difference is to compare the sorts of books that have been written about the last two presidents. Naturally, conservatives write disparaging books about Bill Clinton and adulatory books about George W. Bush while liberals do the opposite. The difference is the strikingly personal tone the conservative books take.

In 1996, the former FBI agent Gary Aldrich published what he called an exposé of the Clinton administration. Between his odd and somewhat disturbing sociological observations — the Clinton staffers, in his recollection, consisted of "pear-shaped" men and "broad-shouldered women in pants" — Aldrich passed on all manner of tawdry gossip. For instance, he reported that Hillary Clinton ordered miniature crack pipes to be hung on the White House Christmas tree, that the president had regular hotel trysts with a Hollywood actress, and other explosive accusations.[43] Most of these claims were second- or thirdhand, and Aldrich later admitted the hotel trip story was "hypothetical."[44] Nonetheless, conservative news outlets like the *Washington Times* and the *New York Post* repeated these stories, and they eventually made their way into mainstream outlets. *Unlimited Access* became a number-one bestseller, with sales eventually topping three-quarters of a million copies.[45]

After this stunning commercial success, Aldrich's screed became a template. Regnery, his publisher, cranked out seven more jeremiads against Clinton over the next four years. Some of these titles ostensibly deal with Clinton's policies (i.e., William C. Triplett's *Year of the Rat: How Bill Clinton Compromised U.S. Security for Chinese Cash*), but their appeal rests on personal scandals, real or (mostly) imagined. Nicholas Confessore, writing in the *American Prospect,* summarized the Regnery line of anti-Clinton screeds thusly: "Each posits a nebulous conspiracy centered around the Clinton White House, a murky stew that typically blends one or more of the following ingredients: shady banking and land deals loosely grouped under the 'Whitewater' rubric; the murder — or induced suicide — of Vince Foster; Filegate and Travelgate; dalliances with prostitutes and nymphets; rampant drug use; treason via Chinese spies; and an Arkansas-based, Clinton-masterminded drug-smuggling outfit."[46] Entire subgenres of books about Hillary Clinton and Al Gore subsequently emerged, generally peddling similar themes of deep personal corruption, lesbian sex, criminal conduct, and other outrages.

The line of conservative Bush books is, not surprisingly, a mirror image of this. George W. Bush comes across as a paragon of virtue, all his political triumphs ultimately emanating from the strength of his character. In *The Right Man,* David Frum, a Bush speechwriter, spoke mostly of Bush's punctuality, his formal attire, and the way he "opened every cabinet meeting with a prayer and scorned the petty untruths of a politician." And his subordinates rightly adored him. Unlike the previous White House, where the staff remained seated when the president entered the room, "the Bush staff rose to their feet with a snap that would have impressed a Prussian field marshal."[47]

The succession of paeans to Bush all followed this formula. They praised his policies, but they inevitably portrayed them as an outgrowth of the great man's personal qualities. Where the Clinton books were characterized by revolting personal detail, the Bush books were characterized by inspiring personal detail. The genre could be called leadership pornography. To wit, John Podhoretz wrote in *Bush Country*, without any hint of irony, that "those closest to Bush say that his extraordinary physical condition has allowed him to maintain a dazzling degree of focus and concentration on the details of the war on terror and the war in Iraq."[48] It puts one in mind of the stories of Mao's swimming the Yellow River.

Ronald Kessler's *A Matter of Character* makes explicit the character-centric case for Bush. Kessler summarizes his thesis when he attributes Bush's success in the war on terror to his "vision, courage, patience, optimism, integrity, focus, discipline, determination, decisiveness, and devotion to America. It was, in the end, a matter of character."[49]

Liberals have produced their own shelf of books about Bush. They are, to be sure, deeply unflattering, and the tone is hardly measured. Unlike the books damning Clinton, though, they generally eschew wild or salacious tales of personal misconduct. (There are, of course, a few notable exceptions, such as James Hatfield's *Fortunate Son*.) These traditional polemics are dedicated to impugning the Bush administration's policies. The table of contents of *The Book on Bush*, by Eric Alterman and Mark Green, begins:

1. Introduction: *The Power of Audacity*
2. Drill and Cough: *W.'s Environmental and Energy Policies*
3. Déjà Vu-doo Economics: *The Real Faith-Based Policy*
4. When Laissez Isn't Fair: *How a Business President Handles Business Fraud*
5. Secrecy and Civil Liberties: *"Watch What [You] Say"*

And so on, marching earnestly through the forty-third president's domestic and foreign agenda.[50]

Even a book with an inflammatory title, *The Bush-Hater's Handbook*, by Jack Huberman, is organized alphabetically, and the beginning lists the issue-based offerings: "Abortion, Birth Control, and Reproductive Health; AIDS; Air Pollution; Ashcroft; Axis of Evil; Biological Weapons; Budget and Taxes," etc. It does allow itself a few quick diversions into the personal, but even these instances are limited to public actions or statements — Bush's mockery of a woman he executed, his crony capitalist business history, and the like — and they are utterly pallid compared with the hysterical charges leveled against the Clintons.[51] Other tomes with more sensational titles — i.e., *The Lies of George W. Bush,* by David Corn, follow the same format.[52] The title may sound similar in tone to the screeds against Clinton, but the difference is substantial. The lies in question concern Bush's public justifications for his program, not (as with the polemics against Clinton) his golf game or things he said to his wife. The lies are presented as an outgrowth of the misguided and failing policies rather than the policies springing from some deeper character flaw.

And the liberal books on Clinton are not even remotely equivalent to the conservative hagiography of Bush but are far more balanced and almost entirely devoid of personal veneration. The closest equivalent to Frum's puff job would be *All Too Human,* by George Stephanopoulos. Like Frum's, it is a White House memoir by a former aide turned sympathetic pundit published in the midst of the presidency it discusses. The title suggests its general tenor — it defends much of Clinton's work but derides his "stupid, selfish and self-destructive" affair, and even questions his general character.[53] Other sympathetic books about Clinton — *The Natural,* by Joe Klein, and *The President We Deserve,* by Martin Walker — have a similar balance. The closest thing to a pure apologia is Sidney Blumenthal's *The Clinton Wars,* and even Blumenthal, once a Clinton aide, devotes far more of his energies to assailing Clinton's enemies than to venerating his former boss.

IF THERE IS one book that epitomizes the conservative embrace of character, it is Peggy Noonan's biography of Reagan, *When Character Was King.*[54] Noonan published this book in 2001, which does not come as a surprise. She pays scant attention to Reagan's triumphs. The title captures its basic assumption — Reagan's success, in her dewy eyes, sprang from his character. Her book is written in the style of a fairy tale, not only in its tone, but also in its depth and moral complexity. Reagan is brave and loyal and decent and modest (and oh, by the way, he enacted a bunch of laws, too). It is one of those biographies that teach you very little about the subject and a great deal about the author. No book like this could have been published before the Clinton presidency. During the 1980s, the conservative analysis of Reagan was mainly ideological. Noonan's book is a reinterpretation of Reagan through the eyes of the post-Clinton GOP.

Indeed, Noonan personifies the character propagandists who have emerged on the right. A beautiful, blonde former speechwriter for Presidents Reagan and Bush, she uses her perch as a *Wall Street Journal* columnist to wax poetic on the moral virtues of leading Republicans and savage the character of Democrats. The closest Noonan has ever come to explaining her ideology came in a column written during the impeachment drama in 1998. Describing the moment that the Republican Speaker of the House Bob Livingston confessed his extramarital affair and resigned, she concluded that the episode showed "different styles, almost characterological differences between Democrats and Republicans these days. The Democrats in Congress now are like the young Chuck Colson, partisan, ruthless and tough. The Republicans seemed like the young William Cohen, thoughtful and stricken."[55] This was during the height of the GOP's impeachment fervor, no less!

Noonan, of course, fell deeply for Bush, whom she called "transparently a good person, a genuine fellow who isn't hidden or crafty or sneaky or mean, a person of appropriate modesty." He was also "respectful, moderate, commonsensical, courteous," not to mention "a modest man of faith." She wrote all this before September 11, 2001. Afterward, her view of Bush rose to even loftier heights. He had "a new weight, a new gravity, a new physical and moral comfort." Also "a sharp and intelligent instinct, an inner shrewdness," and he was "emotionally and intellectually mature."[56]

Noonan is the perfect case study in the inescapable bias of the characterological interpretation. In one column, she attacked Clinton for "unleashing the fierce energy of your hatred into the national bloodstream, and getting all your people out there on television every day to hate for you." In another, she sneered that Democrat Tom Daschle "did his hair up and got made up" to deliver a speech.[57] She seemed honestly to believe that Republicans would never take to the airwaves to launch vitriolic attacks or apply makeup before doing so.

In 2000, she said of the Clinton administration's efforts to suppress leaks: "The code of omerta ran strong and was obviously enforced." The next year she devoted the bulk of a column to praising Bush's staff for the very same thing. ("They are loyal to him, and they are loyal to each other.") When Al Gore's campaign criticized Bush in 2000, she painted it as a monstrous evil. ("Al Gore is surrounded by tough mean operatives whose sole political instinct is to rip out the other guy's guts and dance in the blood.")[58] But after Bush's campaign attacked John McCain during the 2000 South Carolina primary — disparaging his military record and implying that his adopted Bangladeshi daughter was a black love child, among other tough tactics — she took it in with equanimity. "You make the best case possible for yourself and what you stand for, and you paint your opponent in less attractive light," she wrote calmly. "That's what politics is."*[59]

This is the most brainless form of partisanship imaginable. To

---

* By Bush's second term, when his poll numbers sank and conservatives turned sharply against him, Noonan began to discern serious personality flaws in the forty-third president. Of course, this is simply another demonstration of how silly her style of analysis is: her view of politicians is rooted in politics, but she expresses it entirely in personal terms. Bush was a perfectly wonderful man until he became a burden to the conservative movement.

consistently side with one party over the other because you share its ideological goals is perfectly natural. To side with one party time and again because you think its standard-bearers are consistently nicer people is lunacy. But Republican presidents and would-be presidents are seen as having a stronger character than their Democratic counterparts in large part because this sort of thinking so dominates the right. There is no liberal equivalent of Peggy Noonan.

THE DEFINITION OF A FLIP-FLOP

The result of all this image-building is that the impressions the public forms about the character of presidential candidates don't bear much relation to reality. In 2004, for instance, most sentient Americans considered it almost self-evident that John Kerry habitually flip-flopped while Bush clung to his positions come hell or high water. Yet even a casual examination of the facts shows that this was not the case. The debate over comparative flip-flopping was insipid at the time, and since then it has grown no more edifying. But it's worth revisiting if only to show just how far the common impression can diverge from the truth.

Bush's campaign compiled a list of what it deemed thirty-seven flip-flops by Kerry.[60] Of these, a mere six could be counted as unquestionable instances of Kerry's reversing himself. Some of them clearly reflect an attempt to abandon a politically unpopular stance. Kerry opposed capital punishment for terrorists and favored higher gasoline prices, but he later reversed himself on both issues. In 1992, he criticized affirmative action as "limited and divisive" but did not entirely reject it — before later embracing it without qualification. Like almost every presidential hopeful, he went from con to pro on ethanol subsidies. In all these cases, there was no plausible explanation for Kerry's change of heart except political expediency.

On two other reversals, Kerry could at least credibly argue that he reversed positions due to changing circumstances. In 1993, he expressed doubt about how well the Federal Employees Health Benefits System worked. In 2004, he made it a model for his health care plan. He also opposed making companies count stock options as an expense before abandoning that position after the corporate scandals of 2002. In the first case, Kerry probably learned more about the issue at hand, having never had to draft a national health care plan previously. In the second, Enron made Kerry's anti-expensing position look substantively stupid at the same time it made it politically stupid. Whether Kerry was bowing to reason or to expediency is anybody's guess.

Republicans also counted as flip-flops cases in which Kerry emphasized different aspects of his position at different times. In 2000, he called for a reevaluation of the Cuban embargo. Asked in 2003 if he'd lift the embargo, he replied, "Not unilaterally, not now, no." A few months later, he explained that he favored some travel or cultural exchanges but not "opening up the embargo willy nilly." (There's nothing inconsistent about favoring a reevaluation but opposing "unilateral" or "willy nilly" elimination.) In 2006, Kerry appeared before an Arab-American group and criticized Israel's security fence for encroaching too far into Palestinian territory. A few months later, he defended it as a "legitimate act of self-defense." His position was internally consistent — he approved of the fence but not where it was being built — but he obviously went out of his way to give different impressions to different audiences.

The most well known instance of this subtle shading is Kerry's position on Iraq. But here as well, Kerry never altered his underlying stance. He favored a tightened inspections regime and recognized that only the threat of unilateral U.S. action embodied by a congressional authorization for war would spur the United Nations to act. He subsequently opposed the way Bush used that authority.

Bush now says that, by endorsing a use-of-force resolution, Kerry "voted for the war." At the time, though, Bush sold the resolution in exactly the way Kerry saw it. "If you want to keep the peace," Bush argued in 2002, "you've got to have the authorization to use force."[61]

The rest of the Bush campaign's list of supposed Kerry flip-flops was simply phony. He voted for the No Child Left Behind Act but castigated Bush for failing to deliver the promised funds. He voted to develop missile defenses but opposed deploying them immediately on the grounds that they didn't work yet. He voted for a bill to spend $87 billion on fighting and rebuilding in Iraq and to pay for it by repealing upper-bracket tax cuts, but he voted against a bill to spend the same money financed by borrowing. (Thus his famous explanation: "I actually voted for the $87 billion before I voted against it.") And so on. Republicans ridiculed Kerry for his "reversals," but, in these examples and others, there was a clear difference between what Kerry supported and what he opposed.

None of this should be interpreted as a brief for John Kerry or an attempt to paint him as a paragon of consistency. Kerry indeed had flip-flopped on more than one issue. But of course, flip-flopping is one of the things politicians do. The instructive thing is to compare Kerry on this score to his opponent. In 2004, the liberal Center for American Progress compiled a list of what it called thirty Bush flip-flops.[62] Of these, thirteen were indisputable reversals. For instance, when running for Congress in 1978, Bush favored abortion rights, then later he flipped. He opposed the McCain-Feingold Act but later signed it. He insisted on holding a final vote on going to war at the U.N. Security Council in early 2003 — "No matter what the whip count is, we're calling for the vote"[63] — but dropped plans to do so. Bush opposed the creation of a Department of Homeland Security before embracing the idea. He did the same on creating an outside commission to investigate WMD intelligence failures. In turn, he opposed creating the 9/11 Commission, opposed giving it a time extension to finish its work, opposed allowing Condoleezza Rice to testify, and insisted on limiting his testimony to one hour before eventually abandoning each impediment.

One can debate either side of the question of whether Bush or Kerry was more of a flip-flopper. It would not be wildly unreasonable to conclude that Kerry flip-flopped a bit more than Bush. The unreasonable thing is the way flip-flopping came to define the very essence of Kerry's nature — Kerry not merely as a politician who, like most politicians, flip-flops from time to time, but Kerry as "a flip-flopper."

I do not want to take this analysis too far. I am arguing that what we think of as the character of our public figures is *in large part* the product of conscious manipulation. I am not arguing that it is entirely so. If the Democrats in 2008 were to nominate for president a charming, self-made man who rose from poverty to become a war hero and devoted family man while Republicans nominated a cocaine-snorting white-collar criminal, I suspect the public would see the Democrat as the more moral of the two. But the playing field is noticeably tilted. At this writing, I have no idea who will appear on the top of the parties' tickets in 2008. But even without knowing this, I can predict that the Republican candidate will be seen as having the stronger character.

7

THE ABUSE OF POWER

Shortly before the beginning of his second presidential term, President Bush was asked whether his administration ought to be held accountable for some of the mistakes it had made in the course of the Iraq war. He replied, almost contemptuously, "We had an accountability moment, and that's called the 2004 elections."[1]

This phrase, "accountability moment," was at once remarkable and deeply revealing. It was remarkable because accountability in the American political system is not supposed to be a momentary thing. To be sure, the ballot box represents the premier instrument of our elected leaders' accountability, but there is supposed to be some measure of accountability between those biennial November intervals. We do not simply send a president off to the Oval Office and ask him to report back four years later. Our officials are supposed to explain their goals and policies to their countrymen in regular intervals, subject themselves to at least some measure of public scrutiny, and conduct their affairs with reasonable transparency. And Bush's comment was revealing because a persistent (and mostly successful) campaign to limit accountability — to make it a fleeting event that takes place only on Election Day — has become the most prominent feature of the Republican Party's governing style.

The previous chapters showed how the conservative movement has figured out how to win elections despite the unpopularity of its economic agenda. But elections, of course, are not the end of the story. The Republican Party has lost many an election over the last three decades, most recently, of course, in November 2006, yet it has managed to drive the terms of public debate steadily rightward. Part of the trick, clearly, lies in what happens between elections. Here is where the economic right's mastery of the political process truly shines through. Enacting an ambitious agenda is supposed to be tricky, and all the more so if that agenda lacks any popular support. Many an ambitious politician has come to power with hopes of sweeping change, only to see his program dashed on the shoals of Washington. The barriers to change are everywhere in Washington — some of them formal rules in the Constitution, others informal social customs that have developed over the decades.

One of the differences between the two parties is that these barriers have held back the Democrats, but they have not held back the GOP. Republicans have been far more aggressive about using the prerogatives of office to cement themselves into power. Their power to smother accountability may not have been unlimited, as the 2006 elections show, but it was considerable. The Republicans' success at defeating the democratic process explains why it has been able to enact its agenda despite a lack of popular support and, more important, even when Democrats are in power, why they will have such an uphill fight reversing it. Just how the GOP managed this feat is a remarkable story.

THE INFORMATION VOID

Democracy, as everybody knows, means more than simply free and fair elections. It means that the public has ample opportunity to hold its leaders accountable. Don't take my word on this, take the president's. In a 2004 interview with Al Arabiya television, Bush explained that in a democracy, "leaders are willing to discuss [problems] with the media. And we act in a way where, you know, our Congress asks pointed questions to the leadership. In other words, people want to know the truth. That stands in contrast to dictatorships."[2]

As a working definition of democracy, this one was oddly lacking in self-awareness.* The Bush administration has made hostility toward the media a point of pride. During his first term, Bush held fewer solo press conferences than any president since the advent of television.[3] As the formal procedures of accountability dwindled, the informal channels by which information trickled out of the White House dried up as well. "In other Administrations, the chief of staff and key deputies — people like [Michael] Deaver and James A. Baker III, during the Reagan-Bush years, and John Podesta and Leon Panetta, under Clinton — have usually been open with reporters; they've even courted the press," reported the *New Yorker*'s Ken Auletta. "In the current White House, [Andy] Card and [Karl] Rove usually don't return calls, and staffers boast of not answering reporters' questions."[4] Reporters are left with only the official statements of the White House spokesmen.

IN CONTRAST WITH Bush's apparent belief that one of the features of a democracy is a "Congress [that] asks pointed questions to

---

* It also revealed a bit too much about how the government has worked under Bush's presidency. The Constitution makes the legislative and executive branches equal. Bush views Congress as a subordinate branch, as suggested by his defining "leadership" as something Congress is not part of.

the leadership," his administration has persistently refused to field questions it finds politically awkward. In 2004, Attorney General John Ashcroft refused to release the administration's memos on the use of torture — even to offer a legal basis for his refusal. In 2002, the administration denied requests to have the Homeland Security czar, Tom Ridge, testify on Capitol Hill. That same year, Medicare's director, Thomas Scully, refused to appear at a hearing where witnesses with different points of view were going to testify. (Scully offered to appear on his own rather than "mix it up with people who have a gripe about a particular regulation," as if appearing with people who disagree with your actions were inimical to the purpose of a congressional hearing.)[5]

The most famous instance of Bush's belief that he need not answer for his actions was his persistent hostility toward the bipartisan September 11 commission. First, Bush fervently opposed creating the commission. When that failed, he threw up impediments to its work. He sought (unsuccessfully) to prevent the national security adviser, Condoleezza Rice, from testifying. Bush himself initially refused to testify and blocked the commission's access to important documents. Later, after agreeing under pressure to testify, he refused to do so under oath.* He tried to limit his testimony to one hour. He tried to block commissioners other than the co-chairmen from attending his testimony. He demanded that Cheney appear alongside him. (Why did Bush insist on having Cheney at his side? When asked, Bush offered only this nonanswer: "Because it's a good chance for both of us to answer questions that the 9/11 Commission is looking forward to asking us. And I'm looking forward

---

* In the end, Bush had to capitulate on some of his more extreme demands. But this reflected the highly unusual circumstances of the case. The 9/11 attacks captivated public attention unlike any other event in recent history. And the families of the victims, who demanded that Bush testify, were unusually sympathetic and unusually able to command media attention. In almost every other instance of the administration's rebuffing attempts to hold it accountable, it has won unconditionally.

to answering them.") He allowed only a single staffer to take notes. And he barred the presence of a transcriber.[6]

In keeping with its aversion to accountability, the administration has swept vast realms of data out of the public domain. In 2004, the government classified more than fifteen million secrets, a nearly fivefold increase from a decade earlier. "We have never had this kind of control over information," observed Alan Lichtman of American University. "It means policy is being made by a small clique without much public scrutiny."[7]

One might think that the increased security demands following the September 11 attacks account for this massive surge in secrecy, but a huge proportion of it is unrelated to security. In 2003, *U.S. News & World Report* investigated the administration's secrecy. "For the past three years, the Bush administration has quietly but efficiently dropped a shroud of secrecy across many critical operations of the federal government — cloaking its own affairs from scrutiny and removing from the public domain important information on health, safety, and environmental matters," the magazine found. "The result has been a reversal of a decades-long trend of openness in government."[8]

Much of the information would only be missed by hard-core wonks. To take one example, the administration's 2004 budget cut discretionary grants to the states. After statehouses complained, the administration announced it no longer publish *Budget Information for States,* which documents how much states receive from various federal programs. (The administration said it wanted to save on printing costs.) "There's no one place in the public domain for this information anymore," lamented Alysoun McLaughlin of the National Conference of State Legislatures.[9]

It is not only such prosaic data that the administration has withheld. Some of its most prominent initiatives have depended on suppressing information that undermined Bush's argument. In the leadup to the Iraq war, administration officials repeatedly insisted that Iraqi reconstruction would pay for itself with oil revenues. (Deputy Defense Secretary Paul Wolfowitz, for instance, cheerfully asserted that Iraq, through its oil, would "finance its own reconstruction, and relatively soon.")[10] Yet before the war, a secret Pentagon task force had found that Iraq's oil industry was badly damaged and would produce far less oil than the administration was claiming.[11]

Likewise, the administration managed to squeak its Medicare drug benefit through Congress by promising the plan would cost no more than $400 billion over ten years. In fact, the administration's own estimate had found that the actual cost would exceed that by more than $100 billion. Members of Congress asked Richard Foster, the chief actuary of the Department of Health and Human Services and a civil servant for more than three decades, for Bush's own cost estimates. Foster turned to Thomas Scully, the Bush administration's Medicare apparatchik, to see if he could release the information. The questions from Congress, wrote Foster, "strike me as straightforward requests for technical information." Scully's assistant wrote back that he was forbidden to release this information, warning that he must "send [the data] to Tom Scully only. NO ONE ELSE . . . the consequences for insubordination are extremely severe."[12]

The most charitable interpretation of this wanton secrecy is that the Bush administration is fixated on the theory of "executive privilege" — the belief that the Oval Office needs to assert its legal prerogatives — and that the president has carried this fixation to zealous extremes. This is not, obviously, a very flattering interpretation — information, after all, is the lifeblood of democracy. Yet even the charitable explanation is too, well, charitable. In fact, the Bush administration has been notoriously promiscuous about releasing official secrets when doing so suits its own political ends. In 2002, Bush declassified portions of a transcript of a conversation in which

Israel's prime minister, Ehud Barak, asked Bill Clinton to pardon the fugitive tax-evader Marc Rich. (It was the first time in American history that a president's discussion with a foreign head of state was declassified.) Clinton asked that the rest of the conversation be declassified as well, insisting that the context would make him look better. Bush refused.[13] Bush has also declassified numerous documents that either seem to make his administration appear vigilant against terrorism or his predecessor appear lax. "Bush is the first president since Richard Nixon to try to brandish declassification as a political weapon," concluded John Prados, an analyst with the National Security Archive.[14] There is no real executive privilege principle at work here. The only principle is the Bush administration's consistent desire to expand its control over what information makes it into the public discourse.

SEPARATE POWERS, JOINED

Anybody who has taken a high school civics course knows that our political system has a ready cure for these sorts of abuses: checks and balances. If the executive branch oversteps its bounds, as the Founding Fathers wisely decided, the legislative branch will step in to correct it.

Yet, while Republicans controlled both ends of Pennsylvania Avenue, nothing of the sort happened. Instead, Congress made itself a willing appendage of the White House. With vanishingly few exceptions, it simply made Bush's agenda its own. This willful subordination rendered Congress unable and unwilling to correct the errors or excesses of the executive branch. In most cases, the daily workings of this hand-in-glove relationship went unnoticed because it has happened behind closed doors and neither party to the arrangement has had any incentive to divulge it publicly. But some of the outwardly visible aspects give us a sense of how it has worked.

One episode came to light in highly unusual circumstances, and it suggests just how much congressional Republicans subordinated their own instincts to partisan loyalty. In the days after the 9/11 attacks, an anomalous and short-lived sense of bipartisanship broke out on Capitol Hill. Shut out of their offices by anthrax attacks, the ranking members of the House Appropriations Committee, Democrat David Obey and Republican Bill Young, decided to investigate the nation's readiness to repel another terrorist attack. They met with representatives from every major security agency — FBI, CIA, National Security Agency, Centers for Disease Control and Prevention, and so on — and what they found frightened them. Even though Congress had speedily approved $20 billion in homeland security spending immediately after the attacks, prime terrorist targets around the country remained appallingly vulnerable. The two compiled a list of the most urgent needs and agreed that only items approved by both parties would make their list. "We stripped the list down to its bare essentials," Obey recalled. "When that was done, I asked my staff to cut the remaining list in half to make sure there was absolutely no 'soft stuff.'" The list included things like computer upgrades for the FBI, improved security for ports and nuclear facilities, new customs agents, and other top homeland security priorities. The cost ran to around $10 billion.

On November 6, 2001, Obey and Young, along with their Senate counterparts, Robert Byrd and Ted Stevens, secured a meeting with Bush in the White House. The president was immediately and unalterably reluctant to spend any more money than he had already appropriated. Perhaps this reflected his characteristic refusal to revisit his own decisions or his fear that spending even more money would pressure him to scale back his cherished tax cuts. So Bush received his visitors icily. "I understand some of you may want to spend more money on homeland security than we have requested," he told them, according to members of both parties who attended. "My good friend [budget director] Mitch Daniels here assures me that our [$20 billion funding] request is adequate. . . . I want to make it clear that if Congress appropriates one dollar more than we have requested, I will veto the bill."

Bush told the delegation he would permit each of them to make one comment before the meeting ended. In his allotted comment, Obey explained that the funding requests had come from the president's own agency appointees and that he and Young would remove any particular items to which Bush objected. He also described specific federal installations that he had learned were vulnerable and asked if the president had been informed of them. Bush gave no sign that he had been briefed and refused to budge from his stance.

Rebuffed, Obey sought a vote on the House floor. It seemed like a promising place, as Republicans had professed the need to spend more on homeland defense. The administration had to dispatch Dick Cheney to appeal to the Republican loyalties of the House majority. Soon enough, whatever glimmerings of bipartisanship or independence faded away, and Republicans abandoned Obey. The House voted not to permit even a debate on any of the items Obey had proposed. As the *New York Times* reported, "No Republicans challenged any items Mr. Obey said were needed. But Representative Ray LaHood of Illinois said, 'Nobody knows more about this than the commander-in-chief.'" Even Young, Obey's erstwhile partner, was now toeing the line. In a floor speech, he urged his fellow partisans, "Stay in lockstep, stay behind the president."[15]

Perhaps even worse than Congress's abandonment of any corrective role in writing legislation was its total abdication of its responsibility to monitor the presidency. At the heart of our system of checks and balances is oversight, which refers to the congressional practice of holding hearings to investigate scandals and bureaucratic failures or simply make sure the executive branch is doing its job. When Democrats controlled Congress, they regularly conducted investigations that embarrassed Democratic presidents. For instance, Democrats conducted an investigation into environmental malfeasance that chastised Clinton's Justice Department. "We believed we had something to do, to [assure] that public money was being spent appropriately, that laws were being enforced, and we did," recalled John Dingell.[16]

Naturally, oversight continued when Republicans took control of Capitol Hill during the Clinton administration. From 1995 to 1998, Congress conducted thirty-seven investigations into various alleged Clinton scandals.[17] But once George W. Bush took up residence in the White House, the practice ground to a halt. One measure shows the stark difference. In 1993–94, under a unified Democratic government, the House Government Reform Committee held 135 oversight or investigative hearings. In 2004–2005, under a unified Republican government, Congress held just 37.[18]

In 2004, a hurricane struck Florida, and by all accounts the Federal Emergency Management Agency made a hash of the response. The sites of the worst damage received little or no relief, yet counties far from the hurricane's path were lavished with tens of millions of dollars in federal aid. Florida lawmakers from both parties asked the relevant committees in Congress to investigate, to no avail.[19] (The consequences of this carnival of incompetence, of course, came into sharp and tragic focus the next year, when Hurricane Katrina hit.) Such negligence was typical. "This Congress doesn't see itself as an independent branch that might include criticizing an incumbent administration," observed the congressional scholar Norman Ornstein of the American Enterprise Institute in 2005. "Meaningful oversight, because it might imply criticism, has been pushed off the table altogether."[20] Even many Republicans agreed with this sentiment. "Our party controls the levers of government," confessed Ray LaHood of Illinois. "We're not about to go out and look beneath a bunch of rocks to try to cause heartburn."[21]

AN UNPRECEDENTED THREAT

The proximate failure was that of the Republicans in Congress, and that has receded as the opposition party has taken over the majority. But the larger failure is that of the political structure itself. The system of separation of powers is based on the idea that the branches will naturally vie for power against one another. The Founding Fathers did not envision political parties as a force that could potentially unify the branches under a single command. Thus the separation of powers works best under a divided government, and it may not work at all under a unified government. In a 2006 paper, the legal scholars Daryl Levinson of Harvard and Richard Pildes of New York University argue that this amounts to a systemic failure. "Under unified governments," they wrote, "smaller partisan majorities will be able to effect major policy changes without the full range of checks and balances that are supposed to divide and diffuse power in the Madisonian system."[22]

But wait, you may say. We have had this system of government for more than two centuries. We had unified governments many times. Why did a crisis of untrammeled power arise only in 2001?

The answer is that never before did ruling parties in this country have such ideological unity. For most of the twentieth century, ideology corresponded only loosely to partisan affiliation. The Republican Party had a sizable coterie of progressives, descended from the radical abolitionists of the nineteenth century, to go with moderates and hard-core conservatives. Democrats had even less ideological coherence. The South was monolithically Democratic, and among that contingent numbered some of the most reactionary conservatives in Congress. (When conservative Democrats like Jesse Helms and Strom Thurmond switched parties, they immediately found themselves on the GOP's right wing.)

So, even when a party managed to control the White House and both chambers of Congress, the sort of unified power grabs executed by Bush proved impossible. The most striking example is Franklin Delano Roosevelt's plan to add more seats to the Supreme Court, thereby packing it with friendly justices. Roosevelt had ample justification to take radical steps — the Court, on spurious grounds, had struck down a huge share of the New Deal — but his court-packing scheme represented a dangerous precedent for future presidential power grabs. Conservative Southern Democrats — who saw the conservative Court as a bulwark of the states' rights they cherished — rebelled and forced him to back down.

In addition to ideologically fractious parties, there was no centralized control. Since 1910, when rank-and-file members of Congress rebelled against the iron rule of the House Speaker Joe Cannon,* enormous power rested in individual committees. The chairmen of those committees safeguarded their prerogatives, valuing them far more than the success of their party. And party leaders often showed little desire to challenge them. House Speaker Sam Rayburn, asked about unifying his party around a cohesive agenda, replied contemptuously that "a wild man from the North will get up and make a wild speech. Then someone from another section will answer him with a wilder speech. First thing you know, you've got the Democratic Party so divided that you can't pass anything."[23]

These dynamics — the fractious parties, the decentralized control — produced in Washington a distinct culture. Generations of

---

* And since Cannon frequently defied fellow Republican presidents, his iron-fisted rule made it hard for a single party to dominate.

congressmen occupied the Capitol and imbibed the ethos of the town until the culture itself, more than any formal rules, came to shape their thinking. A perfect example of the type is Dan Rostenkowski, who served from his election in 1958 until his fall from grace in 1994. The jowly, bearish Chicagoan is remembered, not altogether unfairly, as a crook more than anything else.

Indeed, he did use his office to enrich himself and employ his cronies. But what animated him most was governing, and governing meant passing legislation. Like many Democrats of his era, he was the product of a political machine, and as such his ideological impulses were weak. As the longtime chairman of the Ways and Means Committee, he was at home raising or lowering the taxes. The important thing for him was that he ran the process. In 1981, when Ronald Reagan proposed large tax cuts, Rostenkowski's highest priority was to ensure that they went through his committee. "I wanted to pass legislation," he later told his biographer, Richard E. Cohen. "The conservative Republicans and liberal Democrats wanted it all their own way . . . But, as Lyndon Johnson said, you have to open the door to get it ajar." Rostenkowski maintained throughout his career a thoroughly bipartisan outlook. He voted for George Bush in 1988, and in 1996 (after he had left Congress), he told friends he'd feel comfortable with Bob Dole as president. As chairman, his goal was to pass legislation that commanded a majority in both parties.[24]

During these years, the notion that Congress would turn itself into a mere cog in the president's political machine was simply unimaginable. Only in rare circumstances — Roosevelt during the Great Depression, Johnson after the Kennedy assassination, each with massive majorities behind him — could a president coax the system into enacting a bold program of change. And even in both those cases, the majority's momentum petered out within a few years. Chronic gridlock was widely seen as endemic to the American system. In 1980, Lloyd Cutler, a powerful adviser to President Carter, wrote a widely discussed essay in *Foreign Affairs* bemoaning

> the structural inability of our government to propose, legislate and administer a balanced program for governing. In parliamentary terms, one might say that under the U.S. Constitution it is not now feasible to "form a Government." The separation of powers between the legislative and executive branches, whatever its merits in 1793, has become a structure that almost guarantees stalemate today.

Carter, of course, enjoyed majorities far larger than any President Bush has ever commanded. But those majorities felt free to buck him. "No member of that majority has the constitutional duty or the practical political need to vote for each element of the president's program . . . ," Cutler lamented. "In the famous phrase of Joe Jacobs, the fight manager, 'it's every man for theirself.'"

This was the world in which Bill Clinton found himself during the first two years of his presidency, when he, like Carter, had substantial Democratic majorities in both houses of Congress. Yet the congressional barons felt no compunction about giving the back of the hand to the first Democratic president in a dozen years. In 1993, the Senate defeated Clinton's economic stimulus bill, which had been a major part of his campaign platform.* In 1994, the House and Senate both held hearings into Whitewater, an act of partisan disloyalty that would be inconceivable in the Bush era. (Just try to imagine Republicans in Congress holding hearings into allegations of insider trading during George Bush's career as an oilman.)

The single event that, more than any other, epitomized Congress's independence was Clinton's failed bid to reform the health care system. The plan died for many reasons. But for anyone who has watched the GOP Congress move in lockstep with President

---

* The stimulus bill was, in my opinion, a bad idea, given that the economy was already growing out of a recession. Still, the point is not that Clinton's ideas were all praiseworthy but that he lacked control of Congress.

Bush, it is stunning to recall the degree to which Clinton failed simply because his fellow Democrats in Congress refused to cooperate. The simplest way to steer a plan through Congress would have been to create a special omnibus committee dedicated to passing a bill. But Democrats did not want to surrender their prerogatives. "By the early 1990s, Congress had an unusually large number of committees (and subcommittees) claiming health jurisdiction," wrote the Harvard health scholar Theda Skocpol. "Each and every one of those expected to have a 'piece of the action.'"[25] So instead of Clinton's creating one committee to shepherd his prized legislation, he had to pass different bills through seven separate committees — five in the House and two in the Senate — each of which offered a distinct opportunity for opponents to stop the bill.[26] Moreover, it subjugated reform to the idiosyncratic whims of each committee chairman.

The most idiosyncratic of them was Daniel Patrick Moynihan, the white-haired, bow-tied chairman of the Senate Finance Committee. Very early in Clinton's tenure, Moynihan privately admitted that he didn't understand health care. For most senators, this would have been a reason to defer to a fellow partisan president who had made the issue a priority. But Moynihan was not the sort to defer on any issue, no matter how little he understood it, and he insisted on putting himself at the center of the issue. He insisted from the beginning that the only way to pass reform was if he cosponsored a bill with Bob Dole, the Senate minority leader.[27] This tactic proved disastrous. After some conciliatory statements early on, Dole moved steadily away from health care reform, in time even repudiating a moderate bill that he had cosponsored.

Meanwhile, Moynihan continuously undermined Clinton. In one appearance on *Meet the Press*, he called the administration's cost projections for Clinton's plan "fantasy" and insisted, "We don't have a health care crisis in America." Each of these statements, coming from a fellow Democrat, hemorrhaged support for the plan. All the Clinton administration could do was to woo the prickly senator in the hope of preventing still more fratricidal outbursts. As the *New York Times* noted, "White House officials find they can do little but simmer in private, fearing that if they strike, Mr. Moynihan will only retaliate."[28] The congressional mentality of the era was aptly expressed by one of Moynihan's staffers, who declared, "Nobody here [in Congress] surrenders ever. You don't fucking win. And you do not have an election against us where there's a vote cast where we have to leave. We are here forever, and we don't fucking surrender."[29]

Perhaps the most incredible thing about the health care debacle is that the Democrats could have avoided the filibuster that ultimately killed the reform if not for the stubborn insistence of one senator — a liberal Democrat, at that. Passage would have been all but guaranteed if the Senate had included health care as part of a "reconciliation bill." This is a Senate term for an annual piece of legislation dealing with the budget. A reconciliation bill, unlike any other, cannot be filibustered and therefore can pass with a simple 51-vote majority. Given that the Democrats controlled 57 Senate seats, the numbers would have allowed for easy passage even with a half-dozen defections.

Yet the Democrats did not do this because West Virginia's Robert Byrd adamantly refused. Byrd was an old-fashioned New Deal Democrat who supported reform but cared more about the traditions of the Senate than anything else. He was given to interminable speeches quoting Cicero and other orators of antiquity, and his sense of his importance may have exceeded even Moynihan's. Byrd objected on the grounds that reconciliation bills could be subjected to a twenty-hour debate limit, and he felt the issue was too important to be so circumscribed.[30] He would not budge in the face of pleas from Clinton and his fellow senators, and his ability to tie the Senate in knots if so inclined deterred the Clinton administration from crossing him. In the end, Dole spearheaded a filibuster that killed the potential reform.

THE NEW PARTY GOVERNMENT

The Clinton health fiasco epitomized everything political scientists believed was wrong with Washington. The system did not work. Government could not take action to solve pressing national problems. Under divided control, neither side could enact its program, and even under unified government the president could not bend Congress to his will. Further, the voters did not know who to hold responsible for this failure because responsibility was so diffuse.

Academics and good-government activists had long advocated a solution: make the parties more responsible. If the parties arranged themselves along ideological lines, and the leadership in Congress had some means of forcing its members to toe the line, then parties could carry out their promises and voters could decide whether they liked the results.

But, as it turned out, the reformers had misdiagnosed the problem. The chronic stalemate the system produced did not result inevitably from the institutions put into place by the Constitution. It was a product of the people who filled those institutions. The ethos of a Congress more loyal to its own power and the institution it served than to its parties grew out of the peculiar history of American politics, with its heterogeneous parties. All it took to transform the culture was for a united party, one not encrusted by chairmen steeped in the culture of self-aggrandizement, to take control

That, of course, is what happened after the Republicans swept to power after the 1994 elections. In many ways, the GOP takeover was a model of the responsible party government that reformers had urged. The Republicans ran on a unified platform, the Contract with America. To keep the committee chairmen from amassing too much power, the GOP leadership eliminated the seniority system — which allocated chairmanships based on tenure — and replaced it with one in which they chose the chairmen on the basis of party loyalty. They further limited the chairmen to six years, so that they could not become ensconced like the old Democratic barons. In addition, they made it clear that the leadership, not the committees, would set policy. (Bill Archer, the Republican who took over for Rostenkowski, noted that decisions were being made at a "higher pay grade.")[31] Newt Gingrich later explained the strategy. "Prior to us power centered in the chairmen and you had a relatively permissive leadership on the Democratic side that could only maneuver to the degree the chairmen would tolerate," he recalled. "We had exactly the opposite model: a very strong leadership that operated as a single team."[32] The result was a Congress governed by a party discipline not seen since the first decade of the twentieth century, and over a period of years, Republicans won a seemingly unbroken string of votes in the House, with only marginally less success in the Senate.

The fruits of this discipline were on display late in the morning of November 22, 2003, when the House took up President Bush's Medicare prescription drug benefit. Although its concept — offering drug coverage to Medicare recipients — was wildly popular, the bill had no natural constituency. Conservatives reviled it as the largest new federal entitlement since the Great Society and an affront to their small-government principles; liberals recoiled from the hundreds of billions of dollars in subsidies it lavished on GOP-friendly industries. The vote was always expected to be close, and the House leadership spent the night wheedling and cajoling members for votes. At 3:00 A.M., believing they had finally corralled a majority, the Republicans' acting speaker, Richard "Doc" Hastings, announced that it was time for members to cast their votes. After fifteen minutes, the time customarily allotted for floor votes by House rules, the leadership was shocked to discover that they had lost, 218–216.

Rather than accept defeat, the leadership decided to hold the vote open. This maneuver, it should be said, was not totally unprecedented. In 1987, the Democrats found themselves one vote short when a member named Marty Russo objected to a small measure, cast what he thought was a symbolic no vote, and immediately left for the airport. Unable to reach Russo in the era before cell phones, the House Speaker, Jim Wright, kept the vote open for some twenty minutes while an aide coaxed a member to change his vote to yes. This was considered a massive scandal, cited for years afterward as evidence of the Democrats' autocratic style. "It was, in my opinion, the most arrogant, heavy-handed abuse of power I've ever seen in the 10 years that I've been here," complained Dick Cheney, then a representative from Wyoming. "You have a Speaker who is . . . a heavy-handed son of a bitch and he doesn't know any other way to operate, and he will do anything he can to win at any price, including ignoring the rules, bending rules, writing rules, denying the House the opportunity to work its will."[33]

This was the one and only time the Democratic leadership had extended a vote, and when the Republicans took control of Congress, the new House Speaker, Newt Gingrich, promised not to repeat this abuse. Over time, though, the Republican leadership found it increasingly necessary to extend voting deadlines to wring out bare majorities. During the first three years of Bush's presidency, they resorted to this tactic some dozen times, going for as long as an hour past the voting deadline.[34] The Medicare vote, though, exceeded anything they had ever attempted before. The vote stayed open for nearly three hours, while the GOP leadership frantically cajoled its rank-and-file members, before they finally made it over the top and closed the vote at close to six o'clock in the morning. The congressional scholar Norman Ornstein called this episode "the ugliest and most outrageous breach of standards in the modern history of the House."

Exactly what promises the leaders made during those frantic hours will probably never be known. Nick Smith, a retiring Republican congressman from Michigan, later complained that "bribes and special deals were offered to convince members to vote yes." The columnist Robert Novak reported that "Smith was told business interests would give his son [Brad, who was running to fill his father's seat] $100,000 in return for his father's vote," and that after Smith voted no, "Duke Cunningham and other Republicans taunted him that his son was dead meat."* Smith told Gil Gutknecht, another Republican House member, that it was "people from leadership" who had promised the money. Smith, who refused to support the bill, seems to have thought that he was merely complaining about heavy-handed tactics. When *Slate*'s Timothy Noah wrote that what Smith described met the legal definition of bribery, Smith clumsily and unconvincingly retracted his story.[35] Ultimately, the Justice Department did not investigate the incident despite clear evidence of bribery, and the House Ethics Department issued only a toothless report. (This is one of the consequences of having all the investigative apparatuses in the hands of the party in power.) Senate Democrats declined to filibuster the bill — the Minority Leader, Tom Daschle, explained that his caucus remained divided on the tactic — and Bush signed it into law on December 8, 2003.

The system that resulted in the Medicare bill would have been unrecognizable to the would-be health care reformers of a decade earlier. The Republicans won on Medicare, and the Democrats lost on health care reform, for many reasons. Chief among them was that Clinton's plan imposed large costs on politically powerful busi-

---

* Brad Smith did lose his primary campaign, and Cunningham was eventually convicted of taking a bribe from a defense contractor, which certainly helps explain his contempt for Smith's refusal to accept a payoff.

nesses and Bush's plan showered business with largesse. But the decisive factor in each case proved to be the GOP's willingness to run roughshod over procedural niceties. Key Democrats had been paralyzed by an exquisite sensitivity to the traditional norms of Congress — its independent fiefdoms, cumbersome rules, and deference to the custom of cooperating with the minority party. Republicans understood that if they controlled the majority, however narrowly, and were sufficiently determined to get their way, almost nothing could stop them. All they needed to cut through the paralyzing thicket of impediments was to summon the requisite will. Once that happened, the checks and balances of the system that had once appeared so imposing were now frighteningly weak.

POLITICS IN THE DEAD OF NIGHT

Here is where the good-government reformers had miscalculated. They imagined that a world of ideologically cohesive parties would throw open the political issues of the day to public inspection. "Proponents of reform assumed that voters, armed with adequate information, would punish those who abused the laws," wrote Julian Zelizer in his history of congressional reform. "The producers of knowledge hoped to fulfill the Progressive Era vision of an 'informed citizen' who would make educated choices about politics without having to depend on parties or experts."[36] What they failed to understand was that those unified partisan majorities could just as easily use their power to conceal an unpopular agenda from the public.

If you look at how contemporary Republicans governed differently from their predecessors (in both parties), the unifying theme is withholding information and obscuring choices from the public. There are two tools they used to great effect. The first was to severely restrict the terms of debate in the House of Representatives.

Unlike the Senate, where minorities can wreak havoc, the House has always allowed the majority party to rule relatively unfettered. The primary locus of the majority's control is an obscure body called the Rules Committee, which sets the terms for debate in the House. Typically, the committee would hold that the House could debate a bill for only an hour and forbid any amendments or alternatives. The practical effect was to spare House members from having to vote against popular legislation. So, to take just a few examples, the Republican Rules Committee forbade the Democrats from proposing votes on more generous unemployment benefits, more funding for homeland security, and a higher minimum wage. (The public supports the latter measure, according to a 2005 Gallup Poll, by a seventy-point margin.)[37] The political scientist Robert Van Houweling has noted that closed rules in the House skyrocketed under GOP leadership.

The Rules Committee is how the majority party sets the terms of debate. For instance, if you ask most Americans if they favor tax cuts without suggesting an alternate use of the money, they say yes. If, however, you give them choices that go beyond a simple yes or no, everything changes. Democrats have favored a smaller tax cut with more money devoted to programs like education or a tax cut that gives a greater share of its benefits to lower- and middle-income taxpayers. Those alternatives, as noted earlier, all command strong majorities. But forbidding anything but a straight up-or-down vote on the Republican tax cut allowed the GOP to frame the debate on its own terms, shoving more popular alternatives off the agenda.

The same dynamic holds true on issue after issue. No doubt the public would have preferred a prescription drug benefit that gives more money to Medicare recipients and less to the pharmaceutical industry, but no such choice was permitted on the House floor. Thus the Republicans were able to stand behind an unpopular agenda without fear of exposure before the voters.

Given the reality of a public that pays scant attention to politics and whose understanding of what Washington does is almost always confined to broad brushstrokes (i.e., "tax cut," "prescription drug bill," etc.), the ability to control the terms of debate confers on the majority almost limitless power. This power has always been formally available to the House majority. Yet only under Republican control has it been used so extensively.

REWRITING THE RULE BOOK

In theory, this should not affect the Senate, where the majority can't easily prohibit votes on legislation or amendments preferred by the minority. In fact, Senate Democrats frequently used their strength to wring concessions from the majority. In response, however, the Republicans came up with another device to protect themselves: the stacked Conference Committee. A Conference Committee is a basic feature of the system. Allow me to give the quick, high school civics text explanation. When the House and the Senate both pass legislation on the same issue and the legislation differs, the two chambers form a Conference Committee to negotiate. The unified bill that emerges from the committee then goes back to the House and Senate for an up or down vote. (End of civics lesson.)

Traditionally, the Conference Committee includes members of both parties, in roughly equal numbers, and seeks to create some middle ground between the two versions. Yet, like the fifteen-minute voting window in the House, it is a matter of custom rather than formal rule. The Republicans in Congress systematically excluded Democrats from Conference Committees, or perhaps allowed one or two of the most pliant Democrats to attend. They would then produce a bill that wiped out whatever concessions the Democrats had won and send it to the Senate, where it could not be amended. In this way they have turned the Senate into a chamber very much like the House: a place where the leadership can control the terms of debate and exclude any moderate alterations.

The typical dynamic during the Bush era has been for the House to pass a measure entirely to the administration's liking, then the Senate passes a measure somewhat less so, followed by a Conference Committee version similar to the House version. This ritual took on almost comical tones at times. In the spring of 2003, Bush proposed another round of tax cuts, worth some $726 billion over a decade. GOP moderates in the Senate, who had signed on to Bush's 2001 tax cuts only after extended professions of reluctance, insisted they would not acquiesce. Their leader, as it were, was George Voinovich of Ohio, a longtime deficit hawk. "We're on the edge of a fiscal crisis in this country if we keep going the way we are, particularly with this war that's hanging over us today," he warned. Indeed, he reflected the majority sentiment on that score. One poll showed that just 38 percent said Congress should pass Bush's tax cut, with 52 percent saying it should not.[38]

Voinovich, along with a handful of fellow moderates, defected from the Republican leadership to pass a budget allowing only $350 billion in tax cuts, less than half of what Bush desired. The news media, almost without exception, treated this as a major blow to Bush's plans. Yet in a Conference Committee Republicans restored all of Bush's tax cuts, simply using a series of transparent fiscal gimmicks to reduce their apparent cost. They made no effort to hide what they were doing. As Tom DeLay gleefully cackled to the *New York Times,* "Numbers don't mean anything." Yet, when the bill returned to the Senate, the moderates meekly submitted, having exhausted their capacity to sustain dissent or never having had any interest in anything deeper than the mere appearance of moderation.

Even on those rare occasions when moderates in the House have defied the leadership, the Conference Committee has usually undone their work. This has usually happened when certain measures gain overwhelming popularity and capture the attention of the news media. So, for instance, Republican moderates teamed with Democrats in both chambers to defeat an administration measure letting employers deny overtime pay to several million workers and weakening regulations against media concentration. These provisions thus made their way into both the House and the Senate versions of the legislation. But the Conference Committees excised them.

A classic example is a measure allowing the reimportation of generic prescription drugs, typically from Canada. The notion is wildly popular with voters but fiercely opposed by the prescription drug industry. Democrats have made a show of accompanying busloads of senior citizens to Canada to buy medicine at prices much lower than those on offer domestically. Eventually moderate Republicans went along.

When the prescription drug bill appeared to be doomed, one Republican representative, Jo Ann Emerson of Missouri, switched her vote from no to yes in return for a written promise from House Speaker Dennis Hastert to allow a vote on reimportation.[39] Hastert relented, and the House later voted for the reimportation measure, 243–186. Although both the House and Senate had expressed a clear preference for reimportation, the Conference Committee left it out of the final bill.

This ploy gave a double victory to the Republican leadership. The moderates were able to stay on the right side of popular opinion on a high-profile issue and at the same time establish their independence by voting against their party's conservative leadership. But the leadership can simply undo their handiwork behind closed doors, rendering these shows of independence cost-free. The Conference Committee's final bill is usually a sweeping measure that moderates can approve with little fear of punishment. Ultimately, the moderates can say they had voted for reimportation. Sure, the prescription drug bill they voted for in the end did not have that feature, but somebody else had taken that provision out. How many voters could possibly have followed the Byzantine legislative maneuvers that produced the final bill?

The Republicans were not the first ones to discover the possibilities of abusing the Rules Committee or the Conference Committee. But they expanded these black tools far beyond anything ever attempted in modern history. "If Democrats, when they were in the House majority, jammed through plenty of bills without Republican participation and turned off moderate Members of the minority, their highhandedness was nothing compared to what House Republicans are doing now," noted Ornstein. The unifying purpose is to shield elected officials from the unpopularity of their actions — what the political scientists Jacob Hacker and Paul Pierson have called "backlash insurance." The Republicans figured out a way to remove the locus of accountability from the vast majority of members — and especially those in moderate districts or states — and into the hands of a tiny coterie of loyalists.

STACKING THE ELECTORAL DECK

Of course, those loyalists must face their own accountability moments every time they run for reelection. Alas, the electoral process itself has become deeply corroded, in part by luck and in part by design. The result is that even if the bulwarks Congress has built to insulate itself from public opinion fail and the voters turn against them, the GOP has a final line of defense at the ballot box.

Two big things have happened in the House of Representatives over the last several decades to protect Republicans. The first is that the field of competitive races has shrunk. In the spring of 1994, the Cook political report — a respected nonpartisan political prognosticator — identified one hundred House races as competitive. At a similar point in 2006, it identified just thirty-five.[40]

This decline in competitive races results, in part, from a natural demographic change. Over the last decade, American politics has increasingly polarized over lifestyle and culture, with the result that people increasingly live among their fellow partisans — NPR-listening Democrats live near other NPR-listening Democrats, gun-toting Republicans live near other gun-toting Republicans. On top of that, both parties have grown increasingly adept (and shameless) about drawing up congressional districts to ensure that one party or another prevails. Increasingly sophisticated software allows state legislatures to identify partisans block by block, or house by house, and draw up congressional districts to ensure a given result. The upshot of all this is that fewer and fewer members of the House have anything to fear from the voters. Which party has more to gain from being insulated from public backlash? The answer, of course, is the party that's most out of step with public preferences.

The second major trend is that, as the House has grown generally less competitive, it has also grown more friendly toward Republicans. Again, part of this is an organic trend. In drawing a political map, the advantage goes to the party with the fewest wasted votes. You want to win a lot of races 55–45. If you're winning 80–20, you have too many partisans that would do more good if they resided in a competitive district. Since Democrats tend to live in cities, they are packed together in districts with huge Democratic majorities. (Black representatives have aggravated the situation, insisting on ultrasafe districts packed with huge black majorities, a demand Republicans have been only too happy to oblige.) Republicans, meanwhile, tend to have less overwhelming majorities in small towns and distant suburbs, hence fewer wasted votes.

But Republicans have also been more effective, and more ruthless, in drawing the map to their advantage. (As even the conservative *Wall Street Journal* editorial page conceded, "Because Republicans have more House incumbents, and more governors, they're likely to get the partisan advantage.")[41] While tradition held that states conducted a redistricting only every decade, following the census, Republicans in 2003 carried out an unprecedented redistricting in Texas and Colorado without prodding from a census. The result is a House heavily tilted toward the GOP. During the 2006 elections, for instance, Democrats won nearly 58 percent of the total vote in House races but ended up with just 53 percent of the seats.[42]

The same is true of the Senate, though the causes are entirely natural. The Senate, of course, gives every state equal representation. Naturally, this gives more voting power to residents of less populous states. (Wyoming gets one Senate vote for every 251,000 people, while California gets one senator for every 1,780,000 residents.) It so happens that Republicans are more likely to inhabit the less populous states, so they have a natural advantage in this chamber. If you assume that each senator represents half that state's population, 58 percent of the population lives in states voting Democratic, but those states only accounted for 51 percent of the Senate.[43]

This means that, in a political equilibrium, Republicans ought to dominate the Senate. Grover Norquist made this point in characteristically gloating fashion, writing: "In the 50–50 election that was 2000, Bush carried 30 states and Al Gore 20. Over time, a reasonably competent Republican Party will tend to 60 Republicans in the Senate."[44]

In 2006, as everybody knows, the Republicans were not reasonably competent. They had presided over a mind-boggling confluence of disasters, chief among them a quagmire in Iraq and numerous personal scandals. And here is where the full weight of their structural advantages came through. Despite almost everything going wrong that could possibly go wrong for the GOP, the Democrats were able to eke out only the barest of majorities in the House and Senate. But this also suggests that were circumstances reversed — if the Democrats presided over a major scandal, a foreign policy disaster, or a recession — Republicans could potentially win huge majorities.

And because the political map remains tilted against the Democrats, their efforts to govern will remain an uphill fight. Their slight majority relies on large numbers of senators and representatives from Republican states and districts, and they face political pressure at home to demonstrate their independence from the national Democratic Party. Even if the Democrats manage to win the presidency in 2008 and sweep up every plausibly contestable seat in the House and Senate, they will have a hard time rolling back even the worst excesses of the Bush era, let alone enacting an ambitious progressive program. The political style displayed by Republicans relied on ironclad party discipline of the sort Democrats are unlikely to match.

NO ACCOUNTABILITY

Perhaps the best gauge of the conservatives' strength is their reaction to the 2006 electoral debacle. In nearly every corner of the conservative movement and the Republican Party, the reaction was the same: Republicans lost because they betrayed the one true faith. Republicans "were punished not for pursuing but forgetting conservatism." In an address after the election, the Republican Party chairman, Ken Mehlman, declared that his party had behaved as if government was "the answer to every question," an assumption that "leads to defeat." He urged the audience to "redouble our efforts to cut taxes."

Now, at some level, this is simply laughable. There's no evidence that Republicans lost because they were insufficiently committed to cutting taxes or other elements of conservative dogma. In 2006, 91 percent of Republicans supported a GOP House candidate, a drop of just two percentage points from Bush's support two years earlier. The proportion of conservatives in the electorate likewise fell just two percentage points. Why did Republicans lose, then? Because independents, who supported Democrats by just one percentage point two years earlier, voted Democratic by a whopping nineteen-point margin in 2006. The GOP defeat occurred in the center, not on the right.

Yet in the end there is a strange logic behind the conservatives' stubborn adherence to their creed. While Republicans obviously did not lose because they failed to muster the requisite anti-tax zeal, there's little evidence their zealotry hurt them, either. The plutocratic agenda may lack popular support, but it was not at the root of the GOP's electoral defeat. The difference between 2006 and the previous three national elections was not a sudden public awakening to the dangers of the Republican agenda. It was scandal and a failed war — things that are not intrinsic to the conservative agenda.

So, in a sense, conservatives are correct to believe that they can recommit themselves to Reaganism — or, as I've already explained, what they believe to be Reaganism — and thrive politically. Unpopular though their economic agenda may be, they have constructed a powerful apparatus to conceal it from the public and insulate themselves from any popular backlash. It is not powerful enough to guarantee they will always win. But it is powerful enough that they can ride out the inevitable downturns and always come back, ideologically undaunted and stronger than ever.

8

THE MAINSTREAMING OF RADICALISM

Twenty years after the end of the Second World War, as we've seen, the basic ideological questions of American government all seemed to have been answered. The sweeping reforms of the New Deal, so radical and controversial when Franklin Roosevelt first proposed them, had hardened into settled fact, and eight years of Republican rule had passed without any major effort to roll them back. Republicans and Democrats still harbored differences, of course. (McCarthyism in the 1950s and the emergence of the New Left in the late 1960s offered glimpses of the kind of splenetic vitriol that is so common today.) But of the bread-and-butter issues that consumed most of the capital's attention, the two sides differed only around the margins. Both accepted a basic middle ground between the preferences of business and labor, which themselves were not generally very hostile, with Republicans closer to the former and Democrats to the latter. In 1960, Daniel Bell wrote *The End of Ideology,* celebrating this great consensus on the role of the state. In 1962, John F. Kennedy told the graduates of Yale University: "The differences today are usually matters of degree. . . . What is at stake in our economic decisions today is not some grand warfare of rival ideologies which will sweep the country with passion, but the practical management of a modern economy."

As we have seen, the conservative movement that dominates the Republican Party today was born out of opposition to this consensus. Modern conservatives trace their intellectual lineage to the *National Review* and their political lineage to the 1964 Barry Goldwater campaign. Both the *National Review* and Goldwater assailed Republican leaders like Dwight Eisenhower for their acquiescence to the swelling welfare state. (Eisenhower's policies amounted to, in Goldwater's memorable phrase, a "dime store New Deal.") They regarded Nixon, if anything, as worse. (The former *National Review* publisher William A. Rusher recently called the decision by conservatives to back Nixon's first presidential campaign "the blunder of 1968.") In the conservative mind, the bipartisan establishment had seduced the Republican Party into abandoning its principles. As the congressman and future House majority leader Dick Armey once oh-so-delicately put it: "Bipartisanship is another word for date rape," a comparison later embraced by Grover Norquist.

The unraveling of the postwar consensus began when conservatives first tasted power under Ronald Reagan, and it reached its completion when conservative insurgents in the House of Representatives took control of their party in the 1990s. The debate in Washington, which once centered on gradations and degrees of emphasis, now centered on philosophical first principles — not on the proper ways to extend the principles of the New Deal but whether the previous accomplishments of the New Deal were legitimate. "We are different from previous generations of conservatives . . . ," explained Paul Weyrich, a critical leader of what was then called "the New Right" who created the Heritage Foundation in 1973. "We are no longer working to preserve the status quo. We are radicals, working to overturn the present power structure of this country."[1]

If you believed, as the conservatives did, that the state had no business taxing the proceeds of accumulated wealth or providing health coverage to the uninsured, then the old ways of splitting the difference became impossible. Inevitably, the friendly tone that had dominated took a sharper turn. As Grover Norquist once told reporters, "We — the conservative activists, the new Republican activists — did not come to Washington to join their establishment." Conservatives correctly understood that the Washington consensus, and the bipartisan style it spawned, was incompatible with the policies they favored. In his 2006 farewell address to the House, Tom DeLay noted, "The common lament over the recent rise in political partisanship is often nothing more than a veiled complaint about the recent rise of political conservatism."

There's nothing inherently wrong in all of this. Consensus is not intrinsically good, and no party ought to feel bound to a consensus it considers misguided. The point here is that the postwar consensus died for the very specific reason that the Republican Party wanted it to die. When political scientists analyze the ways the two parties have changed ideologically, they confirm the obvious. Keith T. Poole and Howard Rosenthal studied every recorded vote in the House and Senate from 1970 to 2003 and found that Republicans have moved sharply to the right while Democrats have scarcely moved left at all. Moreover, even the slight leftward shift among Democrats is accounted for by the disappearance of the party's conservative Southern wing. "Outside the South, Democrats are roughly as liberal, on average, as they were thirty years ago," conclude Jacob Hacker and Paul Pierson. "The typical Republican politician, however, is much more fiercely and consistently conservative than the GOP stalwarts of thirty years ago."[2]

The center has disappeared because the parameters of the political debate have lurched rightward. Politicians who have stayed in national office long enough have found themselves relocated on the political spectrum without having changed their beliefs. In 1976, Gerald Ford needed to placate his party's conservative wing, which had supported Ronald Reagan's insurgent primary campaign. So he dumped his sitting vice president, the moderate Nelson Rockefeller, and replaced him on the ticket with Senator Bob Dole of Kansas, then considered something of a right-wing firebrand. (Dole called his selection "a bridge to the Reagan forces.")[3] Twenty years later, Dole himself won the nomination, but the party dynamics had shifted to the point where *he* was now considered suspiciously moderate and had to nominate the more conservative Jack Kemp to placate the party base. What was once considered hard right is now considered moderate.

In the Democratic Party, it has worked the other way around, at least on economic policy: what was once considered moderate is now considered radical. Twenty or thirty years ago, the measure of a politician's liberalism was how rapidly he wanted to expand government. In 1977, a *Newsweek* story discussed the new breed of Democratic moderates. The paradigmatic examples: Michael Dukakis and Jerry Brown! Today those two are paradigmatic examples of unreconstructed liberalism. But *Newsweek* called them "national symbols of the pragmatic new conservatism — tight-fisted political hybrids who seek to limit the further spread of government and place a balanced budget at the top of the public agenda." By the standards of thirty years ago, favoring balanced budgets did make you moderate. Today, of course, merely seeking to limit the spread of government is not enough to make one a moderate. To qualify, one must favor things like the repeal of the estate tax, a notion once completely far-fetched for even the most hardened conservatives. The poles of the political spectrum may be pulling farther apart, but the right is doing all of the pulling.

NONPARTISAN CHIC

This, however, is not the way most people think of what has happened in Washington. The decline of comity in politics and the erosion of bipartisanship are universally acknowledged phenomena that are almost universally blamed on both parties in equal measure. The consensus that Democrats and Republicans alike have moved toward the extremes is so widely held that objective reporters routinely repeat it as simple fact (e.g., then–CBS News anchor John Roberts: "Both parties have abandoned the middle").

The pox-on-both-their-houses consensus is, indeed, so deeply ingrained that pundits can't seem to assimilate information that contradicts it. Our moderate political commentators resemble pre-Galilean astronomers, so invested in one conception of reality that they must go to ever more implausible lengths to make the facts fit. A 2005 column by Morton Kondracke, the executive editor of *Roll Call* and a fixture of television punditry, is a typical offering, remarkable only as an archetype. The subject of this particular column is the powerlessness of the GOP's moderate wing. Kondracke notes that while there is no institution pressuring the Republican Party to move toward the center, "the Democratic Party has an influential moderate wing, led by the Democratic Leadership Council." The presence of an influential moderating force in one party — in this case, a group that directly shaped or strongly influenced the last three Democratic presidential nominees — and the corresponding absence in the other would seem to strongly suggest a fundamental difference between the two parties. Yet for Kondracke the contradiction between this observed fact and the dogma of partisan symmetry is too great to bear. So, in the same column, he asserts that "there's no question that the Democratic Party is just as much a captive of the left as the GOP is of the right."[4] Cognitive dissonance is banished, and the universal truth once again upheld.

This dogged insistence on blaming both sides for the erosion of the center is, in part, a journalistic conceit. As discussed earlier, reporters and commentators who wish to be seen as nonpartisan are professionally constrained from siding strongly with one party.

But this nonpartisan conceit is not merely an artifice created for the convenience of the Tim Russerts and the David Broders. It also represents an authentic popular sentiment, one that propelled the presidential candidacy of Ross Perot, who avowed that America's deepest problems could be solved simply by forcing both parties in Washington to work together. The antipartisan impulse finds its latest, and perhaps most pure, expression in the form of an Internet political activist group called Unity '08. Its avowed purpose is to elect a presidential ticket consisting of a Republican and a Democrat, or perhaps two independents, running on a platform of what Unity '08 calls "crucial issues." This platform consists, in its entirety, of the following: "Global terrorism, our national debt, our dependence on foreign oil, the emergence of India and China as strategic competitors and/or allies, nuclear proliferation, global climate change, the corruption of Washington's lobbying system, the education of our young, the health care of all, and the disappearance of the American Dream for so many of our people."

The odd thing about this list is that it is a virtual facsimile of the Democratic platform. Some of these issues, to be sure, are shared by Republicans. But most have ranked very low among GOP priorities, whereas every single one has been lavished with attention from Democratic candidates, officeholders, and their affiliated policy intellectuals. Unity '08, though, is determinedly even-handed in assessing blame for the failure of these priorities to seize the national agenda during a period of mostly unified Republican control of government. As its Web site declares: "Unity '08 believes that neither of today's major parties reflects the aspirations, fears or will of the majority of Americans."[5]

And why have these issues not commanded Washington's agenda? Because, Unity '08 says, the two parties have instead campaigned on secondary social questions. In reality, even the most facile observer of American politics could see that in recent years it has been the Republicans who have put gun control, abortion, and gay marriage at the center of the political debate and Democrats who have sought desperately (though unsuccessfully) to deflect attention from them.

A 2006 cover story in *New York* magazine by Kurt Anderson produced a strikingly similar analysis. The article called for the formation of a "Purple Party," a blend of red-state Republican and blue-state Democratic ideas. And those ideas, as Anderson saw them, the ones that combined red and blue impulses? Opposition to the GOP's efforts to criminalize "Middle Eastern democracy as a force-fed contagion," "tax-cutting monomania," abortion, and flag-burning, privatize Social Security, and limit stem cell research. In favor of the government's providing universal health care, a higher gasoline tax, and action to limit global warming. All these positions, obviously, put Anderson deeply at odds with the Republican Party. For balance, he declared himself in favor of "experimentation with charter schools," free trade, and a foreign policy that takes terrorism seriously. It's not terribly difficult to see where this leads. All of these positions are compatible with either significant factions, or the whole, of the Democratic Party.[6] To acknowledge this glaringly obvious truth, though, would undercut the studious neutrality that is the bedrock of the militant nonpartisan worldview and the source of its moral authority. To reside in the center, in the mind of the militant centrist, is to be sensible, independent-minded, and unburdened by dogma.

TO GET A SENSE of the almost inexplicable prestige associated with nonpartisanship, consider the charmed political career of John Breaux. Breaux came into politics as an aide for the legendarily corrupt Louisiana governor (and later convicted racketeer) Edwin Edwards. Louisiana politics was never known for its tradition of good governance, and Breaux certainly did not distinguish himself. He first achieved national attention in 1981, several years after he was first elected to Congress. He broke with his party to support President Reagan's budget in return for the administration's promise not to touch the tax on imported sugar (which falls heavily on the poor but bestows windfall profits on the domestic sugar industry, which is based in Louisiana). His notoriety came not from the vote itself but from his frank explanation that while his vote was not for sale, "it can be rented."

Breaux soon discovered that his penchant for dealmaking would be more favorably received if he portrayed it not as a tawdry exercise in back-scratching but as a noble quest to bring the two parties together. Over time he made himself into the indispensable figure for any bipartisan deal. His essential technique was to stake out a position halfway between those of the two parties and insist that any person of goodwill must join him. This approach was moderately successful at producing legislation and astonishingly successful at burnishing his image as a thoughtful and public-spirited legislator.

In 1999, for instance, the two parties found themselves at an impasse over how large a tax cut they should pass. Republicans desired a large one, in the $800 billion range. Democrats countered with a smaller one, costing just $300 billion. Moderate economists thought that with the economy at full tilt, a tax cut was unnecessary and the money better used to pay off the national debt. Breaux tried to bring the two sides together to pass a $500 billion tax cut.[7] Under the threat of a veto from President Clinton, he failed, but still won praise for his willingness to work with both sides. One news report bemoaned "the frustration these legislative pragmatists are feeling as they see their centrist offering spurned by both parties."

Two years later, with George W. Bush in the White House, the definition of centrist had shifted sharply. Republicans had doubled the size of their proposed tax cut, to $1.6 trillion. Democrats, afraid to be seen as intransigent, raised their offer to $900 billion, more expensive than the tax cut they had previously rejected as unaffordable. Breaux, leading what the *New York Times* called "an eclectic group of party apostates in the political center," once again decided that the Republican proposal was a bit too big and the Democratic response a bit too small. He brokered a compromise tax cut of $1.2 trillion.

Breaux's defense of his handiwork perfectly summed up what had become his governing philosophy: "Is this budget a perfect document? Of course not. But does it advance the cause of governing in a democracy that is almost evenly divided among the two parties? I think the answer is yes, it does."[8] Breaux offered a similar defense of his cosponsorship of the Medicare prescription drug bill two years later when he said, "No one got everything they wanted." (In fact, the insurance, pharmaceutical, and other industry lobbies *did* get everything they wanted, and the result was regarded by policy wonks of left, right, and center as a legislative disgrace.) In this pair of statements we can see the two tenets of Breaux's guiding ideology: first, that passing legislation is almost always better than stalemate, and second, that the sensible position by definition lies halfway between the two parties.

This is, in other words, the belief system of someone without a belief system, a legislative cipher. It happens, though, to dovetail perfectly with the dominant ethos of establishment Washington. And so Breaux's relentless positioning in the center was seen mainly as a noble desire to produce good government. When he announced his retirement in 2003, a *New York Times* story mourned his departure as "a setback to across-the-aisle cooperation, which is increasingly rare these days." In a fawning valedictory interview before Breaux headed off to (inevitably) K Street, Michele Norris of National Public Radio repeated Breaux's line about his vote being for rent, but this time recalled it fondly. "It's a wonderful story," she told him, "but also a snapshot of a time there, a time when you could work both sides of the aisle." Thus the hack was transformed into a statesman.

WASHINGTON'S VENERATION of bipartisanship and coopera-tion is the residue of the great consensus era. During the decades when the two parties agreed on the fundamental ideological ques-tions, it really did make some rough sense to define the center as halfway between the two sides and to assume a bipartisan accord would produce some reasonable outcome. But with the Republican Party racing to the right without a corresponding leftward lurch from the Democrats, the whole mindset has become meaningless. Worse: it has rewarded GOP radicalism. To define the space be-tween the two sides as the center, and the center as reasonable, is to allow the ideological poles to set the terms of the debate. Yesterday's radicalism has become today's moderation.

How does this perverse dynamic work? There is a large segment of popular opinion, and an even larger segment of elite opinion, that sees the center as necessarily occupying the space between the two parties. And since the center is, by definition, the middle ground between Democrats and Republicans, such moderates will never blame one party for abandoning it. (Indeed, to those wedded to centrism, blaming one party for abandoning the center would re-flect the very sort of one-sided partisanship they abhor.) A huge chunk of the center may be *ideologically* disposed to defect to the Democratic Party when the GOP moves too far right, but they are *temperamentally* disposed to cling to their partisan neutrality. They may mourn the end of the postwar consensus, but they cannot lo-cate the source of its demise. And so, paradoxically, the nonpartisan impulse has allowed the Republicans to march steadily away from the center — or at least what used to constitute the center — with relative impunity.

As the Republicans have moved away from the center, Democrats have moved steadily toward it. Since Bill Clinton's first presidential campaign, the essence of the Democratic strategy has been to jettison its unpopular positions and set itself in the center. Clinton ran as a "New Democrat" in 1992 and 1996, in opposition to what he called "the brain-dead politics of left and right." In 2000, Al Gore struck a more liberal thematic note, but he did not repudiate any of the substance of Clinton's positions. In 2004, John Kerry consciously put himself forward as a New Democrat and was eagerly embraced by the Democratic Leadership Council, the primary force for moderation in the party. Most, though not all, of the Democrats in Congress have followed in Clinton's wake. They support Clinton's signature repudiations of old-fashioned liberalism — support for police, disavowing of unlimited welfare, and the like.*

Yet Democrats have not managed to define themselves in the public mind as the party of the center because they no longer have a liberal flank against which to define themselves. Clinton's labels of choice — "New Democrat," "Third Way" — were all intended to contrast him with the Democrats to his left. The Democrats, by this reasoning, would be seen as representing a midpoint between the two poles. But when the party moved to the center, the poles simply shifted along with it.

Clinton, for instance, called his program "the vital center," expropriating a phrase first used by Arthur Schlesinger, Jr., in 1948. Schlesinger, though, saw New Deal liberalism as the center between communism and laissez-faire conservatism. For Clinton, New Deal

---

* Free trade is a more complicated case. Clinton supported free trade agreements that included provisions to protect labor rights and the environment abroad, and he was able to bring many Democrats with him. George W. Bush has advocated trade deals that do not include those concessions, and many previously pro–free trade Democrats have therefore opposed him. Many observers have mistaken this as a wholesale abandonment of free trade principles when in fact it's a revolt against the different kind of free trade deals that have prevailed under Bush.

liberalism was now the left pole, and his vital center now rested between it and the same unreconstructed right.

The definitional erosion continued during Clinton's presidency. For instance, in his first term, Clinton struck what appeared to be a centrist note by spurning single-payer health reform and embracing a hybrid plan that retained a prominent role for private health insurers. But soon this compromise plan came to be seen as the liberal, big-government option. Democrats in Congress who wanted to be seen as moderate embraced even more moderate measures than those Clinton proposed. Indeed, in 1974 Richard Nixon declared, "Comprehensive health insurance is an idea whose time has come in America. Let us act now to assure all Americans financial access to high quality medical care." Twenty years later, such a position would have put him well to the left of many Democrats.

RADICALISM AND RESPECTABILITY

The right's saving grace has turned out to be the natural human impulse to look at any complicated dispute and conclude that the truth must lie in between the two sides. There is an innate presumption that both sides must at least have a point. That a given point of view has authority figures to recommend it must mean, at the very least, that it isn't crazy. Crazy views are the positions held by nutty activists on the political fringe, not major party leaders.

It so happens, though, that what we now consider mainstream conservative thinking was not long ago considered unthinkable, or in some cases virtually insane. Fifty years ago, the word "conservative" applied to politicians whom we would today consider moderate liberals. The forerunners of the contemporary conservative movement — the *National Review* crowd and supporters of Goldwater — went by other terms. Theodore Adorno and Richard Hofstadter called them "pseudo-conservatives," on the grounds that "they are far from pleased with the dominant practical conservatism of the moment as it is represented by the Eisenhower administration."[9] They were more commonly, and somewhat less pejoratively, referred to as "the radical right" and considered a fringe movement. As Daniel Bell put it, "The radical is outside the political pale, insofar as it refuses to accept the American consensus."[10] Hofstadter's famous essay, "The Paranoid Style in American Politics," traced the historical arc of crackpot thinking from anti-Masonites through the Populist firebrands through the radical right of the 1950s.

Hofstadter and Bell dismissed right-wing thought as primarily a series of paranoid delusions. It was, in part. One of the main themes of right-wing thought during the 1950s, espoused by the *National Review* and Joseph McCarthy, held that the liberal establishment had not just unwittingly undermined American security but had deliberately sabotaged it through sinister conspiracy. John Stormer's seminal tract, *None Dare Call It Treason*, charged the existence of "a conspiratorial plan to destroy the United States," reaching to the highest levels of Democratic administrations.

But, as some of their contemporaries complained, Hofstadter and Bell had overstated the degree to which this radical brand of conservatism flowed from disturbed thinking. Not surprisingly, it enraged conservatives. (Buckley famously complained that Hofstadter "analyzed" liberals and "diagnosed" conservatives.) Over time, their analysis fell out of favor with intellectuals across the ideological spectrum. In the late 1960s, the radical, anti-intellectual tendencies that the consensus liberals had identified on the right suddenly emerged on the left. The New Left activists — who later produced their own generation of historians — savaged Hofstadter and Bell as elitists.

The worst thing that happened to the consensus liberal analysis was that the radical right took hold of the Republican Party and displaced the Eisenhower wing as the main conservative force in American politics. It was easy to dismiss the radical right as a lunatic fringe while it simmered around the margins of American politics, much harder when it had settled into the mainstream of American life. Today, the prevailing assumption is that conservatism is more or less a mirror image of liberalism and the GOP more or less the mirror image of the Democratic Party — both sides have their crackpots, both sides have their moderates. But in recent years, as the conservative movement (i.e., "the radical right") has finally vanquished the last vestiges of the Republican establishment and had the chance to wield real power, it has become apparent that the Hofstadters and Bells were on to something.

Radicalism is not merely a function of one's distance from whatever policies hold sway at a given time. (To define radicalism merely as the distance from the center of a political debate is to deny the possibility that a radical party can wield power. Imagine this definition applied universally. In the context of, say, the Soviet Union of the 1930s, an advocate of collectivization and massive state repression would be moderate, an advocate of democracy unthinkably radical.) Extremism does have a meaning that transcends its political surroundings. Radical ideologies have in common with one another certain habits of thought, and this holds true however great their power may be. Which is to say, a radical analysis from the left and a radical analysis from the right will often employ identical modes of thought, even though they obviously reach diametrical conclusions. A radical analysis, from the left or the right, is more Manichean, prone to see the hand of conspiracy everywhere, and liable to insist on the absolute and unbending truth of its vision.

From this obvious truth, moderate-thinking people often conclude erroneously that both liberals and conservatives, or perhaps both Democrats and Republicans, are equally prone to the excesses of radicalism. But in the United States today, the radical left is mostly confined to the margins of the two-party system, and the radical right is ensconced in the corridors of power. The parallelism of the nonpartisans, however comforting it may be, fails to describe reality.

The reality is that conservatives have displayed a political style that is distinctly different from that of the liberals — or, really, of any of the political coalitions that have won national elections over the last three-quarters of a century. It is more radical, more driven by hardened ideology, more beset by paranoid thinking. Given this, the strenuously even-handed practice of seeing the two sides in parallel terms breaks down. The essential nature of the relationship between liberals and conservatives, Democrats and Republicans, is not symmetrical. It is asymmetrical.

POLITICAL ASYMMETRY

Until this point, we have been concentrating most of our attention on the political right. But the ideological evolution on the Democratic side is essential as well. The final piece of the realignment that now leaves us with a radical Republican Party and a moderate Democratic Party fell into place during the Clinton presidency.

When Bill Clinton came into office in 1993, nobody knew which path he would take on the economy. As a candidate, he had promised to halve the deficit, but he had also promised to rebuild the public infrastructure and cut taxes for the middle class. Clinton and his economic advisers devoted weeks to fierce internal debate over which course ought to receive the highest priority. The advisers on the left, like Secretary of Labor Robert Reich, argued that a program of infrastructure investments would give the economy a classic Keynesian boost. Those on the right, such as Treasury Secretary

Lloyd Bentsen, insisted that the highest priority ought to go to deficit reduction, which, they claimed, would keep interest rates low and inject more investment capital into the economy.

Ultimately, Clinton chose the latter course. The decision did not come easily to him, and he accepted it only when his centrist advisers persuaded him that his best hope of economic growth lay in convincing the bond market of his intent to lower the deficit. "I hope you're all aware we're all Eisenhower Republicans," he groused at one point. "We're Eisenhower Republicans here, and we are fighting the Reagan Republicans. We stand for lower deficits and free trade and the bond market."[11] Over the course of Clinton's presidency, though, the economy boomed, and the choice that the bond market had forced on him hardened into a governing doctrine. By 1999, he was boasting of his thriftiness. "In an age of worldwide capital markets," he said, "this is the way a nation prospers — by saving and investing, not by running big deficits."

The historical import of Clinton's embrace of fiscal conservatism was not that he won over all the liberal Democrats to his way of thinking. He did not — liberal magazines like the *Nation* and the *American Prospect* sharply criticized him on the grounds that fiscal conservatism starved the public sector of needed investments and social spending. "A fixation on placating Wall Street has made it difficult to fulfill the original mandate for a new economics centered on helping all Americans adapt to economic change," complained Reich. (More moderate outlets, like the *New Republic,* and most liberal editorial pages supported the thrust of Clinton's approach.) The significant thing is that Clinton brought both wings of the postwar consensus into the liberal coalition. So, first the Republican Party abandoned the consensus, then the Democratic Party had grasped what was once the conservative half of that consensus. Now the whole sweep of it, everything from Eisenhower conservatives on the right to Truman liberals on the left, resides in the Democratic Party. All the conflicting prerogatives that had once seized the domestic debate — fiscal responsibility versus social outlay, support for business versus support for labor — are in one coalition.

The result, made final by Clinton, is a transformation of the nature of ideology in American life. Four decades ago, Daniel Bell noted that neither the Republicans nor the Democrats were particularly ideological, at least not the ones who had any real power. The ideologues could be found among the excluded dissidents. "The right-wing Republicans," he wrote, "have an ideology — perhaps the only group in American life that possesses one today."[12] Now that those right-wing Republicans have taken control of the party, our political system now pits a radical party against a moderate one.

This probably seems like a curious statement. Most of us tend to think of liberalism and conservatism as clashing ideologies, with the former preferring more government and the latter preferring less. What separates the two sides, though, is not just goals but epistemologies. Conservatives do not simply believe that government ought to be limited because it is the best way to achieve certain goals. They believe it as a matter of philosophical first principle. Milton Friedman once explained, "Freedom in economic arrangements is itself a component of freedom broadly understood, so economic freedom is an end in itself."

Most conservatives believe that bigger government has all sorts of harmful side effects on economic growth, employment, and the like. But those beliefs, while deeply held, are not necessarily determinative. Conservatives believe government simply has no right to insert itself into economic life the way it has since the New Deal. As Andrew Sullivan (a libertarian conservative) put it, "If faster growth were caused by a bigger government, a conservative would still back smaller government and individual freedom. Similarly, my hostility to a progressive income tax is because I believe it's hubristic over-reach. Why should a government have the power to penalize some individuals for their relative success while rewarding others for relative failure?" So while conservatives believe, say, that progressive taxes inhibit incentives to work, they would not change this view even if it were proven wrong, because buttressing their position is a deeper belief about the immorality of big government.

Liberal support for bigger government, on the other hand, is entirely rooted in what liberals believe to be its practical effects. They support regulations on pollution because they believe it will improve air quality. They support tax credits for the working poor because they believe they will raise incomes for such workers. If liberals were to be convinced those programs failed to achieve their intended goals, they would withdraw support for them. Increasing the size of government does not, in and of itself, serve any greater purpose. Conservatives regularly cite the size of government as a measuring stick — bigger government means they are failing, smaller government means they are succeeding. Liberals don't think this way. For them, bigger government is a means, not an end.

Conservatism thus has a certainty about it that rarely can be found in liberalism. In this way, the ideological style of conservative discourse resembles that of communism much more than liberalism. It has an air of totalistic ideology. It's no surprise that a disproportionate number of conservative intellectuals were once communists — first, the *National Review* crowd in the 1950s (Whittaker Chambers, James Burnham, Frank Meyer, Wildmoore Kendall), then the neoconservatives of the 1970s (former Trotskyists Irving Kristol and Norman Podhoretz). They simply exchanged the primacy of the state for the primacy of the market.

A CULT, NOT A COALITION

The result of this shift is that economic debates among liberals tend to be more contentious and fluid than those among conservatives.

One window into the contrast is the economic summits the last two presidents have held at the outset of their terms. Bill Clinton in 1992 invited economists, CEOs, union leaders, small-business owners, and others to attend a lengthy, rambling wonkfest, and the outcome sowed the seeds for his pivot toward fiscal conservatism. George W. Bush, on the other hand, limited his audience to business leaders who already support his policies, and he used the occasion as a forum for supporters to heap praise on his program.[13] The way forward was known to all — tax cuts, the more the better — and debate and dissent would only be counterproductive.

It is not that conservatives shy away from internal debate, but rather that those debates have a frantic orthodoxy about them. Conservative debates, unlike liberal ones, begin with the premise that there is a single belief system. The debate usually takes the form of an accusation, or mutual accusations, of ideological heresy. Intramural conservative disputes are almost always confined to those few areas, like immigration or certain foreign policy issues, where the conservative litany is not well defined. As we saw earlier, they usually take the form of rival claimants to the true spirit of Reaganism. Conservatives regularly allude to "the conservative movement." Liberals have no corresponding term. This is because there is no liberal movement in anything like the sense that there is a conservative movement.[14]

Liberals, of course, freely accuse each other of all sorts of ideological sins. The difference is that you virtually never see one of them accuse another of "betraying liberalism" because there is no agreed-on definition of what liberalism means. It is an ideological coalition of the sort that has generally been found at the center of American politics throughout our history. Conservatism is more of an ideological sect.

One of the classic traits of sectarian thought is a belief that failure can result only from doctrinal impurity. This is one of the defining features of modern conservatism. Every conservative setback is invariably followed by a purification ritual, whereby the conservative leader is declared a heretic. As we saw earlier, the most famous such apostate is, of course, George H. W. Bush. But nearly every titular leader of the Republican Party since Reagan has suffered a similar fate. Newt Gingrich, even before he led the GOP takeover of Congress, was the very face of conservative zeal. So ardently did he cling to conservative dogma that he let the government shut down rather than compromise his demands for large cuts in taxes and spending. The Republicans' poll numbers plummeted, and even as they realized they had no leverage to bend President Clinton to their will they persisted — not once, not twice, but thrice allowing disastrous shutdowns before finally relenting.

By 1997, the Republican Revolution, as its adherents called it, was languishing, and restive conservatives turned against their champion. "Where once there was awe and gratitude [toward Gingrich], there is now disdain and disgust," reported the *Weekly Standard*. Talk of insurrection to dispose Gingrich filled the conservative press. The once-fearless leader "conciliatory and timid, some may say obsequious" (Donald Lambro, *Washington Times*), "cowering in the halls of Congress" (William Kristol, *Weekly Standard*), had gone "wobbly in the knee" (Jack Kemp). One GOP member of Congress complained, "Gone is the Contract with America. In its place is an ambiguous agenda . . . carefully crafted to upset no one and accomplish not much of anything." (Note the nearly identical tone of this complaint with William F. Buckley's indictment of Eisenhower: "It has been the dominating ambition of Eisenhower's Modern Republicanism to govern in such a fashion as to more or less please everybody. Such governments must shrink from principle.")[15] Discontented conservatives in the House fomented a coup against Gingrich that year. Narrowly surviving, he clung to power for another year and a half before Republicans finally deposed him after the 1998 elections.

George W. Bush, too, was revered by conservatives before many of them finally decided he was a heretic and a fraud. His descent from the conservative pantheon was steep. In the spring of 2004, the president spoke before the American Conservative Union, which burst into frequent standing ovations. (The *Washington Times* noted that his reception rivaled that of Reagan himself — the highest possible praise.) The *National Review*'s David Frum called Bush "a resolute and even heroic president." Conservative publications advertised, for a mere $2,000, a sixteen-inch bronze bust of the president. It was true that conservatives grumbled at Bush's ideological deviations, but those mutterings were drowned out by fulsome praise.

After his reelection in 2004, Bush's popularity sank and his legislative agenda ground to a halt. In the conservative mind there was only one possible explanation: Bush had abandoned the faith. As the liberal writer Rick Perlstein has observed: "Conservatism never fails. It is only failed." The swift collapse of Bush's presidency after his reelection was therefore evidence that he could not be a true conservative. The conservative press reverberated with denunciations of him as an ideological turncoat. Where once they spoke of Bush in the same breadth as Reagan, they now compared him to Richard Nixon or George H. W. Bush — hated moderates who curried favor with the liberal establishment. A previously unknown and unimaginable genre appeared: the conservative anti-Bush book, with titles like *Imposter* or *Conservatives Betrayed*. The cult of personality dissipated all at once. Bush's ideological transgressions, once dismissed as a mere annoyance, suddenly came to define him. Before, conservatives had insisted that Bush's lack of enthusiasm for budget-cutting mattered little in the face of his passion for cutting taxes. In its enthusiastic endorsement of Bush in 2000, for instance, the *National Review* insisted that his "support for tax cuts and Social Security reform is more important than his spending initiatives — not least because if he succeeds on taxes and Social Security, it will be easier to limit government in the future." The Bush presidency was a test of this starve-the-beast strategy, which is the essential premise of conservative domestic policy. But the conservatives could not admit that their own theory had fallen short, that the strategy and the assumptions behind it had failed. Betrayal was the only explanation.

ONE STRIKING THING about the right's habitual regicide is that it takes place entirely within a self-contained bubble. There are no non-ideological criteria for judging politicians. The concept of a good politician, in the universe of the right, is entirely synonymous with the concept of a conservative politician, and bad is likewise synonymous with "moderate" or "liberal." The standard of doctrinal purity to which conservatives hold their leaders is unforgiving. As Hofstadter noticed: "Being uncomfortable with the thought of any leadership that falls short of perfection, the extreme right is also incapable of analyzing the world with enough common sense to establish any adequate and realistic criterion for leadership."

When conservatives denounce their leaders for an apostasy, they generally feel no obligation to explain what other course was available. George H. W. Bush acceded to a tax hike because he believed the economy faced a collapse without some deficit reduction, and Democrats, who controlled Congress, demanded tax hikes to go along with spending cuts. While conservatives flayed Gingrich for compromising with President Clinton — "Rather than folding, some members ought to exercise leadership, drive a message and fight for principle," scolded the conservative House member David McIntosh — as if that very strategy had not been tried with disastrous results. Gingrich had no way to muster the votes to override a Clinton veto, so he could not achieve any reductions in spending without making concessions to the Democrats.

The denunciations of George W. Bush, too, have an otherworldly quality. The fiercest conservative objections center around Bush's spending in general and his Medicare expansion in particular. They complain not just about the bill's undeniable bloat but its very existence. As Jeff Flake of the Republican Study Committee, a faction of true believers in the House, put it in a typical remark: "I never believed that it was responsible to create this new entitlement." There is, however, the inconvenient fact that in 2000, the public approved of adding prescription drugs to Medicare by an overwhelming margin of 89 to 7 percent.[16] How could Bush have pulled out the election by taking such an unpopular stand? How could he have won reelection without fulfilling this promise? Conservatives do not say.

The belief that they can win without compromising the purity of their beliefs is deeply ingrained in the conservative sect. The truest believers among them are convinced, as radical populists of all sorts tend to be, that they are the only legitimate representation of the popular will. Naturally, this conviction lends itself to paranoid interpretations. Phyllis Schlafly, in her influential 1964 Goldwaterite tract, "A Choice Not an Echo," charged that "there is no way Republicans can lose *so long as we have a presidential candidate who campaigns on the issues.*" Why, then, did Republicans lose elections so frequently at the time? Schlafly maintained that "a small group of secret kingmakers, using hidden persuaders and psychological warfare techniques, manipulated the Republican National Convention to nominate candidates who would sidestep or suppress the key issues." This was no fringe pamphlet. It sold several million copies, and 93 percent of the delegates to the 1964 GOP Convention said they had read it.[17]

I should point out that there's nothing inherently paranoid about believing that a political party can have the better of public opinion and still lose elections, especially close ones. (This book, of course, argues that just that has happened recently.) Elections often hinge on random or fleeting factors and thus belie the national mood. Jimmy Carter's 1976 victory is a classic example — a squeaker of an election, pulled out with the aid of a massive backlash against Watergate and against strong conservative headwinds of public opinion. What's paranoid is believing that one's own party *cannot* lose a fair contest if they remain true to their ideological convictions and that defeat can be brought about only by sinister plot.

SINCE IT HAS gained control of the Republican Party, the right has directed most of its paranoid impulses away from the GOP's moderate wing and toward the Democratic Party. It is with regard to the prospect of electoral fraud that the right's paranoid impulses come into full bloom. Something about the idea of cheating taps deep into the paranoid mindset — it is hidden, it subverts the will of the people, and therefore it is an expression of the enemy's pure malevolence. Electoral chicanery is, of course, an abiding (if marginal) fact in American political life. What makes the right's fixation with fraud paranoid is the belief that cheating is mostly or entirely confined to the other party, serving as an essential and recurrent feature of its electoral strategy. Here the right evinces a kind of paranoid thinking that, as we will see, cannot be found in the mainstream left.

The level of dementia at work here can be seen in two remarkable documents that appeared during the 2000 Florida recount. The first is an editorial in the *Wall Street Journal* bemoaning the Republican Party's "squeamish" lack of determination to prevail. This was itself an exceedingly bizarre complaint, given the party's willingness to massively outspend the Democrats, fly in a phalanx of staffers to disrupt the recount in Dade County, violate its stated belief in upholding technical ballot requirements to allow more military votes, and so on. At one point in the editorial, the *Journal* editors mused, "With further desperation, we would not be surprised to see 1,000 Gore votes appear somewhere in the dead of night." As support for this wild and unsubstantiated allegation, the *Journal* proceeded to offer up the following: "Palm Beach County Commissioner Carol Roberts said the other day she would go to jail to drive the count forward, and someone offered a vote-punching machine on eBay."[18]

An even more delirious editorial appeared around the same

time in the *Weekly Standard*. The point of the editorial was that the first, automatic machine recount of votes added 0.0007 percent to Al Gore's total as opposed to just 0.0002 percent to George W. Bush's, a discrepancy so large it violated all mathematical probability.[19] The "mandatory next-day recount of its ballots," the editorial noted with dark sarcasm, "by purest chance broke 80 percent in Al Gore's direction. No. Virtually impossible." What, then, did happen? Here the editorial elaborates on the conspiracy:

> In our bones, we're pretty sure what happened here. In the middle of the night on November 8, Democratic ultraloyalists like the people who run elections in Volusia, Gadsden, and Palm Beach counties watched a fevered Bill Daley announce that things were still close in Florida — and that his party's campaign would "continue" until the rectification of unspecified "irregularities" in that state made Al Gore president. The ultraloyalists read this hint for what it was. And next, they set about, fast as lightning, before anyone was watching, doing "anything to win." We're pretty sure, too, on whose instructions Daley issued his hint. Every Florida machination, after all, has been engineered by Al Gore personally.

The intellectual methodology of both editorials is strikingly similar. Both rely on unseen and unrecorded acts undertaken "in the dead of night," as the *Journal* put it, or "in the middle of the night," in the *Standard*'s phrase. The facts they use are not concocted whole cloth, they are just stitched together in the manic style common to all conspiracy theories. As much as conservatives object to the way Hofstadter described their thinking as paranoid, their fantasies about vote theft offer a perfect case study. "What distinguishes the paranoid style is not, then the absence of verifiable facts . . . ," Hofstadter wrote, "but rather the curious leap in imagination that is always made at some crucial point in the recital of events." Thus a comment from a Democratic county commissioner and the online sale of an old voting machine are woven into a lurid conspiracy.

The most telling detail is the way both editorials rely on intuition to reach their conclusions, signified by the phrase "we would not be surprised" in the *Journal*'s case and "In our bones, we're pretty sure" in the *Standard*'s. It is unusual, to say the least, for a respected publication to make allegations on the basis of nothing more than a hunch. In the minds of the writers, though, it *is* more than a hunch. One of their foundational beliefs is that liberals are so evil, so out of step with the public, that they must cheat. After the 2000 election, the conservative talk radio host Rush Limbaugh told his listeners: "This is not a liberal country, it is not a country predisposed to voting Democrat and liberal. . . . They've got to cheat in order to win big."[20] (This was after the Democrats had won the presidential popular vote for the third consecutive election!)

These sorts of outburst were not just confined to the white-hot intensity of the 2000 presidential recount. A 1992 essay by Grover Norquist in the *American Spectator* provides a dramatic specimen of this hallucinatory worldview. Norquist wrote that Democrats in Congress "cheated. And so will a Clinton administration." How would he do it? Norquist proceeded to spin an elaborate scenario of the skulduggery that would surely follow Clinton's election: he would pad out the Senate by granting statehood to the District of Columbia and, quite likely, Puerto Rico and the Virgin Islands. He would expand the judiciary in order to flood it with his loyalists. By changing labor law, he would "organize a 1996 war chest that could outspend the Republican campaign by a factor of ten — or more." He would dispatch bureaucrats to shake down businessmen for donations. He would allow the automatic registration of voters — "not necessarily citizens," he noted — at welfare offices and prison induction centers.[21]

Obviously, Clinton never attempted, let alone pulled off, a single one of these fantastical schemes. But countervailing evidence cannot deter such fevered imaginations. In 2004, Hugh Hewitt, another popular conservative talk radio host, published a book titled *If*

It's Not Close They Can't Cheat: Crushing the Democrats in Every Election and Why Your Life Depends on It. In it, he wrote: "Republicans must win by comfortable margins. If it is close, you can count on the Democrats cheating."[22] After the 2004 election, the conservative columnist Michael Barone wrote in *U.S. News & World Report* that Democrats had rigged the exit polls. "My own suspicion is that some Democrats — at the command level, or somewhere below — had an election-day project of slamming the results," he said. "If somebody had slipped some Democratic operative the list of exit poll sites — 40 to 50 sites in each critical state — he or she could have slipped several hundred operatives into the polling places to take the exit poll ballots and vote for Kerry. The results would have shown Kerry much farther ahead than he actually was and, broadcast through drudgereport.com and other sources, could have heartened Kerry supporters during the afternoon and disheartened Bush supporters."[23] That such a conspiracy would have required the participation of thousands of Democratic activists without word leaking did not daunt him.

There are, of course, plenty of liberals plagued with dark suspicions about Republican cheating. The key distinction here, again, is that left-wing paranoia tends to emanate from the political fringe and is usually rebuffed by mainstream liberals. In 2000, for instance, while respectable conservative organs wallowed in lunatic conspiracy theories, mainstream liberal opinion incessantly counseled even-handedness and restraint. "If they are worthy of being president, the goal of both Al Gore and George W. Bush at this stage ought to be more than just winning," urged the *Washington Post* editorial page in a typical offering. "Both need to plan for their presidencies and also look to history for lessons in how to preserve the worthy old idea that whoever is president is president of all Americans," echoed the *New York Times.*[24]

Or take the 2004 elections. In the wake of Bush's late-night victory, after the exit polls showed him losing, e-mails circulated among liberals charging massive Republican fraud in the decisive state of Ohio. Their tone was similar to that taken by conservatives four years earlier — small pieces of data, such as lengthy voting lines in heavily Democratic precincts or seeming anomalies in the vote tabulations, with a sudden leap to ominous conclusions. The difference is that mainstream liberalism dismissed the accusations almost immediately. Even left-wing or rabidly partisan outlets, like the *Nation* magazine or the Daily Kos blog, unequivocally declared the allegations of a stolen election untrue.*

The point here is not that liberals are more intelligent than conservatives or even that all conservatives are paranoid. Many, clearly, are not. The point is that conservatism is a more radical ideology than liberalism, and radical ideologies are inherently more prone to sectarianism and paranoid interpretations.

THE WAR OF THE INSTITUTIONS

The differing intellectual style of mainstream liberalism and mainstream conservatism is expressed in the very different sorts of institution associated with the two sides. Conservatives have long believed the dominant institutions of the American elite to be hopelessly overgrown with liberal bias, so they have determinedly created their own counterinstitutions. The conservative Heritage Foundation would balance the liberal Brookings Institution, the conservative *Washington Times* would counteract newspapers like the *Washington Post* or the *New York Times*, and Fox News Channel would offset CNN.

Sensible centrists view all of these institutions as more or less mirror images of each other. "There are two teams, each with its own

---

* In a December 6, 2004, article, David Corn, writing in the *Nation*, rebutted many of the arguments alleging that the vote in Ohio had been stolen. "Suspicion needs reality checks . . . ," he wrote. "A recount in Ohio is well and good. But it probably won't change the results."

politicians, think tanks, special-interest groups, media outfits and TV personalities," wrote Fareed Zakaria in *Newsweek*. "The requirement of this world is that you must always be reliably left or right."[25] There is, however, something distinctly lopsided about each of these pairings. In every case, the conservative doppelgänger is more partisan and more deeply ideological than its liberal counterpart.

Mainstream think tanks — or, as we now call them, "liberal" think tanks — grew out of the Progressive Era belief in public policy informed by disinterested expertise and social science research. The Brookings Institution is the preeminent example of a think tank that grew out of this ethos, but many others followed. The scholars at such institutions are not omniscient, and obviously they disagree with one another and get things wrong more than occasionally, but their work grows out of Robert Brookings's goal of promoting research "free from any political or pecuniary interest." (Two of Brookings's former presidents, Michael Armacost and Bruce MacLaury, were Republicans.) The scholars at liberal think tanks move comfortably in the world of academia. The worst thing that could happen to them would be to have their research seen as partisan hackwork.

Conservatives, though, deemed this Progressive ethos as but a clever hoax. As we saw earlier, they grew increasingly cynical about the very possibility of objective social science research. The guise of objectivity was merely the New Class's pretext for commandeering the government toward its own ends. In this critique, there was an eerie echo of the same relativism that the far left has deployed against the academic establishment. As Irving Kristol wrote of the social scientists, "Though they continue to speak the language of 'progressive reform,' in actuality they are acting on a hidden agenda: to propel the nation from that modified version of capitalism we call 'the welfare state' toward an economic system so stringently regulated in detail as to fulfill many of the anticapitalist aspirations of the left." There was no objective research, only research that served one set of interests or another. Thus Kristol's insistence that "corporate philanthropy should not be, and cannot be, disinterested" and his blithe admission that he supported the development of supply-side economics primarily to help Republicans win elections, with little interest in whether its claims were correct.

Kristol played a central role in shaping conservative foundations — earning him the nickname "the Godfather" of the right-wing foundation world — and his relativistic view dominated. The conservatives believed the center-left think tanks to be bastions of left-liberal ideology, so they set about to mimic the enemy as they imagined him. The established liberal think tanks strove to cleanse their work of ideological bias, but the conservatives regarded this as a pretense to be dispensed with. James Piereson, the executive director of the conservative Olin Foundation, has made this point with admirable candor. "I've always seen that whenever anybody calls the Ford Foundation 'liberal,' they resist being given that designation. I've always found it kind of odd," he said. "We don't resist being called conservative."[26]

Brookings, for instance, describes itself in its mission statement as "an independent, nonpartisan organization devoted to research, analysis, and public education." The conservative Heritage Foundation, on the other hand, declares that its "mission is to formulate and promote conservative public policies based on the principles of free enterprise, limited government, individual freedom, traditional American values, and a strong national defense."

A conservative might insist that this willingness to forthrightly admit ideological bias proves only that they have a lower capacity for self-deception than their liberal counterparts: both are biased, but only the conservatives admit it. This might make for a confounding objection if there was no other evidence of the asymmetrical relationship between left and right think tanks. Fortunately, self-admission is not all that we have to rely on. Andrew Rich, a political scientist at City College in New York, conducted a mail survey of more than a hundred state-based conservative and liberal think tanks. Three-quarters of the leaders of conservative think tanks listed political ideology as a very important, or the most important, quality they looked for in hiring staff; just over 40 percent of liberal think tank heads said the same thing. Liberal think tank heads, on the other hand, placed a higher premium on hiring candidates with advanced degrees. Conservative think tank leaders were far more likely to cite "influencing public opinion" as an important goal.

THE SAME LOPSIDED dynamic holds true in the case of journalism. On the left, you have a set of institutions steeped in a Progressive Era ethos of objectivity. On the right, you have a set of opposing institutions, founded in the conviction that their counterparts were hopelessly liberal and setting out to match the bias they perceived. One can have interesting arguments about whether, and to what degree, the *New York Times* and the network news tilt leftward in their coverage of politics. The best case conservatives make on this point is that these institutions cultivate a subconscious ideological bias that is manifest below the purportedly objective surface. On the other hand, the *Washington Times* and the Fox News Channel display a flagrant visible bias that no sentient observer could in good faith deny.*

THE MORE INTERESTING contrast is not between the news reporters of the mainstream media and their purportedly objective conservative peers but between liberal opinion journalists and con-

---

* The evidence on this point is massive and fairly well documented. In 1996, while still working as a Fox News anchor, Tony Snow endorsed Bob Dole for president in *Rising Tide*, a magazine published by the Republican National Committee (*New York*, November 17, 1997); Andrew Kirtzman interviewed for a job at Fox News and was asked about his party affiliation ("They were afraid I was a Democrat," he told the *Village Voice* on October 15, 1996). Those still needing persuasion should see the documentary *Outfoxed*, which, among other evidence, has memos from Fox managers describing how news stories ought to be spun.

servative opinion journalists. Most people, after all, realize that Fox News is not a neutral arbiter. Opinion journalism, on the other hand, appears — at least on the surface — to have a balance, with pundits on the left and the right. In fact, it shares the same asymmetrical character as the "balance" between liberal and conservative think tanks.

The institutions of conservative opinion journalism, like the conservative think tanks, were conceived as a counterweight to the perceived monolithic liberalism on the other side. Conservative pundits see themselves as members of a movement in a way that liberal pundits generally do not. "These days, conservatives and Republicans more often think of one another as members of the same team," confessed David Brooks in the *Weekly Standard* in 2001. "There is no longer a bright line separating the pool of conservative intellectuals and journalists from the pool of Republican officeholders. Now there is something of an expectation that activists, commentators, and rank and file conservatives should behave like Republican organization workers."[27]*

Conservative pundits are often indistinguishable from movement foot soldiers. They participate in Grover Norquist's weekly strategy meetings. In the late 1990s, John Fund served as a member of Gingrich's Speaker's Advisory Group even as he wrote editorials for the *Wall Street Journal*. In 2004, Tony Snow — then a Fox News commentator, and later Bush's press secretary — hosted an American Conservative Union dinner celebrating Bush.[28] Conservative intellectuals regularly find themselves subject to loyalty tests. It is considered newsworthy not when they accede but when they resist.

---

* Brooks immediately proceeded from this observation to write, "A similar transformation has occurred on the left — as the Lewinsky scandal made clear, when liberal groups universally betrayed their feminist principles to stand by their party leader." The implication that liberals' principles would normally compel support for impeaching a president for committing adultery is, obviously, absurd. It is typical, though, of a conservative mindset that resolutely insists its movement character merely reflects the same behavior on the other side.

For instance, David Brock, then a conservative, faced the wrath of the movement when his 1996 biography of Hillary Clinton, *The Seduction of Hillary Rodham*, took a less hostile view of its subject than his colleagues expected. Among other sanctions, Brock's invitation to a dinner party held by his fellow conservative Barbara Olsen was immediately revoked in explicit retribution. Nor was the step of debarring a writer from a movement dinner for intellectual heresy considered unusual. Tucker Carlson — himself one of the most independent conservative journalists — shrugged off the slight against Brock: "People get bumped off invite lists every day."[29] Only in the world of a Washington conservative — or, perhaps, a left-wing cell — would the application of a strict ideological litmus test to a dinner list be considered unremarkable.

The cultural spheres in which liberal and conservative opinion journalists operate could not be more different. If you're a conservative pundit, the worst thing that can happen to you is to be seen as currying favor with the liberal establishment. In 1997, for instance, Laura Ingraham — who by any sane standard would be considered a right-wing ideologue — wrote a *New York Times* op-ed piece suggesting that Republicans would have more success investigating Clinton if they replaced the widely ridiculed Dan Burton as head of the Government Reform and Oversight Committee. It was bad enough that Ingraham had attacked a conservative; what compounded the error was that she did so in the *Times* — the very thing a fainthearted conservative looking to get into the good graces of the coastal elites would do. The right-wing syndicated columnist Robert Novak dismissed her as a "so-called conservative." Norquist barred her from his weekly meetings, saying she had to choose "whether to be with us or against us."[30]

If you're a liberal opinion journalist, on the other hand, you're expected to maintain your ideological independence. Liberal opinion journalists tend to come out of the journalism world, unlike their conservative counterparts, who are more likely to rise up through the world of movement politics. As Nicholas Confessore observed in the *Washington Monthly,*

> Among pundits of the broad center-left, it's considered gauche to criticize the right too persistently, no matter the merits of one's argument. The only worse sin is to defend a politician too persistently; then you become not a bore, but a disgrace to the profession and its independence — even if you're correct. . . .
>
> That's because liberal journalists and conservative journalists have different value systems. Most liberal pundits — E. J. Dionne, Ronald Brownstein, or Maureen Dowd — came up through the newsroom ranks, a culture that demands shows of intellectual independence from politicians, especially Democrats. Many conservative pundits, on the other hand — [William] Safire, Tony Blankley, or Peggy Noonan — come straight from political careers, a culture that encourages intellectual fealty and indulges one-sidedness.

Liberal pundits obviously infuse their work with opinion but don't see themselves as belonging to a movement. In the world of liberal opinion journalism, the worst thing that can happen to you is to be seen as too close to the Democratic Party, or "in the tank."

The classic example of such a liberal is Sidney Blumenthal, who wrote for publications like the *New Republic* and the *New Yorker.* Blumenthal befriended Bill and Hillary Clinton and fiercely defended them. While serving as the *New Yorker's* chief Washington correspondent, he refused to write about Whitewater, which he considered (not wholly without reason) a trumped-up scandal. All this was, quite rightly, considered wildly improper even for an opinion journalist. The *New Yorker* removed him from his position, and he became a journalistic pariah. "Sid has certainly burned a lot of bridges by being so openly partisan on behalf of the Clintons," a friend of his observed to the *Washington Post.* And as the *New York Times* noted, "Blumenthal has had notoriously bad relations with many of his former colleagues in the Washington press who saw him as too close to the Clintons." In 1997, Blumenthal went to work for the White House, and the journalistic reaction was summed up by the *New York Observer*, which cracked that the "longtime cheerleader for Bill Clinton will now get paid by the White House for his boosterism." There was no graver sin, and Blumenthal's fate served as a warning to other liberals not to be seduced by partisanship.[31]

The Blumenthal saga is compelling not because we should necessarily admire him or even pity him — he did, indeed, grow too close to the Clintons — but because it demonstrates how deeply embedded the ethos of intellectual independence is in liberal journalism. The equivalent of what happened to Brock or Ingraham would be unimaginable for a liberal. Likewise, the equivalent of what happened to Blumenthal would be unimaginable for a conservative.

Conservative pundits defend themselves against the accusation of hackery by pointing out that they routinely attack Republicans. This is perfectly true. When they do so, however, it is almost always to flay some element of the party for straying from the conservative line. Many conservatives are eager to display their independence by taking sides in disputes among Republicans. On those issues that pit Republicans against Democrats, on the other hand, they offer monolithic and unqualified support for their party.

Now, given that conservatives tend to prefer the GOP over Democrats, one would naturally expect them to side with their party on most issues of the day, like the minimum wage or abortion rights. The way to separate genuine conservative principle from blind partisan loyalty is to set aside policy and look at debates over process. A huge proportion of the day-to-day squabbling between Democrats and Republicans centers on these sorts of issues: Is it appropriate for the president to formulate policy in secret? How obligated is the minority party to let the majority enact its program? Must the majority consult with the other side? These debates tend to be vast, squalid pits of hypocrisy: the two parties routinely flip sides on these questions as exigency demands. For instance, when Democrats hold the White House they decry the alarmingly high vacancy rate in the federal judiciary and demand that Congress confirm more judges while Republicans insist there are more than enough judges already. When Republicans take back the White House, the two sides flip positions immediately and seamlessly.

Conservative pundits, with only a very few exceptions, are notable for their supine willingness to join in this game and tailor their principles to the Republican need of the moment. During the Clinton administration, the *Wall Street Journal's* editorial page repeatedly flayed the White House for making recess appointments. (The term refers to the practice of installing federal officials, such as judges or prominent appointees, while Congress is out of session, thereby bypassing the need for congressional approval.) In one typical editorial, "Abusing the System," the *Journal* assailed recess appointments as a "brazen flouting of the Vacancies Act and Congress's authority to confirm nominees." The editors seemed to believe with genuine passion that the tattered Vacancies Act was all that stood between the fragile republic and incipient dictatorship. Yet, when George W. Bush assumed the presidency, the *Journal* immediately ceased this campaign against recess appointments. When it deigned to mention the issue at all, it was to urge Bush to make *more* recess appointments. ("President Bush will have the opportunity eventually to fill the board with recess appointments," cackled one editorial with evident glee and not a trace of fear for the safety of American democracy.)

One could go on without end about such flip-flops, but it would hardly prove that they don't go on in equal measure. The only way to settle the issue would be to conduct some sort of scientific test of these sorts of process debates and measure how often conservative versus liberal opinion journalists support their party's side. Fortunately for us, somebody did exactly that. In 2003, Michael Tomasky wrote a paper for Harvard's Kennedy School of Government in which he meticulously compared the two most prominent liberal editorial pages, those of the *New York Times* and the *Washington Post*, with their two most conservative counterparts, those of the *Wall Street Journal* and the *Washington Times.*

Tomasky's technique was to pair similar episodes across the administrations of Bill Clinton and George W. Bush — say, Clinton's 1993 budget versus Bush's 2001 budget, or Attorney General Janet Reno versus Attorney General John Ashcroft. Tomasky coded every editorial that appeared in the four newspapers as either supportive of the president, critical, or mixed. He found that conservative papers were somewhat more likely to criticize Clinton than liberal papers were to criticize Bush (89 to 67 percent). He found, more significantly, that conservative papers were more than twice as likely to praise Bush than liberal papers were to praise Clinton (77 to 36 percent).

This distinction was especially sharp on matters of process — the issues that smoke out the knee-jerk partisan. For instance, in 1993, Hillary Clinton faced criticism for holding her meetings to formulate a health care proposal in secret; eight years later, Dick Cheney faced criticism for doing the same with his energy task force. The *Wall Street Journal* and the *Washington Times* crusaded against Clinton's secrecy, publishing between them fifteen editorials, all unremittingly negative. The liberal editorials piled onto the secret meetings as well — the *New York Times* called them "unseemly, possibly illegal and wrong" — publishing five editorials, one of which was mixed and four unequivocally negative. When Cheney held his secret meetings, on the other hand, the dynamic was altogether different. The *New York Times* and *Washington Post* continued to uphold the principle of open meetings, publishing six editorials, five critical and one mixed. The conservative editorials, on the other hand, no longer cared very much about secret meetings. The two papers published a mere four editorials, of which just one was negative, one was mixed, and two were positive(!). The *Journal,* for instance, insisted that the General Accounting Office had no business "vetting the Bush Administration's energy proposals on behalf of the President's political opponents."[32]

TO BE SURE, the enforcers of dogma who patrol the conservative world do have their peers on the left. The difference is that the sectarians of the left have not monopolized liberal discourse the way sectarians of the right have monopolized conservatism's. Liberals do not have their own version of the Reagan cult because they lack any understanding of a transcendent doctrine of universal truth. Liberalism has its eager enforcers of ideological discipline, but they tend to reside in blogs or small lobbying outfits, far from the commanding heights. Liberals engage in a perpetual debate over whether the Democratic Party ought to move farther left or farther right. While conservatives debate tactical questions, none of them entertains the notion that the GOP has moved too far to the right. Their canon is beyond dispute; the only debates are over how best to implement it.

The blogs highlight the contrast between right and left. At first glance, liberal and conservative blogs appear similar. Liberal blogs exhibit classic paranoid and sectarian tendencies — thinking in Manichean terms, speaking in coded phrases understood only by fellow believers, and excommunicating ideological dissidents. Equally deranged discourse can be found on conservative blogs as well.

The telling disparity is how the blogs relate to the institutions that correspond with their side. Liberal bloggers maintain a state of intermittent warfare with important institutions in the liberal intellectual world and the Democratic Party. Conservative bloggers usually describe Republican leaders and conservative intellectuals in friendly, almost worshipful, terms. The rabid partisanship of the blogs represents a genuine wellspring of sentiment among the party bases. The difference is that this sentiment finds its satisfactory expression among the elite institutions of the right but remains excluded from the elite institutions of the left. The grassroots left has the same arms-length relationship with the liberal establishment and the Democratic Party that the grassroots right once had with the conservative establishment and the Republican Party: a sense of frustrated exclusion and betrayal masked by intermittent bouts of election-based tactical cooperation. In the short term, they want to help the party win. In the long term, they want to storm its gates and dethrone its fainthearted leaders.

BARNEY'S WORLD

Another way to look at the asymmetry between liberal and conservative commentators is to consider Fred Barnes, the executive editor of the *Weekly Standard* and a regular commentator on Fox News Channel. In the world of conservative commentary, perhaps only George Will enjoys more prestige.

Barnes is widely and eagerly read by political junkies for the same reason that *Pravda* was devoured by Kremlinologists: he faithfully reflects the thinking of the party leadership, whether or not it has anything to do with conservative principle. In December 2001, for instance, the Bush administration was soaring in opinion polls on the basis of a patriotic upsurge after September 11. It decided to use this political capital to pass through Congress a "stimulus bill," consisting in large part of permanent tax breaks for business favored by K Street long before September 11.[33] Tom Daschle, the Democratic Senate leader, was reluctant to cooperate, and Bush decided to launch a public relations campaign assailing Daschle for his lack of cooperation. As a White House official told the *Washington Times,* another faithful movement organ, "The orders came down from on high to start getting tougher [on Daschle]."[34]

Conservative opinion writers dutifully sprang into action, none more dutifully than Barnes. Barnes wrote a lengthy article laying into Daschle for failing to support Bush's domestic goals. Daschle's theory, Barnes explained disgustedly, was to offer unqualified support for Bush's foreign policy while resisting things like long-term business tax cuts or opening the Arctic Wildlife National Refuge for oil drilling. Barnes labeled this approach "crass maneuvering."

Obviously Daschle's tactic was inconvenient for Bush, who wanted to convert his then-enormous popularity on foreign affairs into victories on issues like taxes and the environment, where he had far less public support. Why, though, was it "crass maneuvering" for Daschle to support Bush in those areas where they agreed and oppose him in those where they did not? (Barnes waxed indignant that Daschle had "intervened to upset bipartisan cooperation." But of course Barnes, and other conservatives, were perfectly happy to upset bipartisan cooperation when it threatened to produce legislation they opposed.) Any search for a principle, conservative or otherwise, reinforcing Barnes's argument would have been futile. It simply represented the partisan mentality at its most simpleminded — when your party maneuvers for advantage it's skillful, when the other party does so it's crass.

Barnes goes beyond the normal conservative suppleness of principle in his willingness to jettison even what would appear to be his own deeply held beliefs. In early 2001, for example, he celebrated Bush's unstated plan to bring about "a breathtaking achievement in reducing the size and role of government." He approvingly quoted Bush's budget director, Mitch Daniels, who said that the administration's view of spending is simply "lower is better."

By the next year, it was clear that Bush was expanding the size and role of government. Barnes happily explained that Bush was a "big government conservative" and as such has "a relatively benign view of government." Barnes even cited Daniels, who this time told him that Bush wanted "a budget of big projects." Some conservatives may have gotten the impression that Bush had set out to reduce the size of government. Not at all, Barnes explained: "It's no secret that Bush has a more positive view of government than do most conservatives. He made that clear in the 2000 campaign."[35]

In the 1930s, communist fellow travelers wrote passionately in favor of Western intervention in World War II, only to then violently reverse themselves when the USSR signed its Nonaggression Pact with Germany and reverse themselves yet again when Germany broke the treaty. Barnes's dispatches have a similarly prostrate feel, and his intellectual pirouettes provide a regular dose of comedy. In 2006, Barnes wrote an op-ed piece urging Bush to make "a sweeping overhaul of his administration . . . it would give him a chance to escape the political doldrums that may otherwise doom his presidency through its final 34 months."[36] Bush spurned Barnes's advice and settled for more limited changes. Barnes then celebrated Bush's wisdom in spurning Barnes's most recent advice, even flagellating himself for his incorrect thinking:

> The changes are not likely to constitute a facelift that gives the Bush administration an entirely new look. Such a makeover would risk making the president appear desperate. A far-reaching transformation had been proposed — by me, anyway — as a way to rejuvenate the Bush presidency, shock the media and the political community, and dominate the news for weeks. Instead, Bolten is taking a more prudent, gradual and, in the cases of Rove and McClellan, sensible approach.[37]

One suspects that Bush, in his infinite wisdom and forbearance, forgave Barnes and welcomed him back into the fold.

To hold up Barnes as the very embodiment of conservative journalism would be unfair to the scribes of the right. While Barnes's partisan fealty is not wildly atypical of that of conservative pundits and (unlike Blumenthal) he has maintained a prestigious place among his peers, he does stand out for his slavish, almost canine devotion to the Republican Party. One measure of how Bush thinks of Barnes is the nickname he has given him: Barney. While this is obviously an intuitive play off Barnes's name, it is also the name Bush gave his pet dog, and given the obsequious nature of Barnes's writing, it is hard to dismiss this fact as pure coincidence.

THE OVERARCHING POINT here is that the partisanship of liberal pundits is constrained by some sense of professional detachment, while the partisanship of conservative pundits is not. The asymmetry is most apparent on debates over process. And, since political reporters take a far deeper interest in process than in policy, such disputes consume an enormous share of the narrative that emerges out of Washington.

The disposition of pundits doesn't matter very much when all of them line up along partisan lines. When one side turns against its own party, though, the effect can be overwhelming. When John Kerry contemplated delaying his formal acceptance of the 2004 Democratic nomination in order to avoid a massive financial disadvantage, or when Al Gore in 2000 sought to limit the vote recount in Florida to a handful of Democratic counties, liberal opinion-makers joined conservatives in condemning them. The Democratic candidates quickly reversed themselves under the pressure of an unmitigated hammering in the twenty-four-hour news cycle.

Democrats thus have less tactical flexibility, having to stay within the good graces of opinion-makers whose loyalty falls short of absolute. Republicans, so long as they stay loyal to the movement's core principles, enjoy almost limitless tactical flexibility. The result is yet another structural GOP advantage.

And, in general, the rightward tilt of the institutions in Washington has redefined the boundaries of what seems normal or correct. In every realm, the relationship between mainstream left and mainstream right is asymmetrical. The Heritage Foundation is not like the Brookings Institution. The *Weekly Standard* is not like the *New Republic*. The *Washington Times* and Fox News are not like the *Washington Post* and CNN. Mainstream liberals inhabit a world whose assumptions about philosophy and political tactics generally encourage moderation; mainstream conservatives inhabit a world in which all the cultural assumptions reward ideological and partisan fealty.

THE TITLE OF Stormer's book comes from the seventeenth-century English poet John Harington, who wrote, "Treason doth never prosper: what's the reason? / For if it prosper, none dare call it treason." Something similar could be said about radicalism. In the salons of establishment Washington it is an article of faith that America is a moderate country, and candidates adopting extreme ideas are doomed to failure. The trouble with this logic is that it's circular. Once ensconced in the debate, an idea is, by definition, no longer extreme.

The right's great triumph has been to take ideas once correctly considered absurd and make them seem normal. The perverse happenings we have seen in Washington are the result of an asymmetrical fight — between a moderate party and a radical one, between one party that clings to the social mores that once prevailed in the capital and another party that brushed them aside.

The ascent of the far right over the last few decades has shown that the conventional bromides are wrong. It may be comforting to believe that a party that veers too far from the center cannot win, and for a long time this was probably true. But it isn't true anymore. The forces that once held the center in place have corroded away.

CONCLUSION

PLUTOCRACY IN AMERICA

In February 2006, the conservative journal *Policy Review* published an essay that was shockingly heretical, though perhaps unintentionally so. In it, Carles Boix of the University of Chicago argued that there is a link between democracy and economic equality:

> In an unequal society, the majority resents its diminished status. It harbors the expectation of employing elections to drastically overturn its condition. In turn, the wealthy minority fears the outcome that may follow from free elections and the assertion of majority rule. As a result, it resorts to authoritarian institutions to guarantee its social and economic advantage.[1]

Of the many taboos that prevail among conservatives, the one forbidding any serious discussion of inequality is perhaps the strictest. Any forthright examination of this topic will lead one quickly to the realization that American society has been spreading apart rapidly for three decades and that Republican economic policies have without a doubt contributed mightily to this gulf. So conservatives usually ignore the subject of inequality, except perhaps to minimize its scale or importance.

Why, then, did *Policy Review,* which is published by the staunchly conservative Hoover Institution, open its pages to such apostasy? Well, it didn't intend to. Boix's essay (which was brilliant and widely discussed) concerned the inculcation of democracy *abroad* and did not deal directly with the United States. And the circumstances Boix envisioned — mainly, developing countries attempting a transition to democracy — are different from those in an advanced democracy. Americans, fortunately, do not have to worry about kleptocrats, political violence, and massive vote fraud.

But while Boix's theory may be less applicable to the United States than it is to the Third World, it is still *somewhat* true. Indeed, this theory offers an uncannily precise description of what has happened in American politics over the last thirty years, and it is exactly what this book has described. The first half showed how the rise of the supply-siders and the business lobbyists have turned the Republican Party into a kind of machine dedicated unwaveringly to protecting and expanding the wealth of the very rich. As it has pursued this goal ever more single-mindedly, the right has by necessity grown ever more hostile to majoritarian decision-making for the obvious reason that it's hard to enlist the public behind an agenda designed to benefit a tiny minority.

The second half of the book revealed how the old ways of conducting politics have broken down in the face of this onslaught. The mores of the old Washington establishment — the assumption of some basic intellectual goodwill on both sides, the focus on character over substance, the belief in compromise — all developed during an era when there were few ideological differences between the parties. The old ways may have done a decent job of safeguarding the national interest when the great moderate consensus prevailed, but they have proven unequal to the challenge of a more ideological time.

All this has happened at the same time as a massive increase in income inequality, which is exactly what Boix's theory would predict. In the same essay, Boix marvels at the fortunes amassed by autocratic ruling elites throughout history:

> In exchange for protection against bandits like themselves, rulers such as the Bourbons, the Tudors, or the Sauds seize an important part of their subjects' assets. For example, at the death of Augustus (14 A.D.), the top 1/10,000 of the Roman Empire's households received 1 percent of all income. In Mughal India around 1600 A.D., the top 1/10,000th received 5 percent of all income.

Presumably, readers looking at these numbers are supposed to gape in astonishment at the sheer inequity of those autocratic regimes. But the numbers are less astonishing when you compare them to those in the contemporary United States, which Boix does not. As of 2004, the top 1/10,000 Americans earned nearly 3 percent of the national income — a somewhat smaller share than that earned by the Mughal elite but several times higher than that enjoyed by the wealthiest Romans.[2]

Meanwhile, the gap between Americans and Mughals is closing rapidly. Since the late 1970s, the share of national income going to the top 1 percent has doubled. The share of the top 0.1 percent has tripled, and the share of the top 0.01 percent has quadrupled.[3] This gulf was widened precisely at the same time that the right, growing ever more plutocratic and suspicious of popular demands, was battering away at the culture of American democracy.

THE CURRENT PREDICAMENT is not altogether unfamiliar to America. A century ago, there were vast disparities in wealth and income, and the political system was dominated by a self-serving elite. What finally turned the tide was a wave of labor violence and radical activism, first around the turn of the century and again during the Great Depression. The business and political elite feared that capitalism itself was under siege and might not survive, and in time it embraced the palliative of moderate liberal reform in order to safeguard the free enterprise system.

The elite of that generation, like the elite of today, was conservative by temperament. But their conservatism meant something else — a sense of social responsibility, a commitment to preserving peace between economic classes. The conservatives of today, on the other hand, have redefined conservatism as an expression of their material self-interest, defined in the narrowest and most short-sighted terms. They have forgotten the lessons of their forebears, and if sanity is to be restored to our political order, they must relearn them.

NOTES

INTRODUCTION

1. David S. Broder, "The Phasing Out of Reaganism," *Washington Post*, January 12, 1983.
2. Charles L. Schultze, "The CEA: An Inside Voice for Mainstream Economics," *Journal of Economic Perspectives*, Summer 1996, 37.
3. Karlyn Bowman, "Gay Pride and Prejudice," *Washington Post*, June 11, 2006.
4. http://www.electionstudies.org/nesguide/toptable/tab4c_1.htm.

1. CHARLATANS AND CRANKS

1. Sidney Blumenthal, *The Rise of the Counter-Establishment* (New York: Perennial Library, 1988), 176–78.
2. Ibid., 186.
3. Irving Kristol, *Neoconservatism: The Autobiography of an Idea* (New York: Free Press, 1995), 35.
4. Blumenthal, *Rise of the Counter-Establishment*, 264.
5. Ron Suskind, *The Price of Loyalty: George W. Bush, the White House, and the Education of Paul O'Neill* (New York: Simon & Schuster, 2004), 291.
6. White House Press Releases, "Remarks by President Bush After Meeting with the Cabinet," news release, November 13, 2002. Federal News Service, "Press Gaggle with White House Spokesman Ari Fleischer," news release, February 7, 2002.
7. Austan Goolsbee, "Evidence on the High-Income Laffer Curve from Six Decades of Tax Reform." Paper presented at Brookings Panel on Economic Activity, September 1999.

8. *National Review,* "The Big Ugly," November 19, 1990.
9. Paul Krugman, *Peddling Prosperity* (New York: W. W. Norton, 1995), 85.
10. *The Economist,* "Cocktail-bar calculations," August 18, 2005.
11. N. Gregory Mankiw, *Principles of Economics* (New York: Dryden, 1998), 29–30.
12. Krugman, *Peddling Prosperity,* 88.
13. Robert L. Bartley, introduction to *The Way the World Works,* 3rd ed., by Jude Wanniski (Morristown, N.J.: Polyconomics, 1989), x–xiii.
14. Henry Allen, "George Gilder and the Capitalists' Creed," *Washington Post,* February 18, 1981.
15. George Gilder, *Wealth and Poverty,* 2nd ed. (San Francisco: ICS Press, 1993), 201, 27.
16. Allen, "George Gilder."
17. Gary Rivlin, "The Madness of King George," *Wired,* July 2002.
18. *American Spectator,* "George Gilder, More Is More!" June 2001.
19. Rivlin, "Madness of King George."
20. Joseph P. Kahn, "The Evolution of George Gilder," *Boston Globe,* July 27, 2005.
21. Gilder, *Wealth and Poverty,* 67–68.
22. Jude Wanniski, *The Way the World Works,* 3rd ed. (Morristown, N.J.: Polyconomics, 1989), 45–47.
23. Ibid., 157.
24. Blumenthal, *Rise of the Counter-Establishment,* 225.
25. Wanniski, fax quoted in Jonathan Chait, "Prophet Motive," *New Republic,* March 31, 1997.
26. Mike McNamee, "For Steve, They Kiss and Make Up," *Business Week,* February 26, 1996.
27. Wanniski, "Bush & Cheney Are Misinformed," Wanniski.com, March 25, 2002.
28. Robert Novak, introduction to *The Way the World Works,* 20th anniversary ed., by Jude Wanniski (Morristown, N.J.: Polyconomics, 1989), xi.
29. Kristol, *Neoconservatism,* 35. Irving Kristol, "American Conservatism 1945–1995: Thirtieth Anniversary Issue," *Public Interest,* September 1995.
30. George Gilder, "Inside the Supply Side," *New York Times,* November 23, 1980.
31. Lou Cannon, "Reagan Scales Down Plan for Patching Up Economy," *Washington Post,* September 10, 1980.
32. David Stockman, *The Triumph of Politics: How the Reagan Revolution Failed* (New York: Harper & Row, 1986), 13.
33. Bartley, characteristically, made both arguments in the same essay, oblivious to the contradiction. "In Mr. Reagan's words on how to curb a spendthrift government, 'We can lecture it about extravagance until we're blue in the face, or we can discipline it by cutting its allowance.' On the evidence so far, the success of this strategy has been, if by no means complete, greater than generally understood." In the same essay — in fact, in the previous paragraph — he wrote, "The deficit is a problem of spending, not of tax cuts."
34. Stephen Moore, "Are Supply-Siders All Washed Up?" *Wall Street Journal,* June 5, 1997.
35. Michael Ruby, "And Pigs May Sing," *U.S. News & World Report,* June 21, 1993.
36. Martin Feldstein, "Board of Contributors: Clinton's Plan to Wider Deficits," *Wall Street Journal,* February 23, 1993. Martin Feldstein, "Tax Rates and Human Behavior," *Wall Street Journal,* May 7, 1993.

37. Daniel J. Mitchell and John M. Olin Fellow, "The Impact of Higher Taxes: More Spending, Economic Stagnation, Fewer Jobs, and Higher Deficits," Heritage Foundation Reports, February 10, 1993. Newt Gingrich, interview by Bernard Shaw, *Inside Politics,* CNN, May 11, 1993.

38. Lawrence Kudlow, "The Seduction of the Fed," *Wall Street Journal,* March 8, 1993.

39. Brigid McMenamin, "Flight Capital," *Forbes,* February 28, 1995.

40. Lawrence Kudlow and Stephen Moore, "Economic Expansion Milestone," *Washington Times,* February 1, 2000.

41. Dinesh D'Souza, "How Reagan Reelected Clinton," *Forbes,* November 3, 1997.

42. *Wall Street Journal,* "The New Orthodoxy," October 5, 1990.

43. Larry Kudlow, "The Tax-Cut Battle Royale: This Is *the* Political Issue of the New Millennium," National Review Online, January 4, 2001.

44. Stephen Moore and James Carter, "Repeal the Clinton Tax Hike; Even He Admits He Raised Taxes Too Much," *Weekly Standard,* May 15, 2000. Lawrence Kudlow, "A Tax Cut Plan with Benefits All Around," *Washington Times,* August 31, 2000. Larry Kudlow, "Looking Up, Down the Road," *National Review,* May 30, 2001.

45. Martin Feldstein, testifying before the House Committee on Ways and Means, February 13, 2001.

46. Goolsbee, "Evidence on the High-Income Laffer Curve."

47. *Wall Street Journal,* "The Deficit Fig Leaf," March 17, 2003. Stephen Moore, "Real Tax Cuts Have Curves," *Wall Street Journal,* June 13, 2005.

2. THE SUM OF ALL LOBBIES

1. Jonathan Weisman, "Congress Weights Corporate Tax Breaks; Lawmakers Look to Help Manufacturing Sector While Averting Conflict Over Export Subsidy," *Washington Post,* October 14, 2003.

2. Jonathan Chait, "Company Man," *New Republic,* June 5, 2000.

3. Thomas B. Edsall, "House Majority Whip Exerts Influence by Way of K Street," *Washington Post,* May 17, 2005.

4. Jonathan Weisman, "Special-Interest Add-Ons Weight Down Tax-Cut Bill," *Washington Post,* April 19, 2004.

5. Edsall, "House Majority Whip Exerts."

6. David Wellna, "Corporate Tax Cut Bill Is Passed in the House After Only Two Hours of Debate," *Morning Edition,* National Public Radio, June 18, 2004.

7. Theodore Levitt, "The Johnson Treatment," *Harvard Business Review,* January–February 1967.

8. John B. Judis, *The Paradox of American Democracy* (New York: Routledge, 2001), 66, 101.

9. David Vogel, *Fluctuating Fortunes* (New York: Basic Books, 1989), 66–72.

10. Ibid., 68–72.

11. Ibid., 54.

12. Judis, *Paradox of American Democracy,* 116–18.

13. Irving Kristol, *Two Cheers for Capitalism* (New York: Mentor, 1978), 134.

14. Judis, *Paradox of American Democracy,* 112.

15. Thomas Byrne Edsall, *The New Politics of Inequality* (New York: W. W. Norton, 1984), 114.
16. Vogel, *Fluctuating Fortunes*, 194–99.
17. Edsall, *New Politics*, 128–29.
18. Thomas B. Edsall, "Right in the Middle of the Revolution; Activist Rises to Influence in Conservative Movement," *Washington Post*, September 4, 1995.
19. Richard Lacayo, reported by Jeffrey H. Birnbaum and Nina Burrleigh, "Newt's Cash Machine," *Time*, December 18, 1995.
20. Kathleen Day and Jim VandeHei, "Congressman Urges Republican Lobbyist; Oxley Staff Pressuring Mutual Funds," *Washington Post*, February 15, 2003.
21. Jeffrey H. Birnbaum, "Going Left on K Street; More Democrats Hired to Lobby Despite GOP Efforts to Shut Them Out," *Washington Post*, July 2, 2004. Brody Mullins, "Studios Take Hit in Tax Bill," *Roll Call*, October 7, 2004.
22. Michael Grunwald, "Trade Groups in Lock Step Behind Bush Energy Policy," *Washington Post*, May 30, 2001.
23. David S. Hilzenrath, "SEC Chief: 'Gentler' Agency; Pitt Reaches Out to Accountants," *Washington Post*, October 23, 2001. David S. Hilzenrath, "Two SEC Views of Industry; Ex-Head Levitt Attacked; New Chief Pitt Vows Respect," *Washington Post*, December 5, 2001.
24. Jacob M. Schlesinger, "Treasury's O'Neill Quietly Tests a Number of Clinton-Era Policies," *Wall Street Journal*, June 21, 2001.
25. Joseph Kahn, "Bush Advisers on Energy Report Ties to Industry," *New York Times*, June 3, 2001. Lowell Bergman and Jeff Gerth, "Power Trader Tied to Bush Finds Washington All Ears," *New York Times*, May 25, 2001. Jonathan Cohn, "Toxic," *New Republic*, December 23, 2002.
26. Jeffrey H. Birnbaum and Jim VandeHei, "DeLay's Influence Transcends His Title," *Washington Post*, October 3, 2005.
27. Jim VandeHei, "GOP Whip Quietly Tried to Aid Big Donor; Provision Was Meant to Help Philip Morris," *Washington Post*, June 11, 2003.
28. Kate Ackley and Paul Kane, "Senate, House Jointly Whip K Street," *Roll Call*, April 12, 2002.
29. Clark Clifford, *Counsel to the President: A Memoir* (New York: Random House, 1991), quoted in Michael Kinsley, "Mr. Fix-it," *New Republic*, April 22, 1991.
30. Tony Blankley, "Keep DeLay or Pay the Price," *Washington Times*, April 13, 2005.
31. John B. Judis, "Tammany Fall," *New Republic*, June 20, 2005.
32. Charles Grassley, "Farm Safety Net Unraveling for Family Farmers," Congressional Press Releases, May 13, 2002.
33. *New Republic*, "Down on the Farm," Notebook, February 25, 2002.
34. Laurence Zuckerman, "U.S. Takes Big Role in Airlines' Crisis," *New York Times*, October 4, 2001.
35. Amy Goldstein, "Medicare Bill Would Enrich Companies; $125 Billion More for Employers, Health Firms," *Washington Post*, November 24, 2003.
36. Louis Jacobson and Peter H. Stone, "Trying Times for Tom Scully," *National Journal*, April 10, 2004.
37. Dan Morgan, "Nursing a Fragile Energy Bill; Protection for Fuel-Additive Makers a Sticking Point in Senate," *Washington Post*, November 24, 2003.

38. Thomas Friedman, "Too Much Pork and Too Little Sugar," *New York Times*, August 5, 2005.

39. *Wall Street Journal*, "GOP Spending Spree," January 20, 2004.

40. *National Review*, "The Endorsement," November 8, 2004.

41. Kristol, *Two Cheers*, 171–77.

42. Robert L. Bartley, "Business and the New Class," *The New Class?* ed. B. Bruce-Briggs (New Brunswick, N.J.: Transaction Books, 1979), 65.

43. Robert Hahn and Scott Wallsten, "Bring the President's Nerds Back In from the Cold," *Financial Times* (London), October 30, 2003.

44. Ron Suskind, *The Price of Loyalty: George W. Bush, the White House, and the Education of Paul O'Neill* (New York: Simon & Schuster, 2004), 170–71.

45. Robert Novak, "Still Logrolling for Pork," *Washington Post*, June 19, 2006.

46. Christopher Rowland, "Medicare Bill a Study in D.C. Spoils System," *Boston Globe*, October 5, 2004.

47. David Pace, "Billions in Federal Spending Shifted to GOP Districts After 1994," Associated Press, August 5, 2002.

48. David E. Rosenbaum, "At $500 an Hour, Lobbyist's Influence Rises with G.O.P.," *New York Times*, April 3, 2002.

49. Michael Crowley, "A Lobbyist in Full," *New York Times*, May 1, 2005.

50. Jack Abramoff, e-mail to Daniel Lapin, September 15, 2000, included in exhibits released by Senate Committee on Indian Affairs, *Oversight Hearing on In Re Tribal Lobbying Matters, June 22, 2005, Part I*, 109th Cong., 1st sess., 43.

51. Crowley, "A Lobbyist."

52. Ryan Lizza, "The Insider," *New Republic*, July 30, 2001.

53. Mike Soraghan, "Norton Assailed for Clearing Aide Senator: Secretary Ignore Troubling Facts About Griles," *Denver Post*, May 2, 2004. Susan Schmidt, "Abramoff Cited Aid of Interior Official; Conflict-of-Interest Probe Is Under Way," *Washington Post*, August 28, 2005.

54. Michelle Cottle, "Cajun Dressing," *New Republic*, October 6, 2003.

55. Morton M. Kondracke, "Tauzin Denies Charge He Sought Job While Working on Drug Bill," *Roll Call*, March 6, 2006.

56. US Fed News, "Rep. Barton Issues Statement on Signing of Energy Policy Act of 2005," August 8, 2005.

57. Brody Mullins, "Reliant's Power Connection on Capitol Hill," *Wall Street Journal*, August 4, 2005.

3. DRIVING OUT THE HERETICS

1. Peter Kirsanow, "Shining Countenance on a Hill," *National Review*, June 10, 2004.

2. Anthony Ramirez, "Will the Gipper Ever Get a Piece of the Rock?" *New York Times*, February 11, 2001.

3. Social Security Administration Online, "Popular Baby Names," updated May 12, 2006, http://www.ssa.gov/OACT/babynames/.

4. Michael Mechanic, "Sugarcoating Reagan," *Mother Jones*, March 1, 2001.

5. Dinesh D'Souza, "Divided Parties; Reagan's Misguided Heirs Forget What He Stood For," *Washington Post*, November 23, 1997.

6. Peggy Noonan, "Why Did They Do It?" *Wall Street Journal,* April 24, 2000.
7. Craig Shirley, "How the GOP Lost Its Way," *Washington Post,* April 22, 2006. *Wall Street Journal,* "Reagan on Immigration," May 16, 2006.
8. Stephen Moore and James Carter, "GOP Budget Still Geared for Spending," *Washington Times,* March 24, 1999.
9. William Kristol, "Remember Tax Cuts?" *Weekly Standard,* July 4–11, 2005.
10. Ron Suskind, *The Price of Loyalty: George W. Bush, the White House, and the Education of Paul O'Neill* (New York: Simon & Schuster, 2004), 291.
11. John W. Sloan, *Eisenhower and the Management of Prosperity* (Lawrence: University Press of Kansas, 1991), 61–65.
12. *National Review,* March 21, 1956, quoted in John B. Judis, *William F. Buckley, Jr.: Patron Saint of the Conservatives* (New York: Simon & Schuster, 1988), 136.
13. Sherman Adams, *First Hand Report: The Inside Story of the Eisenhower Administration* (London: Hutchinson, 1962), 135.
14. Joan Hoff, *Nixon Reconsidered* (New York: Basic Books, 1994), 115–32.
15. *National Review,* "Has Reagan Deserted the Conservatives?" April 20, 1982.
16. Heritage Foundation Policy Review 1984.
17. *Washington Times,* "Reaganomics," June 9, 2004.
18. Walter Isaacson, "Scoring on a Reverse: With Blocking from the Democrats, Reagan Wins Another Showdown," *Time,* August 30, 1982.
19. Jim Luther, "Paying No Federal Income Tax," AP, October 5, 1984.
20. Donald Regan, *For the Record: From Wall Street to Washington* (New York: Harcourt, 1988), 212–13, quoted in Lou Cannon, *President Reagan: The Role of a Lifetime* (New York: Public Affairs, 1991), 499–500.
21. Cannon, *President Reagan,* 489–500.
22. Ramesh Ponnuru, "The Perils of Tax Reform," *National Review,* December 13, 2004.
23. Jeffrey H. Birnbaum and Alan S. Murray, *Showdown at Gucci Gulch* (New York: Vintage Books, 1988), 200.
24. Bruce Bartlett, "Bush's High Five," National Review Online, February 10, 2003.
25. Rowland Evans and Robert Novak, *Washington Post,* February 5, 1982, quoted in Paul Craig Roberts, *The Supply-Side Revolution* (Cambridge, Mass.: Harvard University Press, 1984), 202–3.
26. Roberts, *Supply-Side Revolution,* 4.
27. Cannon, *President Reagan,* 225.
28. George W. Bush, interviewed by Brit Hume, Fox News Network, full text online: http://www.foxnews.com/story/0,2933,98006,00.html, September 22, 2003.
29. David Stockman, *The Triumph of Politics* (New York: Harper & Row, 1986), 81.
30. Kenneth M. Duberstein, "Reagan's Second-Half Comeback," *New York Times,* November 2, 2005. Jennifer Loven, "Unlike Previous Administrations, Core of Bush White House Staff Remains Largely Intact After 5 Years," AP, December 30, 2005.
31. Fred Barnes, "The Gergen Temptation; Will Bush Fall for the Advice of the Establishment?" *Weekly Standard,* November 14, 2005.
32. Cannon, *President Reagan,* 78–93.
33. Richard Darman, *Who's in Control?* (New York: Simon & Schuster, 1996), 272–73.
34. Helen Dewar and Tom Kenworthy, "Conservative Republicans Assail Budget Pact; Democrats Skeptical," *Washington Post,* October 1, 1990.

35. Robert MacKay, "Tax Hike? Tax Reform? Tax 'Correction,'" UPI, August 23, 1982.
36. Elaine S. Povich, "Congress Gives Final Budget Approval," *Chicago Tribune,* October 28, 1990.
37. John King, "Tax Opposition Unifies Republicans, But Risks Obstructionist Image," AP, August 9, 1993.
38. John Cassidy, "The Ringleader," *New Yorker,* August 1, 2005.
39. Darman, *Who's in Control?* 35–39, 195–97.
40. Daniel J. Mitchell, "Darman's Disaster — Bush's Responsibility," *National Review,* December 17, 1990. *National Review,* "Darmageddon," November 10, 1990.
41. John Harwood, "Dad's Adviser Darman Is Far from Inner Circle," *Wall Street Journal,* August 2, 2000.
42. David Frum, *Dead Right* (New York: Basic Books, 1994), 8.
43. Thomas B. Edsall, "GOP's Line of Succession Leads to Dole; 'I'm Willing to Be Another Ronald Reagan,' Front-Runner Tells RNC," *Washington Post,* July 16, 1995.
44. *Wall Street Journal,* "Bob Doe, Optimist," August 6, 1996.
45. Grover G. Norquist, "Happy Kempers," *American Spectator,* October 1996.
46. Donald Lambro, "Clues to Misguided Campaign Strategies," *Washington Times,* November 7, 1996.
47. Fred Barnes, "Bush Scalia," *Weekly Standard,* July 5–12, 1999.
48. Cal Thomas, "George W. as Reagan III," *Washington Times,* November 28, 1999.
49. Robert L. Bartley, "Checking In with the Frontrunner," *Wall Street Journal,* December 1, 1999. *Wall Street Journal,* "The Right Direction," December 1, 1999.
50. Ed Kilgore, "Starving the Beast," *Blueprint,* June 30, 2003.
51. Julie Kosterlitz, "The Ownership Society," *National Journal,* January 24, 2004.
52. Richard Leiby, "The Reliable Source," *Washington Post,* November 4, 2004.
53. Bob Thompson, "Sharing the Wealth?" *Washington Post,* April 13, 2003.
54. Jacob Weisberg, "The Conintern," *Slate,* June 29, 1997.
55. Nina J. Easton, *Gang of Five* (New York: Simon & Schuster, 2000), 360.
56. Ibid., 276–79.
57. Cassidy, "The Ringleader."
58. Easton, *Gang of Five,* 399.
59. Ramesh Ponnuru, "Our Enemy, The States," *National Review,* April 11, 2005. Cassidy, "The Ringleader."
60. Dale Russakoff, "Alabama Tied in Knotts by Tax Vote; Riley Stuns GOP by Stumping for Hike," *Washington Post,* August 17, 2003.
61. John Maggs, "Grover at the Gate," *National Journal,* October 11, 2003.
62. Louis Jacobson, "Anti-Tax Cry: Crush the Heretic!" *National Journal,* September 6, 2003.
63. Adam Nagourney and Janet Elder, "Bush's Backing, Still Strong, Shows Steady Decline," *New York Times,* January 24, 2003. Adam Nagourney and Janet Elder, "Americans Show Clear Concerns on Bush Agenda," *New York Times,* November 23, 2004.
64. Pew Research Center, "Beyond Red vs. Blue," May 10, 2005.
65. Ibid.
66. Irwin M. Stelzer, "War on the Cheap," *Weekly Standard,* September 5–12, 2005.
67. Thomas B. Edsall, "Right in the Middle of the Revolution; Activist Rises to Influence in Conservative Movement," *Washington Post,* September 4, 1995.

68. Jesus of Nazareth, "Sermon on the Mount" (speech, delivered in mountainous region near Galilee, c. A.D. 30).

69. *Washington Post,* The U.S. Congress Votes Database.

70. Jeffrey Rosen, "Stare Decisis," *New Republic,* September 19, 2005.

71. Adam Nagourney and Janet Elder, "Nation's Direction Prompts Voters' Concern, Poll Finds," *New York Times,* March 16, 2004. Pam Belluck, "Maybe Same-Sex Marriage Didn't Make the Difference," *Washington Post,* November 7, 2004.

72. Jim VandeHei and Michael A. Fletcher, "Bush Says Election Ratified Iraq Policy; No U.S. Troop Withdrawal Date Is Set," *Washington Post,* January 16, 2005.

73. John F. Harris and Dana Milbank, "Details Cloud Support for Social Security Plan," *Washington Post,* December 22, 2004.

74. The estimate comes from Brian Riedl, a budget analyst for the Heritage Foundation. Riedl, of course, has not drawn from this fact the conclusion that the 1990 budget deal worked; rather, he cited it only to bemoan the paucity of current efforts to cut spending.

75. King, "Tax Opposition."

76. Carl Hulse, "Messy Congressional Finale," *New York Times,* December 23, 2005.

77. Jonathan E. Kaplan, "No Pay-Go on Tax Cuts: House GOP," *The Hill,* May 19, 2004.

78. Jonathan Rauch, "Stoking the Beast," *Atlantic,* June 2006. Sebastian Mallaby, "Don't Feed the Beast; Bush Should End This Tax Cut Myth," *Washington Post,* May 8, 2006.

79. Jonah Goldberg, "Tax Cuts & Revenues," The Corner, National Review Online, May 8, 2006.

80. Jonathan Chait, "This Man Is Not a Republican," *New Republic,* January 31, 2000.

81. Ibid.

82. Eric Pooley, James Carney, John F. Dickerson, and John Cloud, "Giving McCain the Boot?" *Time,* February 7, 2000.

83. *Washington Times,* "Class Warfare Hits GOP," January 18, 2000.

84. Donald Lambro, "McCain's Compass," *Washington Times,* February 10, 2000.

85. *Los Angeles Times,* "Campaign 2000: Ad Watch: A Look at the Candidates' Commercials," February 26, 2000. Sean Scully, "McCain Cloaks Himself in Reagan's Mystique; Senator, However, Violates Former President's '11th Commandment,'" *Washington Times,* March 6, 2000.

86. Edmund L. Andrews, "Bush Budget Plan Would Eliminate Tax on Dividends," *New York Times,* January 6, 2003.

87. Robert Novak, "McCain and Taxes," *Pittsburgh Tribune Review,* September 6, 2005.

88. Donald Lambro, "After Flips, Will McCain Flop?" *Washington Times,* March 6, 2006.

89. Ramesh Ponnuru, "The Full McCain: An Interview," *National Review,* March 5, 2007.

90. Robert Novak, "McCain Inc.?" *Washington Post,* December 14, 2006.

4. THE NECESSITY OF DECEIT

1. FDCH Political Transcripts, "President George W. Bush Addresses a Joint Session of Congress," February 27, 2001.

2. Will Lester, "Poll: Public More Enthusiastic About Bush Than His Tax Cut," AP, February 22, 2001.
3. *Newsweek*, "Recession Anxiety Takes Hold," *Newsweek* Web Exclusive, March 17, 2001. *Hotline*, "Gallup: Bush Job at 56 percent," May 16, 2001.
4. Michelle Davis, e-mail to Paul O'Neill, February 27, 2001, "Re: Tomorrow's Press Conference Unveiling the Budget," made available online by Ron Suskind, "The Price of Loyalty: The Bush Files," http://thepriceofloyalty.ronsuskind.com/thebushfiles/archives/000058.html.
5. Andrew Sullivan, "Downsize," *New Republic*, May 14, 2001.
6. Kevin Phillips, *The Emerging Republican Majority* (New York: Arlington House, 1969), 287.
7. James A. Stimson, professor of political science, Univ. of North Carolina at Chapel Hill. Graph can be found at www.unc.edu/~jstimson.
8. Juliet Eilperin and Dan Morgan, "Something Borrowed, Something Blue," *Washington Post*, March 9, 2001.
9. Karen Gullo, "Bush, Cheney, Wrap Up Train Tour of Swing States," AP, August 7, 2000. Mary Matalin, interviewed by Bernard Shaw, *Inside Politics*, CNN, February 27, 2001.
10. White House Press Releases, "President Discusses Homeland Security and the Economy with Cabinet," news release, November 13, 2002. White House Press Releases, "Remarks by President Bush After Meeting with the Cabinet," news release, November 13, 2002.
11. Mitch Daniels, interviewed by Ted Koppel, *Nightline*, ABC News, February 27, 2001.
12. White House Press Releases, "President Discusses New Economic Numbers and Middle East," news release, April 26, 2002.
13. Mike Allen, "Card Sees 'Cloud' over U.S. Economy," *Washington Post*, March 25, 2001.
14. William Kristol, "Back to Basics," *Weekly Standard*, October 3, 2005.
15. FDCH Political Transcripts, "Governor George W. Bush (R-TX) Delivers Acceptance Speech at Republican National Convention," August 3, 2000. FDCH Political Transcripts, "George W. Bush Addresses African-American Leaders," March 29, 2001.
16. Richard Armey, *Flat Tax* (Westminster, Md.: Ballantine Books, 1996).
17. Robert E. Hall and Alvin Rabushka, *Low Tax, Simple Tax, Flat Tax* (New York: McGraw-Hill, 1983), 67, 58.
18. David E. Rosenbaum, "With a Passion for Tax Cuts, and in Power," *New York Times*, April 4, 1995. William March, "Presidential Hopefuls Experienced Life on Dole," *Tampa Tribune*, July 23, 1995.
19. Tony Snow, "The Tax Cut Tinkerers," *Washington Times*, February 11, 2001.
20. John Cassidy, "The Ringleader," *New Yorker*, August 1, 2005.
21. Bill Archer, "Cutting Taxes Will Be Harder the Next Time," *Wall Street Journal*, May 29, 2001.
22. Steven R. Weisman, *The Great Tax Wars* (New York: Simon & Schuster, 2002), 136.
23. Arthur M. Okun, *Equality and Efficiency: The Big Tradeoff* (Washington, D.C.: Brookings Institution Press, 1975).
24. Richard L. Berke, "Clinton Rebuffed on Plan to Reduce Election Spending," *New York Times*, February 4, 1993.

25. Citizens for Tax Justice, www.ctj.org.
26. Jonathan Chait, "A Very Special Kind of Math," *Los Angeles Times*, April 29, 2005.
27. Ibid.
28. Glenn Kessler, "Tax Cut Debate's Division Problem," *Washington Post*, May 17, 2001.
29. Dana Milbank, "Tax Cut Statistics Disputed; White House Rejects Conclusion That Rich Are Favored," *Washington Post*, March 2, 2001.
30. Elizabeth Bumiller, "Bush Pushes Tax Cut as Small-Business Aid," *New York Times*, January 23, 2003. *New York Times*, "High-Stakes Politics: The Race to Rule the Nation," February 18, 2001.
31. Scott Lindlaw, "President's Stump Speech Gets Constant Adjustment in Campaign's Final Days," AP, October 30, 2004.
32. Dana Milbank, "Official Work for the Politician in Chief," *Washington Post*, April 28, 2001.
33. *Wall Street Journal*, "Fat-Cat Calvary Rides in to Rescue High Taxes," February 16, 2001.
34. Jonathan Chait, "Oh, Now That's Rich!" *Los Angeles Times*, October 1, 2004.
35. Larry Kudlow, "Crossing the Tax-Cut Aisle," *National Review Online*, January 22, 2001.
36. Jim Saxton, press release, "New Study Shows Why Tax Distribution Should Not Drive Tax Policy," study, December 19, 2003.
37. E. J. Dionne, Jr., and Thomas B. Edsall, "Bush Caught Between Conflicting Constituencies," *Washington Post*, October 20, 1990.

5. MEDIA: THE DOG THAT DIDN'T WATCH

1. Kurt Andersen, "The '80s: The Decade That Wouldn't End," The Breakfast Table: Kurt Andersen and Nora Ephron, *Slate*, September 15, 1999.
2. Frank Rich, "Journal; J. Crew vs. Banana Republic," *New York Times*, March 11, 2000.
3. Joe Klein, "Grand New Party," Talk of the Town, *New Yorker*, August 14, 2000.
4. "Bottom-Line Pressures Now Hurting Coverage, Journalists Say," Pew Research Center for People and the Press, May 23, 2004. "National Survey of the Role of Polls in Policymaking," Henry J. Kaiser Family Foundation in collaboration with *Public Perspective*, June 2001. Paul S. Voakes, "The Newspaper Journalists of the '90s," American Society of Newspaper Editors, October 31, 1997.
5. Dana Milbank, "Boehner Makes His Political Comeback," *Washington Post*, February 3, 2006.
6. Alfred M. Landon, "I Will Not Promise the Moon," Milwaukee, Wisconsin, October 15, 1936.
7. Steven Thomma, "Social-Security Overhaul Is Longstanding Conservative Dream," Knight Ridder/Tribune News Service, February 6, 2005.
8. Peter J. Ferrara and Michael D. Tanner, *A New Deal for Social Security* (Washington, D.C.: Cato Institute, 1998).
9. Glenn Kessler, "Paving the Way for Privatizing Social Security," *Washington Post*, June 26, 2001.

10. Dick Durbin, interviewed by Tim Russert, *Meet the Press*, NBC News, March 6, 2005.

11. Ted Koppel, interviewed by Larry King, *Larry King Live*, CNN, October 4, 2000.

12. Michael Scherer, "The Making of the Corporate Judiciary," *Mother Jones*, November 1, 2003.

13. "Presidential Candidates Al Gore and George W. Bush Debate Foreign and Domestic Issues," NBC News Decision 2000: Presidential Debates, NBC News Transcripts, October 17, 2000.

14. Sam Donaldson, *This Week*, ABC News, October 22, 2000.

15. Dan Balz, "Stands on Education Cost GOP Among Women, Governors Told," *Washington Post*, November 27, 1996.

16. "In His Own Words," *National Review*, December 31, 1999.

17. "Clinton's Challenges of '92 Confront Bush Today," *USA Today*, April 4, 2000.

18. "A Question of Character: How the Media Have Handled the Issue and How the Public Has Reacted," Project for Excellence in Journalism and Pew Research Center for the People and the Press, September 2000. Jane Hall, "Gore Media Coverage: Playing Hardball," *Columbia Journalism Review*, September/October 2000.

19. James Carney, "Faith of His Father," *Time*, August 2, 1999.

20. James Carney, "The Bush Tax Tango," *Time*, August 9, 1999.

21. Eric Pianin and Terry M. Neal, "Bush to Offer $483 Billion Tax-Cut Plan," *Washington Post*, December 1, 1999.

22. Jackie Calmes, "Bush's Big Income-Tax-Cut Plan Lowers Rates from Top to Bottom," *Wall Street Journal*, December 1, 1999.

23. Lou Waters, *CNN Today*, CNN, December 1, 1999.

24. David Bloom, "George W. Bush Outlines His Tax Cut Plan if Elected," NBC Nightly News, December 1, 1999.

25. Robert Pear, "The President's Budget: The Overview; First Bush Budget Proposes to Raise Aid for Education," *New York Times*, April 10, 2001.

26. Carolyn Skorneck, "Conferees Agree on AIDS Funds, Move Closer to Deal on Aid Spending Bill," *Congressional Quarterly*, November 21, 2003.

27. Lisa Cox Barrett, "Jim Lehrer on Billy Bob, Reports of Rain and Stenography as Journalism," *CJR Daily*, June 2, 2006.

28. Adam Clymer, "Americans Reject Big Medicare Cuts, a New Poll Finds," *New York Times*, October 26, 1995.

29. Michael Weisskopf and David Maraniss, "Republican Leaders Win Battle by Defining Terms of Combat," *Washington Post*, October 29, 1995.

30. Ibid.

31. Adam Clymer, "An Impasse of Bipartisan Appeal," *New York Times*, January 14, 1996.

32. Kevin Sack, "Public Hospitals Around Country Cut Basic Service," *New York Times*, August 20, 1995.

33. Ronald Brownstein, "Clinton's Target Audience: Married, with Children," *Los Angeles Times*, June 13, 1996.

34. John F. Harris, "Clinton Pulls Punches; Ads Land Them," *Washington Post*, September 11, 1996.

35. Decision 2000 Debate Coverage, NBC News, October 3, 2000.

36. Burt Solomon, "Militant Moderates," *National Journal*, October 7, 2000.
37. David E. Rosenbaum, "Doing the Math on Bush's Tax Cut," *New York Times*, March 4, 2001.
38. David Noonan et al., "A Voter's Panic Guide," *Newsweek*, November 6, 2000.
39. Calvin Woodward, "A Forgotten Timber Concern and Other Casualties in Factual Claims of Bush-Kerry Debate," AP, October 9, 2004.
40. Judy Woodruff, Inside Politics, CNN, October 6, 2004.
41. Richard W. Stevenson, "Steady on the Right, Bush Pitches to the Center," *New York Times*, September 6, 2004.

6. HOW WASHINGTON IMAGINES CHARACTER

1. Julie Hirschfeld Davis and David L. Green, "Voters Opting for Bush in Two Battleground States; Many Say the President Is the 'Lesser of Two Evils,'" *Baltimore Sun*, September 13, 2004.
2. Dan Balz and Vanessa Williams, "Poll Shows Bush with Solid Lead; Despite Worries, Voters Cite Lack of Clarity from Kerry," *Washington Post*, September 28, 2004.
3. Adam Nagourney and Janet Elder, "Poll Shows Tie; Concerns Cited on Both Rivals," *New York Times*, October 19, 2004.
4. Ronald Brownstein, "The Times Poll; Voters Still Split Sharply, and Evenly," *Los Angeles Times*, October 26, 2004.
5. CNN, "The World Today," September 22, 2000.
6. R. W. Apple, Jr., "The Democrats: The Contest; Retooled Lieberman Sticks by Master," *New York Times*, August 17, 2000.
7. *Newsweek* poll conducted by Princeton Survey Research Associates, October 18–20, 2000.
8. Fox News/Opinion Dynamics poll, August 9–10, 2000.
9. Dan Quayle, speech, Fort Worth, Texas, September 23, 1992.
10. George H. W. Bush, second presidential debate in Richmond, Virginia, October 15, 1992. Ruth Marcus, "For Bush, a Breakfast of Champions Is a Dish Dripping with Symbolism," *Washington Post*, October 22, 1992.
11. George J. Church, "Questions, Questions, Questions," *Time*, April 20, 1992.
12. Michael Kelly, "The Matter of Trust: Clinton's Big Burden," *New York Times*, October 18, 1992.
13. Ronald Brownstein, "Clinton Maintains Lead; Fight for Congress Is Tight," *Los Angeles Times*, October 29, 1996.
14. Richard Hofstadter, *Anti-Intellectualism in American Life* (New York: Random House, 1963), 158–60.
15. Ibid., 226–27.
16. Jeane Kirkpatrick, speech to the Republican National Convention, Dallas, Texas, August 20, 1984. Myron S. Waldman, "Bush: Dukakis Is Product of Elitism," *Newsday*, June 11, 1988.
17. Larry Rohter, "Unrepentant, Marilyn Quayle Fights for Family and Values," *New York Times*, October 28, 1992.
18. George H. W. Bush, speech, Enid, Oklahoma, September 17, 1992.

19. Rich Lowry, "Al Gore, Pointy Head," *National Review Online*, www.na tionalreview.com/lowry/lowry101100.shtml, October 11, 2000.

20. Ben Stein, *Imus in the Morning*, WFAN-AM, October 6, 2000.

21. Adam Nagourney and Richard W. Stevenson, "Bush's Aides Plan Late Sprint in '04," *New York Times*, April 22, 2003.

22. Naomi Wolf, "Female Trouble," *New York*, September 27, 2004.

23. George W. Bush, first presidential debate, Boston, Massachusetts, October 3, 2000.

24. Daniel Walker Howe, *The Political Culture of the American Whigs* (Chicago: University of Chicago Press, 1984), 85–91. Robert Vincent Remini, *The House: A History of the House of Representatives* (New York: HarperCollins, 2006), 236.

25. Larry J. Sabato, "Media Frenzies in Our Time," *Washington Post*, www.washingtonpost.com/wp-srv/politics/special/clinton/frenzy/frenzy.htm, March 27, 1998.

26. Rush Limbaugh, interviewed by Ted Koppel, *Nightline*, ABC News, April 19, 1994.

27. Paul Baskin, "Poll Boosts Clinton Health Plan Supporters," UPI, March 10, 1994.

28. Alison Mitchell, "House Republicans, in a Shift of Focus, Begin a Public Campaign Against Gore," *New York Times*, May 19, 1999.

29. Michael Duffy, "What It Took," *Time*, November 20, 2000.

30. Richard L. Berke, "Tendency to Embellish Fact Snags Gore," *New York Times*, October 6, 2000.

31. Nancy Phillips, "Democrats Join Town Meeting," *Philadelphia Inquirer*, August 12, 2003. Brit Hume, Political Grapevine, *Special Report with Brit Hume*, Fox News Network, August 12, 2003.

32. Dana Milbank, "Steak Raises Stakes for Kerry in Philly," *Washington Post*, August 13, 2003.

33. George W. Bush, speech, Ridley Park, Pennsylvania, August 17, 2004.

34. Kathleen E. Carey, "Essington Eatery Fills Executive Food Order," *Daily Times* (Delaware County, Pa.), August 18, 2004.

35. "Gore's Summer Surprise," *Newsweek*, November 20, 2000.

36. Richard L. Berke, "Democrats See, and Smell, Rats in G.O.P. Ad," *New York Times*, September 12, 2000.

37. Jack W. Germond, *Fat Man Fed Up* (New York: Random House, 2004), 207–10.

38. Michael Powell, "Forbes Reveals Little but His Ideas," *Washington Post*, November 12, 1999.

39. John Harwood, "Kerry's Early Win! Narrowing the Gap in Fund Raising," *Wall Street Journal*, May 26, 2004.

40. David Brooks, "The Responsibility President," *Weekly Standard*, May 28, 2001.

41. Bob Dole, speech to the Republican National Convention, San Diego, California, August 15, 1996.

42. Mark Helprin, "The Uses of Honor," *Wall Street Journal*, March 6, 2000.

43. Gary Aldrich, *Unlimited Access* (Washington, D.C.: Regnery, 1998), 30, 105, 137–39.

44. Howard Kurtz, "Who Are You Calling a Liar?" *Washington Post*, May 20, 1997.

45. Best Sellers, *New York Times*, August 4, 1996. Linton Weeks, "All Right Already," *Washington Post*, September 22, 2002.

46. Nicholas Confessore, "Hillary Was Right," *American Prospect*, January 17, 2000.

47. David Frum, *The Right Man* (New York: Random House, 2003), 13–15.

48. John Podhoretz, *Bush Country* (New York: St. Martin's Press, 2004), 24.
49. Ronald Kessler, *A Matter of Character* (New York: Sentinel, 2004), 290.
50. Eric Alterman and Mark Green, *The Book on Bush* (New York: Viking, 2004).
51. Jack Huberman, *The Bush-Hater's Handbook* (New York: Nation Books, 2003).
52. David Corn, *The Lies of George W. Bush* (New York: Crown, 2003).
53. George Stephanopoulos, *All Too Human* (New York: Little, Brown, 1999), p. 4.
54. Peggy Noonan, *When Character Was King* (New York: Viking, 2001).
55. Peggy Noonan, "The Good Guys Finally Won," *Wall Street Journal*, December 21, 1998.
56. Peggy Noonan, "Something to Prove," *Wall Street Journal*, September 1, 2000. Peggy Noonan, "Gore's Behavior Contradicts His Message," *Wall Street Journal*, October 19, 2000. Peggy Noonan, "Bush, a Modest Man of Faith," *Wall Street Journal*, November 2, 2000. Peggy Noonan, "God Is Back," *Wall Street Journal*, September 28, 2001. Peggy Noonan, "Plainspoken Eloquence," *Wall Street Journal*, January 31, 2002. Peggy Noonan, "2001: A Bush Odyssey," *Wall Street Journal*, January 4, 2002.
57. Peggy Noonan, "Memo to Bill Clinton," *Wall Street Journal*, August 11, 2000. Peggy Noonan, "Eeek! Eeek!" *Wall Street Journal*, May 29, 2001.
58. Peggy Noonan, "Write-Wing Conspiracy," *Wall Street Journal*, March 1, 2001. Peggy Noonan, "A House Undivided," *Wall Street Journal*, April 20, 2001. Peggy Noonan, "The Hurdler and the Hitter," *Wall Street Journal*, August 7, 2000.
59. Peggy Noonan, "Senator, You're No Ronald Reagan," *Wall Street Journal*, February 22, 2000.
60. Horace Cooper, "The Massachurian Candidate?" UPI, May 11, 2004. David Paul Kuhn, "Kerry's Top Ten Flip Flops," CBSNews.com, www.cbsnews.com/stories/2004/09/29/politics/main646435.shtml, September 29, 2004. Jonathan Chait, "Fictional Character," *New Republic*, October 18, 2004.
61. George W. Bush, press conference with Colin Powell at the White House, Washington, D.C., September 19, 2002.
62. "President Bush: Flip-Flopper-in-Chief," Center for American Progress, www.americanprogressaction.org/site/pp.asp?c=klLWJcP7H&b=118263, September 2, 2004.
63. George W. Bush, press conference at the White House, Washington, D.C., March 6, 2003.

7. THE ABUSE OF POWER

1. *Washington Post*, January 16, 2005.
2. Interview with Al Arabiya television, May 5, 2004. www.whitehouse.gov/news/releases/2004/05/20040505-2.html.
3. *Boston Globe*, August 9, 2005.
4. *The New Yorker*, January 19, 2004.
5. Susan Schmidt, "Ashcroft Refuses to Release '02 Memo; Document Details Suffering Allowed in Interrogations," *Washington Post*, June 9, 2004. Alison Mitchell, "Letter to Ridge Is Latest Jab in Fight over Balance of Powers," *New York Times*, March 5, 2002. Ceci Connolly, "Medicare Official Defies Subpoena to Appear at a Hearing with Critics," *Washington Post*, April 11, 2002.

6. Jonathan Chait, "Power from the People," *New Republic*, July 26, 2004.

7. Jim VandeHei, "GOP Tilting Balance of Power to the Right," *Washington Post*, May 26, 2005.

8. Christopher H. Schmitt and Edward T. Pound, "Keeping Secrets," *U.S. News & World Report*, December 22, 2003.

9. Dana Milbank, "Seek and Ye Shall Not Find," *Washington Post*, March 11, 2003.

10. House Appropriations Committee hearing, March 27, 2003.

11. Jeff Gerth, "Report Offered Bleak Outlook About Iraq Oil," *New York Times*, October 5, 2003.

12. David Rogers, "Medicare's Chief Actuary Reveals E-Mail Warning," *Wall Street Journal*, March 18, 2004.

13. Don Van Natta, Jr., "Bush Policy on Releasing Records Differs in Case of Clinton Ones," *New York Times*, February 1, 2002. Joshua Micah Marshall, "Bush's executive-privilege two-step," *Salon*, February 7, 2002.

14. John Prados, "Declassifixation," New Republic Online, April 21, 2004.

15. The details of this episode come from a story I wrote in the *New Republic*, "The 9/10 President," March 10, 2003. It can be found at www.tnr.com/doc.mhtml?i=20030310&s=chait031003. The quotes from Obey came during an interview with the author in February of 2003.

16. Susan Milligan, "Congress Reduces Its Oversight Role," *Boston Globe*, November 20, 2005.

17. Ronald Brownstein, "Life in the Time of Scandal," *U.S. News & World Report*, April 27, 1998.

18. Susan Milligan, "Congress Reduces Its Oversight Role," *Boston Globe*, November 20, 2005.

19. Shailagh Murray, "Storms Show a System out of Balance," *Washington Post*, October 5, 2005.

20. Ibid.

21. David Nather, "Congress as Watchdog: Asleep on the Job?" *Congressional Quarterly Weekly*, May 21, 2004.

22. Daryl J. Levinson and Richard H. Pildes, "Separation of Parties, Not Powers," *Harvard Law Review*, April 2006.

23. Julian Zelizer, *On Capitol Hill* (Cambridge: Cambridge University Press, 2004), 44.

24. Richard E. Cohen, *Rostenkowski* (Chicago: Ivan R. Dee, 2000), 128, 131, 137.

25. Theda Skocpol, *Boomerang* (New York: W. W. Norton, 1996), 101.

26. Zelizer, *On Capitol Hill*, 253.

27. Haynes Johnson and David Broder, *The System* (Boston: Little, Brown, 1996), 350.

28. Richard L. Berke, "Prof. Moynihan and His Political Pupil," *New York Times*, January 14, 1994.

29. Johnson and Broder, *The System*, 355–56.

30. Helen Dewar, "Shortcut for Health Care Plan Blocked," *Washington Post*, March 14, 1993.

31. Richard E. Cohen, "The Means Test," *National Journal*, April 22, 1995.

32. Juliet Eilperin, *Fight Club Politics* (Lanham, Md.: Rowman & Littlefield, 2006), 16.

33. James A. Barnes, "Partisanship," *National Journal*, November 7, 1987.

34. Norman Ornstein, ". . . and Mischief," *Washington Post*, November 26, 2003.

35. Robert Novak, untitled column, *Chicago Sun-Times*, November 27, 2003. R. Jeffrey

Smith, "GOP's Pressing Question on Medicare Vote," *Washington Post,* December 23, 2003. Timothy Noah, "Nick Smith Recants," *Slate,* December 5, 2003.

36. Zelizer, *On Capitol Hill,* 88.

37. Gallup Poll, November 7–10, 2005.

38. NBC News broadcast, "Results of NBC/*Wall Street Journal* poll about Iraq war," March 31, 2003.

39. Amy Goldstein and Helen Dewar, "Hill Negotiators Rethink Reimported Drugs," *Washington Post,* November 6, 2003.

40. Ronald Brownstein and Janet Hook, "GOP Can Win by Limiting Losses," *Los Angeles Times,* May 8, 2006.

41. Editorial, "The Gerrymander Scandal," *Wall Street Journal,* November 10, 2001.

42. http://en.wikipedia.org/wiki/United_States_House_elections%2C_2006#Preliminary_results.

43. Editorial, "Rejoice," *New Republic,* November 20, 2006.

44. Grover Norquist, "Step-by-Step Tax Reform," *Washington Post,* June 9, 2003.

8. THE MAINSTREAMING OF RADICALISM

1. John Soloma, *Ominous Politics: The New Conservative Labyrinth* (New York: Hill and Wang, 1984).

2. Jacob S. Hacker and Paul Pierson, *Off-Center* (New Haven, Conn.: Yale University Press, 2005), 28–30, 118.

3. Interview, Henry Hubbard, "'A Bridge to Reagan,'" *Newsweek,* August 30, 1976.

4. Morton Kondracke, "Can GOP Moderates Exert Power in Party Dominated by Right?" *Roll Call,* August 8, 2005.

5. Unity '08's beliefs are spelled out at www.unity08.com.

6. Kurt Anderson, "Introducing the Purple Party," *New York,* April 24, 2006.

7. Peter Kenyon, "Senate Continues to Debate Tax-Cut Bill," *Morning Edition,* July 30, 1999.

8. CNN, *Inside Politics,* May 10, 2001.

9. Richard Hofstadter, *The Paranoid Style in American Politics and Other Essays* (Cambridge, Mass.: Harvard University Press, 1964), 43–44.

10. Daniel Bell, *The Radical Right,* 3rd ed. (New Brunswick, N.J.: Transaction, 2002), 41.

11. Bob Woodward, "Clinton Felt Blindsided over Slashed Initiatives; 'We're Losing Our Soul' in Cutting Deficit," *Washington Post,* June 5, 1994.

12. Ibid., p. 1.

13. Dana Milbank and Glenn Kessler, "Bush, with Executives, Hails Action and Pushes Tax Cuts," *Washington Post,* January 4, 2001.

14. This fact has begun to change with the rise of liberal Internet activists. The netroots have come into existence precisely because of the absence of any coherent liberal movement. Despite its rapid ascent, it has not come close to replicating the conservative movement's influence over mainstream politics.

15. William F. Buckley, *Up from Liberalism* (New York: Hillman, 1961), 114, 126–27.

16. ABC News poll, May 7–9, 2000.

17. Elizabeth Kolbert, "Firebrand," *New Yorker,* November 7, 2005.

18. Editorial, "The Squeamish GOP?" *Wall Street Journal,* November 21, 2000.

19. Jonathan Chait, "Losing It," *New Republic,* December 11, 2000.
20. Robin Toner, "From the Anti-Gore Right, a Battle Cry of 'Stop, Thief!'" *New York Times,* November 26, 2000.
21. Grover Norquist, "The Coming Clinton Dynasty," *American Spectator,* November 1992.
22. Hugh Hewitt, *If It's Not Close They Can't Cheat* (Nashville: Thomas Nelson, 2004), 55.
23. Michael Barone, "The Second Bush Term," *U.S. News & World Report,* November 11, 2004.
24. Editorial, "A Time to Act Presidential," *Washington Post,* November 14, 2000. Editorial, "Stabilizing the Presidency," *New York Times,* November 26, 2000.
25. Fareed Zakaria, "TV, Money, and 'Crossfire' Politics," *Newsweek,* November 1, 2004.
26. Andrew Rich, "War of Ideas," *Stanford Social Innovation Review,* Spring 2005, 22.
27. David Brooks, "The China Lineup; You Can't Tell the Player Without a Scorecard," *Weekly Standard,* April 30, 2001.
28. Jacob Weisberg, "The Conintern," *Slate,* June 29, 1997. Christian Toto, "Nation's Right Turn Cheered," *Washington Times,* May 17, 2004.
29. Tucker Carlson, "Dialogues: Right-Wing Journalism," *Slate,* June 25, 1997.
30. Jacob Weisberg, "The Conintern"; Ingraham's op-ed piece, which appeared on November 20, 1996, under the headline "The Wrong Man for a Sensitive Job," does not appear in Nexis or the *Times'*s online archive. But it is cited in Weisberg's article and in a subsequent letter to the editor by Jonathan Paul Yates that the *Times* published on November 25, 1996.
31. Howard Kurtz, "The Clintons' Pen Pal," *Washington Post,* June 16, 1997. Alison Mitchell, "Clinton Looks for Inspiration from the Left," *New York Times,* August 17, 1997.
32. Editorial, "Cheney's Private Discussions," *Wall Street Journal,* December 11, 2002.
33. Jonathan Chait, "The Home Front: K Street Tries to Exploit September 11," *New Republic,* October 11, 2001.
34. Donald Lambro, "White House Attacks Daschle as Roadblock; At Issue Is Bush's Tax-cutting Stimulus Bill," *Washington Times,* December 7, 2001.
35. Fred Barnes, "Bush's Stealth Budget Strategy; The Budget Director's Plan to Shrink Government," *Weekly Standard,* April 30, 2001. Fred Barnes, "Bush's Big Budget Conservatism; The Era of GOP Big Government Begins," *Weekly Standard,* January 21, 2002.
36. Fred Barnes, "A Third Term for Bush," *Wall Street Journal,* March 20, 2006.
37. Fred Barnes, "Shakeup; What the Changes in the Bush Administration Mean for 2006," *Daily Standard,* April 20, 2006.

CONCLUSION: PLUTOCRACY IN AMERICA

1. Carles Boix, "The Roots of Democracy," *Policy Review,* February/March 2006.
2. "The rich, the poor, and the growing gap between them," *Economist,* June 15, 2006.
3. Jonathan Chait, "Freakoutonomics," *New Republic,* November 6, 2006.

INDEX